Contemporary Arab Scholarship in the Social Sciences, Vol 1

# Democracy, Human Rights and Law in Islamic Thought

*By Mohammed Abed al-Jabri*

I.B.Tauris Publishers
In Association With
The Centre for Arab Unity Studies

مركز دراسات الوحدة العربية
CENTRE FOR ARAB UNITY STUDIES

مؤسسة محمد بن راشد آل مكتوم
MOHAMMED BIN RASHID
AL MAKTOUM FOUNDATION

The translation and publication of this book was made possible by the generous financial support of the Mohammed Bin Rashid Al Maktoum Foundation.

The opinions and ideas expressed in this book are those of the author and do not necessarily reflect those of either the publisher, the Centre for Arab Unity Studies or the Mohammed Bin Rashid Al Maktoum Foundation.

Published in 2009 by I.B.Tauris & Co Ltd
6 Salem Road, London W2 4BU
175 Fifth Avenue, New York NY 10010
www.ibtauris.com
Published in association with the Centre for Arab Unity Studies

In the United States of America and Canada distributed by
Palgrave Macmillan, a division of St. Martin's Press
175 Fifth Avenue, New York NY 10010

Centre for Arab Unity Studies
'Beit Al-Nahda' Bldg. – Basra Street – Hamra
PO Box: 113-6001 Hamra
Beirut 2034 2407 – LEBANON
www.caus.org.lb



Contemporary Arab Scholarship in the Social Sciences, Vol 1

ISBN: 978 1 84511 749 8

A full CIP record for this book is available from the British Library
A full CIP record is available from the Library of Congress

Library of Congress Catalog Card Number: available

Designed and Typeset by 4word Ltd, Bristol, UK
Printed and bound in Great Britain by CPI Antony Rowe, Chippenham

# Contents

VOLUME I:
RELIGION, STATE AND THE APPLICATION OF ISLAMIC *SHARĪʿAH*

## Volume II: Democracy and Human Rights

## Part Four: Enhancing Awareness of Human Rights in Islam

VOLUME I

# RELIGION, STATE AND THE APPLICATION OF ISLAMIC *SHARĪʿAH*

# Introduction

## 1.

There has been much discussion in recent years concerning 'religion and the state' in Islam, and the 'application of Islamic *sharīʿah*'. In most of the works on the subject, regardless of their authors' different approaches, motives or points of view, there has been a noticeable belligerent tone, explicit in some, implicit in others. This belligerent discourse is usually motivated by a desire to invalidate the rival opinion more than anything else. It is a discourse of equivocation and refutation, which ultimately attains no new knowledge and proves no fact. Some authors have tried to avoid open controversy and have sought instead a 'new point of view' or a 'contemporary reading'. In so doing, they mostly start from hypotheses with no basis in the religious texts or in the historical Arab-Islamic experience, or they resort to a far-fetched interpretation of some texts.

Some of these controversies and readings ignore, intentionally or otherwise, the difference between the cognitive and the ideological; between historical facts and mere whims or personal desires, whether in their own discourse or in that of the opponent; in the discourse of creeds, sects, 'intellectuals' or *mujtahidūn* (jurisprudents who derive legal rulings through the interpretive process of *ijtihād*), both past and modern.[1] This is a serious methodological fallacy. The subject of religion and state, and the application of the Islamic *sharīʿah*, is influenced by politics and its related needs and logic. It may be said most authorities referred to by contemporary scholars have been geared, one way or another, to suit their modern political situations. When the scholar has certain political persuasions to affirm, the truth will certainly be lost in a labyrinthine political wilderness of the past and the present.

My aim from these cursory remarks is to emphasize the necessity of establishing an authority more advanced and credible than sectarian authorities or those which were basically formulated as a point of view in support of a certain political stand. The most advanced and original of all authorities, in the historical Arab-Islamic experience, is the conduct of the Companions at the time of the Rāshidūn (Orthodox) Caliphs. Just as the texts of the Qur'ān and *sunnah* did not legislate for the concerns of government and politics, nor did they address the relation between religion and state in the same clear-cut and precise manner as they did other matters, such as marriage and inheritance. It follows that the basic authority, if not the only one, in the field of the relation between religion and state, and the application of the Islamic *sharī'ah*, is based on the conduct of the Companions. It was they who practised politics, established the state and applied *al-sharī'ah* on the basis of a genuine understanding of the spirit of Islam, prior to all other types of understanding which accompanied the various types of contention in the history of Islam, beginning with the one which flared between 'Alī bin Abī Ṭālib and Mu'āwiyah. It may be said that the era of the Rāshidūn was not free from conflicting politics and opinions. This is true as no conduct is free from differences. Yet differences and their solutions form a basic factor in what I call 'the conduct of the Companions'.

To adopt the conduct of the Companions at the time of the Rāshidūn as a basic authoritative referent (*marja'īyah*)[2] – or the only one when necessary – does not condemn as incorrect or devious all other authorities established by the *mujtahidūn* who enjoyed a high degree of knowledge, fairness and objectivity. Rather, what is needed now is to view these men as having established for themselves certain authoritative referents to address the new developments in their ages, on the one hand, and, on the other, to regulate *ijtihād* and define its rules. Since our own age is greatly different from the previous ages, with all the new problems and developments that could never have occurred in the time of the early *mujtahidūn*, the need calls for a return to the original source, when it was open to the laws, and not restricted by them, before the 'surge of conflict' and the rise of creeds and sects, namely, as it was at the time of the Rāshidūn Caliphs.

The rules and foundations of the *uṣūl* (the source principles or 'origins' of Islamic law and interpretive jurisprudence, e.g. *uṣūl al-fiqh*) laid down by the *mujtahidūn* to regulate the discipline of *ijtihād* in their times were a useful, probably necessary means: first, to initiate jurisprudential knowledge (in both religion and politics); and second, to protect such knowledge from confusion and subjectivity. But should those rules and principles be taken as necessary and useful at all times? Like all methodological rules, the rules and principles which regulate knowledge are, generally, no more than means. If such means do not match the development of learning and knowledge, they become impediments which fossilize that knowledge, thus fostering imitation (*al-taqlīd*) and killing the spirit of *ijtihād*.

To illustrate this point, we may look at two rules of jurisprudence which recur in common discussions these days. One states: 'Reliance is on the general [meaning of the] term, not on the particularity of the cause'; the second states: 'Rulings depend on their causes (*ʿillal*), not on their legal consequence (*ḥukm*).' These are two methodological rules laid down by jurisprudents and fundamental savants of religion which we do not challenge under any circumstances. However, I would view them as they are in reality: namely, as related to the method laid down by the *mujtahid* for himself, and not as a part of religion itself. Nonetheless, as methodology is a matter of choice, some *mujtahidūn* have chosen methods which do not adhere to these two rules. The Companions did not abide by any such rules, nor were these terms known in their times. The concepts of the particular (*al-khāṣ*) and the general (*al-ʿām*), and the distinction between the cause (*al-ʿillah*) and the [legal] consequence (*al-ḥikmah*), were logical terms unknown to the Arab-Islamic culture before the first 'Abbasid era, when tradition was put on record. It is true that one may find in the 'conduct of the Companions' what may appear as applying one rule or another, yet it is also true that the Companions did not always abide by any one rule. The only principle they observed consistently was the public good (*al-maṣlaḥah*) above all else. Therefore, we often see them acting in accordance with the dictates of that good, irrespective of the text, no matter how decisively clear-cut it is, when special circumstances demand a deferment of the text, as we shall see below.

Our present age has its own needs and concerns, different from those which dictated to the early *fuqahāʾ* (Muslim jurisprudents, scholars of *al-fiqh*) and *uṣūlīyūn* (scholars of the original sources – *al-uṣūl*), their rules and methods. To address these concerns and problems, we need to relinquish the restrictive methods which shackled the religious knowledge in the past and handle them instead with flexibility, while looking at those methods from a relative and historical perspective. I am calling for the deferment of previous interpretative judgments and for resorting directly to the 'conduct of the Companions', because the subject under discussion is of a religious nature, in the first place, which makes it mandatory to return to the 'source', and secondly because the 'conduct of the Companions' in this field was characterized by relativity and historical perspective. This rendered their action open and inspiring, making room for renewal (*al-tajdīd*) and *ijtihād*, as shall be made clear by the examples that follow.

## 2.

I have spoken of the necessity of rebuilding jurisprudential authority by referring to the conduct of the Companions as the guiding line. By the 'conduct of the Companions' I mean the whole of their political and legislative practices, whether oral or applied, on every level. The matter, therefore, is related to a historical experience, which had, like other experiences, its own political, social, economic and cultural elements that formed the historical and social framework at the time. Therefore, I have to begin by highlighting those historical and social realities, which at the time encompassed the subject of 'religion and state', then I shall discuss the application of *al-sharīʿah*.

At the time of the mission of Muḥammad, the Arabs had no monarch or state. The political-social system in Mecca and Medina was a collective-tribal one, not rising to the level of 'state' (*dawlah*), which is defined as a land of known frontiers, inhabited by a group of people, with a central authority representing those inhabitants in managing their communal affairs, according to certain laws and traditions, and by using force when necessary, a type of force monopolized by that authority in the name of everyone and for the good of everyone. The peninsular Arabs before Islam did not have such authority, neither in the townships nor outside them. That is the meaning of '*al-jāhilīyah*', which describes the life of the Arabs before the mission of Muḥammad. The word does not only mean 'ignorance' and absence of knowledge, but it also covers the state of affairs accompanying such ignorance, especially the lack of abiding by law or discipline, and the absence of a comprehensive outlook which places the public good above any other consideration.

With the mission of Muḥammad, the Muslims began to practise the new religion, not only as an individual attitude towards the worshipped Lord (Allāh), but also as an organized collective behaviour. This developed and became more disciplined as the mission of Muḥammad developed, reaching its peak after the emigration to the Medina. Although the Prophet was actually the head, the leader and the guide of the Muslim group, he repeatedly and unequivocally refused to be called a 'king' (*malik*), or be considered a head of state (*raʾīs dawlah*). He considered himself, and was considered by the Muslims, a prophet and a messenger, as described by the Qur'ān. He took part in wars, led campaigns, organized the affairs of the Muslim community, upheld their unity, sent envoys and appointed rulers, etc., not in the capacity of a political leader or a military commander, but as a man with a mission and a promulgator of a new religion. The difference between the two cases is that political leaders and military conquerors limit their intention to worldly affairs alone: those related to rule, politics and other economic, social and cultural matters which are all connected with the human existence in this world. The Prophet and Messenger centres his concern and mission on the call to the one God, the destiny in the afterlife and the affairs of the hereafter. No other efforts undertaken in order to organize worldly affairs, whether this means worship or transactions, *jihād* (war in the cause of Islam in this case), or relations with other religions and nations, are intended as ends in themselves, but all are for the cause of the religion, promulgating and defending it.

The situation created by the development of the call (*al-da'wah*) of Muḥammad, which effected the organization of all worldly affairs at the time of the Messenger and his Companions, had reached by the time of its completion a degree of expansion, precision and institutionalization that caused the Companions and those close to the Messenger to feel that his absence would create an institutional void. The call had concluded with the establishment of a state (*dawlah*) or what resembled a state. Religion is a divine revelation which cannot be inherited from the Messenger or by any of his successors, but the political-economic-social system which developed with the call would require someone to shepherd it and to put it on the best course after the death of the Messenger. That system did not have a political name, since the Messenger refused to be called 'king'. The Arabic lexicon had no term for 'political presidency' except that of 'king', a term rejected and condemned by Islam, since the only king is Allāh. Therefore, the Companions devised the general term '*amr*' (affair) to signify 'kingship'. So, the question 'Who will be in charge of the *amr*?' has the same meaning as the modern 'Who will head the state?'. Similarly, the phrase 'he has nothing in the *amr*' meant 'he has no right to kingship or presidency'. In Arabic stylistics, this is called 'naming the thing by its function'. The root '*amr*' also means 'command'; so the function of the head of state is to issue an order – *amr*; or orders – *awāmir*.

We have seen that there was a general feeling among the Companions, before the death of the Messenger, that there was a need to know who will be in charge of the *amr* after him. Early historians mention that al-'Abbās, the paternal uncle of the Prophet, raised this question with 'Alī bin Abī Ṭālib during the last illness of the Prophet. He said to 'Alī, 'Go in and ask the Prophet to specify whether the *amr* would be in our hands, or, if in other hands, to recommend us to the others.' It is said that 'Alī refused, for fear he would get a negative answer from the Prophet, so the Hashemites would be deprived of the caliphate for ever. This incident clearly shows that the Companions felt that the call of Muḥammad had actually developed into a state.

The Qur'ān speaks repeatedly and in no uncertain terms of the *ummah* (nation), the *ummah* of Islam and the Muslims: 'You were the best nation (*ummah*) brought forth for people' (2, Āl 'Imrān, 110). Yet, the Qur'ān refrained from specifying the political-social-economic system which characterized that *ummah* as a state. True, it is the Qur'ān that specified legislations and limits, prescriptions and proscriptions, duties to be carried out individually or collectively, and others (namely the *amr*) that would require someone to be in charge of them. The Qur'ān has called on Muslims in clear terms to obey those who 'are in charge of the *amr*': "O you who believe! Obey Allāh and obey the Messenger, and those given authority (*amr*) among you' (4, al-Nisā', 59).

The Qur'ān also condemned tyranny and arrogance, and commended consultation, charity and justice. But the Qur'ān did not specify that the nation of Islam should correspond with the 'kingship' or the 'state' of Islam; nor did it specify who should succeed the Messenger in managing the affairs of this *ummah* (community) or even that there should be such a successor. The Qur'ān left the issue for the Muslims to decide, as if it were subsumed under the [implications of the] Prophetic *ḥadīth*: 'You are better informed of your worldly affairs.'

The first initiative mentioned by historians in this connection is what is related to al-'Abbās, the paternal uncle of the Prophet. He said to 'Alī bin Abī Ṭālib, when the Prophet was pronounced dead, 'Open your hand and I shall pledge allegiance to you, so it would be said that the paternal uncle of the Messenger of Allāh pledged allegiance to the cousin of the Messenger of Allāh, and your kith and kin will follow suit.' 'Alī answered, 'And who else should claim this *amr*?!' The story adds that al-'Abbās had previously asked Abū Bakr and 'Umar whether the Messenger had left any will or instructions to that effect, and the answer was in the negative. Whether this story is verifiable or not, it is historically testified that the Anṣār (Medinan supporters of the Messenger) hurried to a meeting in the bower of Banī Sā'idah to choose someone from among themselves to be in charge of the *amr*, and that Abū Bakr, 'Umar and other Muhājirūn (immigrants who were the first Muslims in Mecca) challenged them in this *amr*.

The discussion in the bower of Banī Sā'idah, which ended with choosing Abū Bakr to succeed the Messenger as a caliph (meaning to manage the *amr* of the Muslims after him), was a purely political discussion, decided by the political-social balance of power (the tribe). I have detailed that discussion in a different work and come to the conclusion that the Companions handled the issue of succession to the Prophet as purely a political matter.[3] Moreover, they handled it as a case of *ijtihād* and with regard to the balance of power, capability, efficiency and the good of the nascent Muslim society. All that was governed by the logic of the 'tribe', i.e. a consideration of the balance of power, as is the case in a tribal society in general, and not for the cause of the faith where both Muhājirūn and Anṣār were on the same footing. The decisive declaration was that made by Abū Bakr: 'The Arabs do not follow except this quarter of Quraysh [i.e. the Prophet's tribe].' This is an objective judgment, specifying a reality, which the Anṣār accepted when they were motivated by the narrow tribal motive (as they recalled the contention between the 'Aws and Khazraj tribes); and also when they found the logic of the Muhājirūn tipping the balance to the side of mutual good. It is irrelevant here to discuss what is relevant about the hesitation and the reluctance of some relatives of the Messenger in endorsing the choice of Abū Bakr, such as 'Alī, Fāṭimah, al-'Abbas, al-Zubayr ibn al-'Awām and some of the weak and oppressed among the Companions, such as al-Miqdād, Salmān al-Fārisī, Abū Dharr, 'Ammar bin Yāsir, and others.[4] There is also no need of a reminder of the way 'Umar bin al-Khaṭṭāb, 'Uthmān bin 'Affān, and Alī bin Abī Ṭālib were chosen for the caliphate, which again depended on discussion, consultation and the balance of power. It was politics and not religion that was the centre of discussion and controversy, and it was within that framework that the decision was made.[5]

These historical facts show decisively that the issue of the relation between religion and state was not present at the time of the Prophet nor that of the Rāshidūn Caliphs. At the time of the Prophet, all efforts were geared towards promulgating and defending the faith. The entire *amr* in all this belonged to the Messenger, to the revelations that came to him, and to his personal interpretation and that of his Companions. No one then regarded this *amr* as 'kingship', as this was an unpleasant and rejected term. Nor was it considered a state, since the word *'dawlah'* meant, according to the *Lisān al-'Arab* lexicon, 'the remainder or aftermath of wealth and war', which is changeable. Hence the *tadawwul* (alternation) of wealth among various hands, the *tadawwul* (exchange) of news among people; and also the expression 'days are *duwal*', meaning that times change from one state to another. About the exchange of money and wealth, the Qur'ān says: 'In order that it [wealth] may not [merely] make a circuit (*dawlah*) between the wealthy among you' (59, al-Ḥashr, 7). About war, we read: 'These days [of varying fortunes] We give to people by turns (*nudāwil*)' (2, Āl 'Imrān, 140); namely that victory alternates between any two opponents.

Muslims at the time of the Companions did not look at Islam as a *dawlah*, state, in the sense of a thing that passes from hand to hand, and subsequently disappears. They rather looked at Islam as the religion that came to end and replace all previous religions and which would remain in operation until the Day of Resurrection. Therefore, they associated it with 'the *ummah*',[6] and ascribed that *ummah* to Islam and the Messenger of Islam, hence the *ummah* of Islam, the *ummah* of Muḥammad. In this sense, the *ummah* is a social–spiritual entity whose existence is not dependent upon any political system. Thus, while previous nations were initiated as 'states', namely political-military systems set up by the conquerors, the Muslim *ummah*, according to the Muslims, grew out of the call of Muḥammad and took its shape before that call developed in the end into that political system which we now call 'state'. The term 'state' (*dawlah*) as a political term did not appear before the success of the 'Abbasid revolt, when the 'Abbasids and their supporters started to say that it was their state, to denote that the *amr* had come into their hands from the Umayyads. Then we begin to see historians speaking of the Umayyad state or the 'Abbasid state, the state of Mu'āwiyah or the state of Hārūn al-Rāshid. These terms denote the transfer of *amr* from one dynasty to another, or from one king to another, terms which find their original meaning in the Qur'ānic verse: 'These days [of varying fortunes] We give to people by turns (*nudāwil*)' (2, *Āl 'Imrān*, 140).

The relation between religion and state was, therefore, not contemplated, either at the time of the Prophet or at the time of the Rāshidūn Caliphs. But when the Messenger suffered his last illness, thought and concern focused on what the *mutikallimūn* (Muslim theologians) later on termed as *imāmah* (leadership by an *imām* – '*imāmate*') or *khilāfah* (vicegerency – 'caliphate'). This is a purely political issue, and it was the first major controversial question in Islam. At the beginning of his book, *Assertions of the Islamists and Differences among People Who Pray* (*maqālāt al-islāmīyīn wa ikhtilāf al-muṣalīn*), Abū Ḥasan al-Ash'ārī says, 'After the Prophet, people differed on many points, accusing each other and denouncing each other. They became conflicting sects and divided parties, Islam was the only common element among them.' Then he adds, 'The first disagreement that occurred among the Muslims, after the death of their Prophet, was their disagreement about leadership.' He goes on to relate the discussion in the meeting at the bower of Banī Sā'idah.

In his *Denominations and Sects* (*al-milal wa al-niḥal*), al-Shahrastānī enumerates the points of disagreement among the Muslims during the time of the Prophet and thereafter. He says, 'The greatest disagreement in the *ummah* was that about leadership *(al-imāmah)*. No sword in Islam was raised in the face of any religious question as it was against leadership in every era.' Then he relates the disagreement between the Muhājirūn and the Anṣār about choosing a caliph after the Prophet, and the complaint of some Companions against ʿUmar, who was chosen by Abū Bakr to succeed him: 'You have appointed a rough, boorish person over us.' Then comes the disagreement among the six 'consultants' appointed by ʿUmar to choose a caliph from among themselves after his death, so ʿUthmān was chosen by a majority, and not by consensus. Subsequently, there is the disagreement among people towards the end of ʿUthmān's caliphate about certain reservations they had against him, a disagreement which developed into a bloody revolt where ʿUthmān himself was the victim. Finally, al-Shahrastānī describes the disaffection of Ṭalḥah, al-Zubayr and 'Ā'ishah with Alī bin Abī Ṭālib, and the war which ensued; and the conflict between 'Alī and Muʿāwiyah and the war between the two, in addition to 'Alī's war against the Khawārij (the dissenters).[7]

These disagreements, and the resulting clashes and wars, were only incidental political conflicts provoked by kinship and interests. Religion was not a point of contention, nor was it ever an element in these conflicts. All the contenders, competitors and combatants were Companions, and all of them understood their religion, practised it and abided by it in their personal conduct. In other words, religion was not an authoritative referent in this contention, as the disagreement was political in the general sense of the word. It was neither in the name of religion nor against religion.

This was the case before the situation was settled in the interest of Muʿāwiyah and the establishment of the Umayyad state. During the Umayyad era, the system of government changed from 'appointment' after consultation to a hereditary system confined to one dynasty. Armed struggle continued, with the revolts of Khawārij and Shīʿites throughout the Umayyad era, in addition to the Shīʿite revolts after the rise of the 'Abbāsid state. However, immediately after the situation was settled in the interest of Muʿāwiyah, the controversy about leadership developed from a mere incidental political issue to reach the level of political theorization. Because the religious text in the Qur'ān, and whatever was known of the *a ḥadīth* before they were compiled and edited, did not address the issue of rule and government, the only referential authority in this field was the conduct of the Companions, at the time of the Rāshidūn Caliphs. Since the political question, as we have seen, was a matter of various disputes in that era, there arose differing theories and even contradictory opinions about the leadership and the caliphate. This is because each one would choose an incident from the time of the Rāshidūn Caliphs that might serve as an authoritative referent to support his opinion and justify his political stand on the question of rule in his own time.

When we consider the entire spectrum of these theories and opinions proposed by the *mutakallimūn* and the *fuqahā'*, from the perspective of religion and state, three main schools of thought can be identified.

The subscribers to the first school of thought believed that the appointment of *al-imām,* and the consequent establishment of the state in the Islamic society, was one of the duties and bases of religion. The leadership (*imāmah*) according to this group, namely the Shī'ite group, was 'not a question of interest, entrusted to the public by whose authority the *imām* is "installed"'. In the words of al-Shahrastānī, 'It is rather a fundamental issue, and a basis of religion, that the messengers cannot afford to ignore or delegate to the public'; namely, leave it to the public without prior designation. al-Shahrastānī explains the Shī'ite point of view in this statement: 'They agree on the necessity of appointment and specification, on the mandatory infallibility of prophets and *imāms*, and their immunity against minor and major sins.' Accordingly, the Shī'ites said, 'The Prophet specified 'Alī bin Abī Ṭālib should be the Caliph and *imām* after him; and that 'Alī specified and recommended, and so did the *imāms* from descendents after him.'

The followers of the second school of thought took a totally opposite stand. They said the *imāmah* (and the state) were not mandatory, as religion does not specify the necessity of their establishment or their abandonment. All was left to the Muslims. If they could appoint a just leader without causing bloodshed, wars or insurgencies, it would be preferable. If they failed to do so, and each Muslim could take care of himself and his kin, and apply the *sharī'ah* as specified in the Qur'ān and *sunnah*, it would be acceptable, and they would have no need for an *imām*. This opinion was entertained by some of the early Khawārij, and the Najdat, who follow Najdat al-Ḥanafi, a leader of a sect of the Khawārij; and it was also held by a sect of Mu'tazilites, best known among whom were Abū Bakr al-'Aṣṣām, Hishām bin 'Umar al-Fūṭī and 'Ibād bin Sulaymān.

In his commentary on the opinions of the group that constitutes this second school of thought, al-Shahrastānī says:

> The Najdat, of Khawārij and a group of *al-qadariyyah* (meaning the Mu'tazilites), like Abū Bakr al-'Aṣṣām and Hishām bin 'Umar al-Fūṭī, believe that the *imāmah* is not specified as a duty in *sharī'ah* in a manner that if the *ummah* did not observe it they would deserve reproach and punishment. *imāmah* (leadership) is based on the conduct of men. If they cooperate in piety and good deeds, each performing his duty, they will have no need for a leader to rule them. Each *mujtahid* is equal to the other in faith, Islam, knowledge, and *ijtihād*. As people are equal to one another, 'why should one obey another who is his equal!'

al-Shahrastānī summarizes the argument of this group:

> The obligation to obey one of the members of the *ummah* [the *imām*] should either be specified by the Messenger, and you have proved that there is no such text (addressing the Sunnis, followers of the third opinion explained below); or, it should be a choice by the *mujtahidūn* themselves. But a unanimous choice (by *ijmā'*) by all *mujtahidūn*, namely by every member of the *ummah*, without disagreement, is not possible in theory and in practice.

Events proved that unanimity among the Companions was not possible in the case of the first Caliph. The immigrants and Anṣār disagreed, and 'Umar nominated Abū Bakr 'on the spur of the moment' and without consultation, as the Anṣār were in a hurry. The following day, when the *bay'ah* was sworn, Banu Umayyah and Banu Hashim hesitated and tried to convince 'Alī ibn Abi-Talib to claim the *bay'ah* for himself as he was the nearest of kin to the Messenger, hence more deserving of the caliphate, as they believed. Therefore, the second school of thought argued: 'When unanimity could not be reached by the early Companions, how could it be reached by others?'

Among the arguments advanced by this group was their assertion that 'the installation of the *imāmah* by choice is a double contradiction'. First, when people chose the *imām*, they must obey him. But how can they be obliged to obey him when they were the ones who chose and installed him? Second, any one of the *mujtahidūn* who installed the *imām* may have disagreed with him on questions of *ijtihād*. There is no question in this line of reasoning wherein the *mujtahid* cannot disagree with the *imām*, so how could they insist that the *imām* was obeyed on condition of disagreeing with him if *ijtihād* necessitated it? Writers on sects mention other arguments, too. For example: 'To make one man a leader and a guide above another man who is his equal, and to judge his actions as right and wrong, is definitely harmful.' By this they mean that the installation of the *imām* and state would undoubtedly lead to a restriction and limitation of people's freedom, and this was an inadmissible harm to them. Another argument was that people would protest against such restrictions and limitations, 'as it is often the case, which would lead to strife (*fitnah*)'.

Another argument was that the *imām* was not infallible, as infallibility is a characteristic of the prophets alone. Hence, the *imām* may perjure his faith or go astray: 'If he is not deposed he will hurt the *ummah* by his blasphemy; if he is deposed, that may lead to strife.' Hence, to abandon the installation of *imāmah* was the safer and more beneficial option.[8]

It should be pointed out here that this party did not mean by their arguments that *imāmah* was prohibited. They only meant to emphasize such installation was not obligatory. In other words, the institution of *imāmah* (or the legal caliphate) was neither prescribed nor prohibited in *sharīʿah*, but it was one of the permitted procedures which may be observed or disregarded. Therefore, this group always reiterated that, when it became necessary to install an *imām*, people may do so, provided he be just and remain just. al-Shahrastānī explains their conviction by quoting from them:

> When [people] feel the need for a leader to protect Islam and rally the people, and when a person's *ijtihād* recommends him to that position, he may be installed, provided he abide by justice and fairness in his conduct. But when he deviates from justice against an individual, it becomes necessary to depose him. This is what the people did to ʿUthmān and ʿAlī. As ʿUthmān was instrumental in some [undesirable] events they deposed him. When he refused to be deposed they killed him. So it was with ʿAlī, when he accepted arbitration and his *imāmah* became questionable, he was deposed and killed.[9]

The third school of thought was generally a disapproval of the two previous ones. It was adopted by all the Sunnis, and the majority of the Mu'tazilites, the Khawārij and the Murji'ah. They all believed that *imāmah* was obligatory on the one hand, but that it should be by choice, not by specification, on the other. On other matters, they disagreed greatly among themselves. Some believed that the necessity of *imāmah* was perceptible by reason, and some say it was known through *sharīʿah*. Yet others joined the two beliefs together. The disagreement on this point was actually due to the origins of these schools of thought and not to the issue itself. The Mu'tazilites had a principal conviction that the mind can perceive good and evil of its own accord. So, reason had it that the good of the *ummah*, namely, the management of the people's interests and their protection against harm, required the establishment of a ruling system among them. The Companions realized that good by their reason, and that led them to choose a caliph to succeed the Prophet as soon as he was pronounced dead.

The Sunnis opposed the Mu'tazilites, who said that reason perceived good and evil before *sharīʿah*. Instead, they believed that *sharīʿah* was the authoritative referent to distinguish good from evil, because it is through *al-sharīʿah* that we know commands and proscriptions. Therefore, the Sunnis said that the necessity of *imāmah* is realized and known through *al-sharīʿah*, not through reason. The basic *sharīʿah* proof, if not the only one in this connection, was the 'consensus' (*ijmāʿ*) of the Companions to appoint a caliph to succeed the Messenger. It is known that *ijmāʿ* was a source of legislation in Islam to all Sunnis; but it was not specified as such until al-Shafi'i did so, which was about a century and a half after the death of the Messenger. It is clear that the Sunnis resorted to *ijma'* to support their stand on this issue, despite differences among the *mujtahidūn* concerning the binding authority, the time and the form of that 'consensus'. It is clear that this party resorted to *al-sharī'ah* to support their argument, because they could not find anything to that effect in the Qur'ān or the *sunnah*. In other words, the reference here is the historical experience of the *ummah* and not the religious text. As Muslims disagreed on the issue of the necessity of *imāmah*, they also disagreed about the issue of choice: Who chooses the *imām*, and how many people are needed to install him? Little can be said here, since the only reference in the question of choice is the historical experience of the *ummah*, an experience so resourceful and so colourful that it can accommodate any of the various points of view. But we have to see how the advocates of *imāmah* employed this experience.

Generally speaking, we can categorize the practice of the *mutakallimūn* about the *imāmah* concerning the historical experience of the *ummah* to three:

(i) To justify previous choices and incidents, especially those belonging to the era of historical authority, namely, that of the Rāshidūn Caliphs. Some Shī'ite and Khawārij factions questioned the method by which the Rāshidūn Caliphs were 'appointed', advancing the issue of priority. Some believed 'Alī was better than Abū Bakr, 'Umar and 'Uthmān. Yet these were chosen before 'Alī, which was the choice of the lesser over the better. This is a principle accepted by the Shī'ite *imām* Zayd ibn 'Alī and his followers, known as the Zaydis, who were moderate Shī'ites. The majority opposed and rejected this principle and came to be called Rawāfiḍ, 'rejectors', who were the *imāmi* Shī'ites. The Sunni discussions of *imāmah* were aimed at refuting those doubts expressed by the Shī'ites in particular, and turned the argument into political theories to justify what had happened, and not to explain what the case should be.

(ii) To justify and legitimize the present, by choosing some incidents of the past as criteria for comparison and justification of present incidents. They used the initiative taken by 'Umar ibn al-Khaṭṭāb to pledge the *bay'ah* to Abū Bakr at the Bower of Banī Sā'idah as a source for justifying their claim that the *imāmah* may be installed through the pledge of one person, and for justifying the absence of consultation in their times and those before them. They also used the declaration made by Abū Bakr to settle the issue at the Bower, namely 'The Arabs would not obey except this quarter of Quraysh', to justify the legitimacy of the powerful to seize the reins of power after the Rāshidūn Caliphs, on the assumption people follow the more powerful ruler.

This led to endorsing the theory of 'might is right', and the complete omission of consultation (*al-shūrā*), replacing it with the principle: 'Obedience is obligatory to the mighty.'

(iii) To prefer the 'state situation'. Even if this state falls short of the Islamic ideal, it is preferred to the 'no-state situation'. The *mutakallimun* highlighted the dangers threatening the *ummah* and the faith in the case of strife and revolt against the *imām*, citing the contention between 'Alī and Mu'āwiyah, and the Siffīn war in particular as an example to support their argument. They also cited the homage paid by al-Ḥasan ibn 'Alī to Mu'āwiyah, and the handing of power over to him, as a referential source to prove the necessity of political consensus and its preference to any disagreement, even if the disagreeing party were in the right. The phrase 'the People of the Consensus' (ahl al-jamā'ah), which was connected with the Sunnis later on (to become 'the people of the *sunnah* and consensus'), relates to this incident in particular. That was the origin of the confusion and contradiction in which the Sunni theorists about the *imāmah* were trapped. They entirely agreed that the caliphate had turned into a 'voracious kingship' with Mu'āwiyah, yet they considered the authoritative referent for political consensus the stepping down of al-Ḥasan to pay homage to Mu'āwiyah as caliph, followed by the rest of the Companions and their followers in this *bay'ah*. They even called that year 'The Year of Consensus'. It is clear that connecting the two incidents, which are connected historically and politically, makes the 'conversion of the caliphate into kingship' a process achieved by a political consensus in the 'Year of Consensus (*'ām al-jamā'ah*)'.

To alleviate some of the tragic effects of this conclusion, a *ḥadīth* was popularized and ascribed to the Prophet, saying, 'The caliphate in my *ummah* lasts for 30 years, followed by a kingship.' The four Rāshidūn Caliphs ruled for that 30-year-period. There is another ascribed *ḥadīth*, more telling in this connection: 'The Prophet said, this *amr* began as a prophethood, mercy, and a caliphate. Then it will turn into a voracious kingship, then into a tyranny, oppression and corruption of the *ummah*.' Such *ḥadīth*, which carry a political implication serving the interest of a certain party, the Umayyads in this case, are highly doubtful, and most probably fabricated. If such *ḥadīth* can be taken as a criticism of the situations experienced by their propagators, they can nevertheless give direct support to the conversion of the caliphate into a 'voracious kingship' as a process 'prophesied' by the Messenger. The political significance of such exploitation of history and *ḥadīth* together is to approve of and endorse the principle: 'Nothing could have been done better than what was done.'

This categorization of the historical experience of the *ummah* in the Sunni political jurisprudence renders the relation between religion and state rather ambiguous. But the absence of clear texts in the Qurʾān and *sunnah* that regulate the affairs of rule and state does not mean that Islam, in general, is not concerned with the question of rule. The historical experience of the nation proves the contrary. The *daʿwah* of Muḥammad at the time of the Prophet himself had developed into a state, and Muslims guarded that state, one way or another, as a necessity for the protection of the faith and for defending the land of Islam. On the other hand, the Qurʾān and *ḥadīth* contain at least what may be considered the moral principles of rule in Islam, such as commending consultation, establishing justice and providing for the poor and needy.

It is clear that realizing these moral principles in the state requires rulers who are 'conversant' in religion and sincere in its application and service. The relation between religion and state cannot hold except when the leader (*imām*) represents the unity of religion and state, as the representative and spokesman of the *ummah*. To be conversant in religion does not merely mean to know the religious rules; it more importantly demands an ability and authority to interpret and employ those rules in a manner compatible with progress and responsive to the public interest in various times. Therefore, the early *mutakallimūn* stipulated 'knowledge' in an *imām*.

While combining religion and statesmanship in the person of the *imām* was achievable at the time of the Rāshidūn Caliphs, it became more difficult to achieve with time, and some of the eminent *ʿulamāʾ* of religion saw in that development a sign *qaḍāʾ wa al-qadr* (divine predestination) which could not be averted. The eminent Andalusian Ashʿārī jurisprudent Abū Bakr bin al-ʿArabī said:

> In the early days of Islam, the leaders (lit., princes) were the *ʿulamāʾ*; the subjects, the soldiers. Then the public became one group; the leaders another. Then God's supreme wisdom predestined that the savants be one group, the leaders another, and the public one group, the soldiers another. Thus disruption set in and people deviated from the right path. Then they tried to resume righteousness but could not find it, and they will never do, as the one who deviates from his intention will never achieve it.

While Ibn al-ʿArabī saw in the division between the leaders and the *ʿulamāʾ* after the times of the Rāshidūn Caliphs a divine predestination, with no hope of returning to the original situation as it was in the early days of Islam, he saw that the leaders should consult the *ʿulamāʾ* and follow their advice in their exercise of authority and rule. Commenting on the Qurʾānic verse 'O you who believe! Obey Allāh and obey the Messenger and those given authority among you' (4, *al-Nisā'*, 59), Ibn al-'Arabi said:

> ...those given authority amongst you, has two interpretations: The older of the two sees the phrase as denoting those undertaking campaigns – that is the military leaders appointed by the Prophet to lead his campaigns and armies. The later one endorsed by the [generation of] Followers and those who came later says the reference is to the *'ulamā'*.

Ibn al-'Arabi added:

> I believe what is meant is both the leaders and the *'ulamā'*; the leaders because the origin of orders is with them and rule is in their hands. As for the *'ulamā'* people should seek their council too, their answer is obligatory and people should abide by their order.

However, the question 'Who can oblige the rulers to consult the *'ulamā'* and abide by their edicts?' remained without answer. Would advice suffice to make the leaders consult the *'ulamā'*? Experience points to the contrary. Or was it necessary to make them do that by force, through mobilizing the public against them (which is the only power in the hands of the *'ulamā'*)? In this case, who could guarantee that the situation would not turn into a civil war (*fitnah*)? The *'ulamā'* realized, more than anybody else, the dangers of strife, and they were most careful to avoid it.

These queries lead directly to the second part of this study: 'The application of *al-sharī'ah*.'

## 3.

The relation between religion and state in Islam is not defined in the texts of the Qur'ān or *sunnah*. Neither specifies whether it is [legally] necessary (*wujūb*) to install the *imām* (and establish the state) and, in the case of such necessity, there is no text to describe how to choose the *imām* and what his authorities are. Yet there is the undeniable fact that Islam is a creed (*'aqīdah*) and a law (*sharī'ah*) together. The creed is concerned with the belief in the one God, His angels, His scriptures, His messengers and the Day of Judgment, which all define the relation between man and his God. There is yet the *sharī'ah*, which includes, in addition to the forms of worship that in their turn relate to the relation between man and God, rulings of a social nature, which regulate the mutual relations among the people. This makes it necessary to have an authority to carry out those rulings, such as punishments. In addition to this, there is the duty of defending the land of Islam, which is the religious duty of *jihād*. The *fuqahā'*, however, are not in agreement about whether this is a conditional 'collective duty' (*farḍ kifāyah*) or an absolute 'individual duty' (*farḍ 'ayn*). In both cases nonetheless there is a need for a military leadership to manage recruitment, logistics, planning, strategies, etc. It may be said, generally, that the state in Islam was established at the time of the Messenger and was consolidated and expanded in the time of the Rāshidūn Caliphs by virtue of these two factors: the application of the *sharī'ah* rulings on the one hand, and *jihād* and conquests on the other.

Therefore, whether we believe in the necessity of installing the *imām* and establishing the state, from a religious point of view, or not, there are still the rulings of *al-sharī'ah* which need to be applied by an authority. The question now is: How were the *sharī'ah* rulings applied during the historical experience of the Islamic nation, irrespective of the form of authority that applied those rulings? (Is a state with a legal system, as it is the case in the Islamic states, or a spiritual or a jurisprudential authority, in a non-Muslim state where the Muslims form only a minority?)

The first point to consider in this connection is that the Islamic *sharī'ah* was not revealed to the Prophet all at the same time. It was revealed gradually and step by step: gradually, to match the development of the Muslim community and in consideration of the change in political, economic and social situations; and step by step in order to suit the progressive influence of the faith on the souls of the people, and the extent to which they have realized the intents and the benefits of that *sharī'ah*. Hence, we have the abrogating and abrogated verses in the Qur'ān. Many of the rulings specified in the Qur'ān were abrogated by later verses. Not only that, but all the *sharī'ah* judgments mentioned in the Qur'ān were actually revealed in connection with events or incidents which happened to some individuals, or they were answers to questions posed by them. Hence, the connection of nearly all of the rulings with the so-called 'occasions of revelation' or the occasion with which the ruling was connected when revealed first. It must be added here that all *sharī'ah* rulings in Islam are regulated by one principle: the public good (*al-maṣlaḥah al-'āmah*). They exist either to bring some benefit or avert some harm. Thus, the *sharī'ah* rulings in Islam are grouped under three principles: abrogation (*al-naskh*), occasions of revelation (*asbāb alnuzūl*), and intents (*al-maqāṣid*).

This close connection between the *sharī'ah* rulings and the development of humanity, realized and supported by the above three principles (abrogation, occasion of revelation and [public] good or benefits), was clearly felt in the role taken by the Companions in legislating at the time of the Prophet. Many problems were brought to the attention of the Prophet when there was no revelation to solve them. So the Prophet used to consult the Companions, who would advise him according to their experience and evaluation of the good. When the Prophet approved of the advice, it became legislation. A revelation could come at the same time or shortly after, to endorse the advice of the Companions.

ʿUmar bin al-Khaṭṭāb was well known in this connection. He outshone the other Companions, and his *fatwās* (legal opinions) and advice were so often endorsed by the revelations that some scholars called these incidents 'ʿUmar's correspondences', and books were written on the subject. Some scholars mention certain *ḥadīth* celebrating these incidents. Ibn ʿUmar quotes the Prophet as saying, 'Allāh has put the truth on ʿUmar's tongue and in his heart'. He is also reported to have said, 'Each time the *ummah* was faced with a controversial case the revelation would descend to correspond with ʿUmar's view of it.' Mujāhid is reported to have said, 'ʿUmar used to express an opinion and the Qur'ān would have it as a new revelation'. It is also said that ʿUmar himself was aware of this and was undoubtedly proud of it. He is reported to have said:

> I was in agreement with my Lord on three occasions: I said, 'O Messenger of Allāh, what if we take Abraham's station as a prayer-place?!' The verse was then revealed 'And take Abraham's station a prayer place' (2, al-Baqarah, 125). I also remarked, 'O Messenger of Allāh, your wives are visited by good and evil men. What if you order them to take cover and veil?!' The verse on the *hijāb* was then revealed. Then the wives of the Messenger began to feel jealous of each other and I said to them, 'May he divorce you and his Lord will requite him with better wives'. So a verse was revealed to that effect.

Another story tells that ʿUmar had a certain opinion about the captives of the battle of Badr, and a later verse was revealed to correspond to ʿUmar's view. Other verses in the Qur'ān were revealed in the same version spoken by ʿUmar earlier. These verses were categorized as 'What was revealed of the Qur'ān on ʿUmar's tongue'.[10]

These correspondences of ʿUmar indicate that Islamic *sharīʿah* was revealed in accordance with the requirements of the current social situation; that is, to concur with the public good. The revelation did not come to ʿUmar, but his social experience, his subtle legal sense and his care to seek the good in his view of affairs were qualities that made his insight into social affairs correspond with the intents of *sharīʿah* which, in turn, has one basic objective, namely the public good. Hence, *ijtihād* was established as a source of legislation in Islam, as the *mujtahid* inevitably starts from a genuine desire to seek what is good and avoid what is evil in the issue under consideration. This principle of observing the public good was the basis on which the Companions relied in their application of *al-sharīʿah*, whether or not there existed a relevant text. The following are only a few examples of the many that give a clear idea of how the Companions went about the application of *sharīʿah*. We shall see how this was an interpretative experience *(ijtihād)* which stemmed from a consideration for the benefit of the *ummah*. When this benefit contradicted the text, the Companions preferred the benefit and ruled accordingly, thus deferring the application of the text.

The Messenger had adopted what nowadays would be called 'decentralization' in his relation with parts of the Arab peninsula, which had nearly all embraced Islam before his death. In the territories which accepted Islam by conquest, such as the Hijaz and Najd, he appointed his own rulers, but he left the other territories to their own chieftains as soon as they declared their acceptance of Islam. Since *al-zakāt* (mandatory Islamic alms tax) was the only duty that could be taken as a social and political criterion of those chieftains' commitment to Islam, the Prophet specified that *al-zakāt* should be paid to him. Thus *al-zakāt,* in this context, became a symbol of political allegiance, in addition to its religious and social significance. As a symbol of allegiance, many tribesmen considered the *zakāt* an imposed tribute on them, payable to the Prophet personally, as a chieftain to whom they owed allegiance. Therefore, many of them refused payment to Abū Bakr when he became Caliph, on the pretext that they used to pay *zakāt* in compliance with a contract or an agreement with the Prophet. Since those tribesmen continued to declare their commitment to Islam, their conduct was inevitably a cause for question among the Companions: Should they be considered 'apostates', like some tribes which declared their apostasy and renunciation of Islam, led by their chieftains and false prophets? Or, should they be given a special dispensation as they were still declaring their commitment to Islam?

That was the first question faced by the Companions about the application of *sharīʿah*, immediately after the death of the Prophet. Some Companions said, 'We should not fight them as unbelievers and apostates', and others said, 'We should'. ʿUmar favoured the party which would not fight, while Abū Bakr favoured fighting. Sources tell us of an argument between the two men, as ʿUmar objected strongly, saying, 'How can we fight them when the Messenger of Allāh said: "I was ordered to fight them until they declare there is no god but Allāh; and when they say it, they attain to sanctuary from me in their lives and property?".' It is reported that Abū Bakr replied, 'But has not the Prophet added after this, "except in what truth demands"?! Is it not among what "truth demands" to perform the *ṣalāt (prayers)* and pay *al-zakāt*?!' Then he added, 'By

Allāh, if they deny me so much as a piece of rope they used to turn over to the Messenger of Allāh I will fight them for it.' And he did.

Thus, the Companions found themselves at odds, to a contrariety, concerning this dangerous matter. Both sides presented justifiable arguments: the first side looked at the matter from a purely religious point of view; these were people who were still declaring their commitment to Islam. The text was clear on this matter: fighting them was not permissible. But the second side looked at the matter from the point of view of the 'state' only. *al-zakāt* was not merely a religious duty, which a person may pay himself to those who were entitled to it, as specified in the Qurʾān. It was, moreover, a symbol of political allegiance. Therefore, to continue paying *al-zakāt* to Abū Bakr meant a continued recognition of the head of the Muslim community (the state). Stopping it meant repudiating that recognition.

Abū Bakr held to his opinion and ʿUmar succumbed to the decision of the caliph who fought the apostates, including those who stopped payment of *al-zakāt*. Abū Bakr was victorious and he restored to the state its dignity and authority. It seems that ʿUmar remained throughout the caliphate of Abū Bakr, at least in his own deep conscience, of the opinion that it was not right to fight those who refused payment of *al-zakāt* as they remained committed to Islam. Therefore, as soon as he assumed the caliphate, after the death of Abū Bakr, he restored them to their previous esteem. He decided to 'return their captives and property and set free their prisoners and detainees'.

Thus, we find that the Caliph ʿUmar al-Khaṭṭāb applied *sharīʿah* according to his own *ijtihād,* even after Abū Bakr had applied it before him in the same case, in a different manner. No one, including the Companions, was disconcerted about applying the *sharīʿah* in two different ways to the same question. They understood the issue as it should be understood: Abū Bakr preferred the interest of the state when the state was in danger, so he fought those who refused to pay *al-zakāt*. ʿUmar assumed the caliphate when the state was well established, so he found it advisable to act in a spirit of reconciliation and to turn over a new page, in accordance with the principles of 'religion' and the text of the *ḥadīth* he quoted. Thus, here, the public good was observed in the application of *sharīʿah*. This does not mean that *al-sharīʿah* must change with the change of interests. Definitely not, as *al-sharīʿah* is fixed and absolute, due to its divine origin. But since the Legislator intends to realize what is beneficial and to protect against the harmful, and since the beneficial and the harmful are relative and they change according to changeable situations, the 'application' alone should change in accordance with the change of interests. The question is not a 'suspension' of the text, but a 'deferment' pending another manner of interpretation.

Another measure taken by ʿUmar, where he advanced the good of the *ummah* over the letter of the text, was his decision not to divide the land of Iraq among the victorious warriors, but to impose a land tax (*al-kharāj*) as a substitute. Here, again, we find ʿUmar giving the priority to the [public] good over the text: the future interest of the Muslims rather than the interest of some of them at that moment in time. The Qur'ān clearly specifies that movable and immovable booty should be divided among those who take part in the conquest, including the land. But when the Muslims occupied the fertile land of Iraq, there ensued an argument among the Companions. Some of them wanted to follow the Qur'ānic text to the letter, but ʿUmar bin al-Khaṭṭāb was thinking of the future and successive generations; so he objected and said, 'What about the Muslims of tomorrow who will come to see the land and the property divided and inherited from the fathers? That is not the right opinion!' 'Abd al-Raḥmā bin 'Auf said to ʿUmar, 'And what is the right opinion?! The land and the property are gifts from God to the warriors!' ʿUmar answered:

> It is so! But I am not of your opinion. By God, no territory should be conquered after me to form a great gain, but be a burden on the Muslims. If we were to divide the land and the property of Iraq and Syria, how are we going to provide for the towns and the forts? What is going to be left for posterity and the widows in these countries of Syria and Iraq?

Discussion heated up between ʿUmar and the supporters of division. So he consulted the Companions, saying, 'I suggest that we exempt the land and the property and impose the land tax, instead', pointing to the public good in his opinion. Then he added:

> Do you not see that these towns and forts need men to manage their affairs? Do you not see that these great cities in Syria and Iraq such as Damascus, al-Jazirah, Kufa, Basra, and Cairo need to provide other forts and territories with men and provide for their sustenance, to guard against the return of the unbelievers to those lands?!

The Companions he consulted said, 'We see your point'. And the land tax was imposed.[11]

It is well known that the Qur'ān mentioned 'those whose hearts are reconciled [to the Truth]' among those who deserve *al-zakāt*. The Messenger used to offer a portion of *al-zakāt* to some Qurayshi chieftains who were late in accepting Islam, and even to some who had not yet embraced Islam, in order to encourage them to do so. It is on record that he said, 'I would like to offer to this man and that to have their hearts reconciled.' When Abū Bakr assumed the caliphate, he followed in the steps of the Messenger in this respect and answered the request of two such men 'whose hearts were to be reconciled' to allot a piece of land to them. When 'Umar heard of that, he became angry and said to the two men: 'When the Messenger of Allāh used to try to incline your hearts to Islam, the Muslims were a minority. But Allāh has enriched Islam. Go about your business and exert yourselves!' This shows clearly that Abū Bakr applied *sharī'ah* according to a Qur'ānic text and emulated the Prophet in this respect. But 'Umar was of the opinion that there was no longer any need to give anything to those 'whose hearts were to be reconciled'. This should not be looked upon as a suspension of the text; it was rather a return to what may be considered the 'original benefit' of *al-zakāt*, which is to alleviate the plight of the poor and needy. Moreover, it discards a 'subsidiary benefit', which is to attract those whose hearts ought to be reconciled [to Islam], an interest which was only temporary and is then valid no longer.

Among the issues where the Companions applied the *sharī'ah* with a consideration for the circumstances, not in accordance with the letter of the text, is the issue of amputating the hand of the thief. It is well known that 'Umar prohibited such amputation in the 'Year of Famine'. It is reported that some young boys stole a female camel from a man, who went complaining to 'Umar. The Caliph called in the employer of those boys and reprimanded him by saying, 'I find that you are starving these boys!' Then he asked the owner of that camel how much the animal was worth and ordered the employer of the boys to pay the price to the owner, letting the boys to go unpunished. Then he said to the employer, 'If I did not think that you use and starve them to the extent that when they find themselves before what Allāh has proscribed they would eat it, I would have cut off [their hands]. But, by Allāh, since I let them alone, I will fine you in a manner most painful.' A similar anecdote is related about Ibn 'Abbās when a slave was brought to him, having stolen a donkey and slaughtered it. The slave said, 'I feared I would starve to death!' Ibn 'Abbās released the slave without amputation and ordered the slave master to pay for the stolen donkey. It was also related that 'Umar was told of a man who stole from the *bayt al-māl* (public treasury). 'Umar said, 'His hand should not be amputated, as he has some right to that *bayt al-māl*.' Again, when a slave stole the mirror of his master's wife, 'Umar said, 'No amputation! Your servant stole your own property!'

It is also reported of the Prophet that he said, 'No hand amputation should be performed during a journey' or 'during a campaign', in a different report. Zayd bin Thābit is reported to have said, '*Ḥudūd* punishments are not to be enforced in wartime, for fear those punishable may desert to the ranks of the enemy.' Hudhayfah is reported to have ordered that the penalty for drinking should not be imposed on an army leader, for fear the enemy might use that for their own benefit. This is what *fuqahāʾ* call 'deferring the penalty due to a contingency'. A similar measure is taken when a woman is pregnant or breastfeeding, when a person is sick and in severe cold or hot weather, as enforcing *ḥudūd* penalties in such conditions may lead to harming the person concerned in a manner not intended by *sharīʿah*. This is acting for the good of the person penalized. Thus, [public] good should always be given priority in the application of *sharīʿah*.

Wine drinking has no specified revealed penalty. Once a drunk man was brought before the Prophet, who said to the Companions who happened to be with him, 'Give him a beating!' Some hit the man with their hands, some with the tail of their garments, others with a slipper! When the man went away, some of those present shouted behind him, 'May Allāh put you to shame!' The Messenger reprimanded them: 'Do not say that. Do not support Satan against him!'

The punishment for drinking continued along the lines of reprimanding and beating without specifying the number of strokes. During the caliphate of ʿUmar, his army general Khālid bin al-Walīd complained to him that people had taken to wine drinking, finding the punishment of beating too light to worry about. ʿUmar consulted the Companions and 'Alī bin Abī Ṭālib said, 'When a man is drunk he begins to talk nonsense, and when he does that he begins to tell lies. A liar is given 80 lashes.' So ʿUmar said, 'Let him be given 80 lashes like a liar'. So, when wine drinking was not widespread, the penalty was light. But when it increased and became a threat to social relations, and a cause of disruption and quarrelling, the penalty became more severe, as it was necessary to guard against harm.

Similar to that, marrying women from the 'People of the Book', namely Jewish and Christian, is permitted in the Qur'ān. Nonetheless, certain situations led ʿUmar to prohibit such marriages. It is said that Hudhayfah married a Jewish woman, and when ʿUmar heard of it he wrote to Hudhayfah asking him to divorce his Jewish wife. When Hudhayfah enquired about the reason, as the Qur'ān permits such marriage, ʿUmar said, 'I fear that others may have contact with the prostitutes among them.'

Another report says ʿUmar's answer was, 'I fear that other Muslims may follow suit and choose their wives from among the People of the Book for their beauty, to the detriment of Muslim women.' ʿUmar did not apply the Qur'ānic text in this matter because he preferred the original aim, which is avoiding harm. Although harm had not occurred yet in that case, the possibility was there, especially that the times were those of recruitment and conquests. Muslims returned to the text when circumstances changed and the expected harm from marrying a non-Muslim woman became minimal or improbable.

These are samples of *sharīʿah* application at the time of the Companions, all of which prove that they looked at the 'application' from the point of view of the ensuing benefit or harm. al-Juwaynī, *imām* of the Two Sanctuaries, says:

> If we look into the conduct of the Companions, who are the example to be emulated, we cannot see in their consultation councils any reference to an origin (*aṣl*) or significance to base the incident upon [as the *fuqahā'* do in their analogical reasoning (*qiyās*)]. They used to study the various aspects of opinion without reference to the origins (*uṣūl*), whether they existed or not.

By 'origins' he means the principles laid down by *fuqahā'* for their schools of legal thought (*madhāhib*). Then he adds:

> The Companions of the Messenger did not use procedures similar to those devised by the dialecticians of these [our] days in order to identify a source (*aṣl*) and deduce a ruling there from, thus emulating a familiar pattern. Instead, they used to make their own judgments and relate them to the public interests in their councils of consultation.

Public interest was the only 'source' adopted by the Companions in their application of *sharīʿah* judgments. When jurisprudence developed along 'theoretical' lines, superseding the actual events and incidents, it moved to the possible and probable. Hypotheses and imaginary cases were put forth, and *fuqahā'* were obliged to define principles for jurisprudential judgments, with branches and details, whether realistic or hypothetical. Then some branches became origins for other branches, and so on. All those realistic and hypothetical cases were governed by situations and dominant circumstances, all of which were closely alike.

Now that social and economic situations have developed to such an extent that make modern life fundamentally different from what it was like in the past, the application of *al-sharīʿah* requires a reorganization of the origins based solely on a consideration of the public good, as the Companions used to do. In other words, to apply *al-sharīʿah* in a manner compatible with the present age requirements demands founding a new authority for application. The only authority that should supersede all others is that of the Companions' conduct. It is the only authority that could bring all the Muslims together, around one opinion, because it was prior to all schools of thought and conflicting opinions. It is also suitable for every time and place, because it is based on the public good.

## Notes

1. The Arabic root j-h-d connotes 'struggle' or 'effort' and from it derives the term *jihād* – which connotes a struggle – military or other. *ijtihād* is a process of independent reasoning whereby a *mujtahid* (pl., *mujtahidūn*) struggles to interpret the original source materials (*al-uṣūl*) of Islamic law (*al-sharī'ah*) and derive a new ruling in conformity with what he determines to be the original intents (*maqāṣid*) of the law most often with consideration of historical precedents in Islamic jurisprudence (*al-fiqh*).

2. The term *marja'īyah* coming from a root which means 'to return' or 'to go back [to something]' connotes in its usage here an 'authoritative referent' or 'point of reference' – wherein a historical personage or even provides the basis for judgment in regard to a particular issue, problem or model. In *fiqh*, *al-marja'īyah* has become 'institutionalized' (to varying degrees) where a religious scholar or jurisprudent (*'ālim or faqīh*) has attained to a rank where he may be consulted on matters of Islamic law and subsequently 'imitated' as an 'authoritative recourse for imitation' – *marja'al-taqlīd*. The author uses it extensively throughout this text generally in reference to historical precedents and events which can be taken as 'authoritative referents' for various concepts and ideas wherein, for example, the European Renaissance serves as such for many seminal, modern Western concepts.

3. al-Jabri, M.A., *The Arab Political Mind*, in Arabic (Beirut: Arab Unity Research Centre, 1990), Part I, Ch. 4.

4. Ibid, para. 3.

5. In the year 622CE, the 12th year of revelation, Muḥammad and his followers were forced to 'emigrate' from Mecca to the city of Yathrīb – later to become known as al-Madīnah (Medina) – 'the city [of the Prophet]'. The year of the immigration (*al-hijrah*) later served as 'year one' in the Muslim calendar, and those first Muslims 'who emigrated' came to be known as the Muhājirūn, whereas those who became Muslims among the tribes of Medina and who were 'helpers' came to be known as the Anṣār. Previous to the *hijrah*, Muḥammad concluded two pacts known as the first and second treaties of al-'Aqabah (621CE) with emissaries from the city of Yathrīb, who sought his arbitration in the relentless ongoing blood feud between two of its most powerful tribes al-Aws and al-Khazraj. On the day of the Prophet's death (the 12th of Rabī' al-Awwal 11AH/8 June 632CE) members of the Anṣār convened a meeting in the bower (saqīfah) of one of the Medinan tribes to choose a new leader. Abū Bakr and 'Umar bin al-Khaṭṭāb hastened to prevent such a decision, and while ultimately the '*amr*' remained in the hands of the Muhājirūn, the seeds for the great schism in Islam were planted between those who would read history from that day forward as a *khilāfah* (caliphate) of the Rāshidūn ('rightly-guided') – that is, Sunnī Muslims, and those who did not recognize the legitimacy of that pledge (*bay'ah*) and would become known as the *shī'at* 'Alī (partisans of 'Alī) or simply al-Shī'ah.

6. The term *ummah* may be translated as 'nation' or as 'community' – which is often the preferred term, especially given its modern usage where the Muslim *ummah* often refers, at least conceptually, to the international trans-border 'community of believers'. The term derives from the same root as the Arabic word for mother *umm*; and Mecca is referred to in the Qur'ān as *umm al-qurā* – 'the mother of villages'.

7. The 'first *fitnah*' (period of strife) in Islam is that in which Muslims shed the blood of other Muslims beginning with the assassination of the third caliph of the Rāshidūn 'Uthmān bin 'Affān in his house in Medina on the 19th of Dhū-l-Hijjah 35AH/17 July 656 CE as a result of numerous disputes including conduct of governors he had appointed in Egypt and Iraq. The following day, Alī bin Abī Ṭālib was declared caliph in the Prophet's mosque and he set out several days later for Kufah, Iraq which he made his new capital. For whatever reasons, 'Alī did not prosecute

'Uthmān's assassins and this led to a dispute of his caliphal office, led chiefly by 'Uthmān's cousin Mu'āwiyah, the governor of Damascus. The matter was further complicated when the Prophet's favourite wife 'Ā'ishah went (on the back of a camel) into battle against 'Alī along with two of Muḥammad's closest Companions Ṭalḥah and Zubayr, who were killed in the so-called 'Battle of the Camel' outside Basra. Between the 8th and 10th of Safar, 37AH/26-28 July, 657CE, forces of Mu'āwiyah fought the major engagement against those of 'Alī in the Battle of Ṣiffīn. When Mu'āwiyah's commander 'Āmr bin al-'Āṣ ordered his fighters to raise copies of the Qur'ān on their lances, 'Alī called off the fighting and agreed to submit to arbitration (ultimately inconclusive when held in Ramadan 37AH/February 658CE) but which precipitated a split in 'Alī's forces who 'went out' and thus became known as al-Khawārij. They asserted that 'Alī's claim to the caliphate was indisputable and that he should never have submitted to negotiation. Ultimately, the Khawārij would adopt the position that 'there is judgment except Allah's' (*lā ḥukmah illā li-lāh*), and that any upright Muslim was fit to rule. Their rebellion went to the extreme that 'Alī was obliged to fight them and decimate their ranks in the Battle of al-Nahrawān (9th of Safar, 38AH). One of the survivors Ibn Muljam would inflict a mortal wound on 'Alī 19th of Ramadan (661CE) who died two days later. The legacy of the Khawārij would, however, survive in contributing an alternative theory of political rule to those of the major Sunnī and Shī'ī schools of thought.

8. al-Shahrastānī, A.F.M.A.K., Summa in al-'ilm al-Kalām (*nihāyat al-iqdām fi ḫilm al-kalām*), in Arabic; also al-Ījī, A.F., *The Positions* (*al-mawāqif*).
9. al-Shahrastānī, op. cit.
10. al-Suyūṭī, *Perfection of Qur'ānic Knowledge* (*al-itqān fi 'ulūm al-qur'ān*).
11. Abū Yūsuf, *The Book of Excise* (*kitāb al-kharāj*), p. 14.

# Part One
# The Question of Religion and the State

CHAPTER 1

# Religion and the State in the Authoritative Cultural Referent

## Execution of Rulings

Nothing can obscure the vision like spurious questions which lead to emotional bewilderment and intellectual aberration. Such questions, like those asked by children, pose fantastic hypothetical problems, yet they are perceived as real problems. The danger of the spurious question is it demands an equally specious answer, which, in turn, raises further intractable problems. This is because every question asked carries implicitly with it an initiative for an answer. But when a question is posed in the form of a dichotomy, such as 'Is Islam a religion or a state?', it puts the person asked, and consequently the mind, before a binary conceptual division, constrained to either the proposition that 'Islam is a religion, not a state' or that 'Islam is a religion and a state'. The third possibility, 'Islam is a state, not a religion', is inconceivable, because Islam, by definition, is a religion.

Spurious questions, in most cases, do not stem from problems in reality but rather from problems conjured by the imagination or informed by abstract metaphysical thoughts. Such questions may obtrude upon a certain field a problem which derives its content and definitions from another. The dichotomy of religion and state, in modern Arab thought, falls into this category of problem. The question of whether Islam is a religion or a state had never been asked in Islamic thought from the rise of Islam until the mid-nineteenth century. It was brought forth in the context of [the Arab revival], foreign to Islamic thought, with roots and terminology found in the European civilizational model which the Arabs were and are yet still aspiring to emulate in their own countries, especially in that which pertains to progress and revival.

It is true that problems may not be transferred from one field to another, except when the other field offers something to somehow justify that transference. In other words, external influences cannot be effective except where there is a prior 'internal' readiness. Yet, even in that case, the transferred object remains alien and causes problems and frictions inside the new sphere, except when the new sphere is fully and successfully acclimatized. The problem of 'the relation between religion and the state', as it was transferred to the Arab sphere in the nineteenth and early twentieth centuries, has not yet been acclimatized to suit the Arab intellectual and civilizational reality to a degree that makes it really expressive of the aspirations of that reality, and not the aspirations of the European reality from which it was transferred.

I will try, then, to achieve a liberation from the tethers of the spurious question by subjecting the question itself to a process of questioning. Once cleared of falsifying factors, that question can be restated in a manner expressive of the Arab reality: its distinctive past and present givens, and of the future aspirations of the Arab nation. To do that, I will address the subject in four stages. Each stage will deal with one aspect of the problem as it has been addressed in modern and contemporary Arab thought. First, I will explore how the problem should be addressed within the context of the traditional authoritative referent, in order to find the [endemic] solutions sought within that authority. Second, I will analyse the answer of that traditional authority. Third, I will examine the way the problem has been addressed from the standpoint of the authoritative referent for the modern and contemporary Arab renaissance. Fourth, and finally, I will examine the relation between this problem and the current Arab reality and its future horizons.

I do not intend to make an academic analysis of the problem of traditional authority, but rather define the problem in a manner that makes it easy to understand. I believe the most serious impediment to communication among the various currents of contemporary Arab thought is that each is isolated within its own authoritative point of reference, ignoring or repudiating any other authority, or categorizing the other as 'ideological' and thus nullifying rival opinion.

The traditional authoritative referent (*al-marjaʿīyah al-turāthīyah*) for the relation between 'religion and the state' emanates from Islamic intellectual and political history, especially the official analects – in the period from the rise of Islam to the early nineteenth century. It is the period when Islam formed a self-sufficient civilization, where there were no problems except those that stemmed from within and so indigenous solutions were found therein. This self-sufficient 'closed circuit', with its own internal problems, is the isolated world of the majority of Arab intellectuals, including both the old religious *ʿulamāʾ* and the young intellectuals. The foundation principle of this referential authority, which directs all its movements, is that whatever is placed in apposition to Islam is alien to

Islam. When the dichotomy of 'religion and state' is posed in its original, European context, which calls for a separation between religion and state, the perception engendered by our traditional authoritative referent would deem it a 'violation of Islam' and an open conspiracy to destroy Islam.

To understand why this is the case, rash accusations of fanaticism and narrow-mindedness have to be avoided. These can do more harm than good. In addition, such accusations betray a lack of understanding of the dimensions of thought based on the traditional referential authority.

Let us look, therefore, into the way this separation between religion and state is seen through our traditional authoritative referent which cannot entertain such dichotomy, since throughout Islamic history 'religion' (*al-dīn*) was never separate from the 'state'(*al-dawlah*), nor existed as a state which accepts having religion separated from it. It is true that some rulers were criticized for being lenient about certain religious duties such as *jihād* or fighting heresies. But no ruler in Islamic history dared declare his dissociation from religion, as no ruler could find legitimacy for his rule without declaring that his duty was to serve the religion and uphold its cause. On the other hand, in no period of Islamic history was there any religious institution separate from the state. The jurisprudents did not form an institution by themselves. They were individuals who interpreted religion and gave consultative opinions about incidents and issues, or problems caused by certain social developments.

The phrase 'separating religion from state', or 'separating state from religion', would mean, in the context of the traditional referential authority, the setting up of an atheist, non-Islamic state, or the deprivation of Islam from the 'authority' which must execute the judgments or both. It is possible to convince someone who thinks within the context of the traditional referential authority alone that the matter is not concerned with setting up an atheistic state or the de-Islamization of society. You may do your best to convince them that it is neither this nor that, but all they would say is, 'Only God knows!' Then they would fall silent. But you can never convince such a person that separating religion from state does not mean depriving Islam from the 'authoritative body' which must be entrusted with the execution of judgments. Therefore, I must begin by distinguishing the authority which executes the *sharī'ah* rulings from that social institution which is called 'state'. This is because religion in the eyes of such a person involves rulings (*aḥkām*) which must be executed, and the state is the authority which should handle that implementation. Therefore, the initial question, 'Is Islam a religion and a state?', cannot be significantly answered from within the Islamic cultural experience except when rephrased by replacing the word 'religion' with the word 'rulings', and the word 'state' by the word 'authority' (*sulṭah*). How, then, should we understand this new version of the question?

## The Caliphate and the Balance of Power

The relationship between religion and state, in the traditional referential authority, is defined by the following historical fact: Islam appeared in a society that had no state. The Islamic Arab state rose gradually, but rather fast: first, due to the expansion of Islam and the victorious campaigns of the Prophet, especially the conquest of Mecca; and, second, because of the expansion of conquests and the rise of the Arabs as a world power who consequently entered into far-reaching international relations.

This is an indisputable historical fact. But it is not easy to explain this fact and derive one legislative result therefrom. The evidence that might support one point of view is tantamount to that which could support a contrary point of view. Therefore, on the one hand, it is not possible at all to be certain whether the Prophet had among his aims, early in his call (*al-da'wah*), the establishment of a state. There is no evidence in the *ḥadīth*, or in what is reported of the Companions, that may indicate such a desire. On the contrary, there is recurrent evidence that the Prophet rejected repeatedly the offer made by the Meccans, at the start of his mission, to make him their chieftain if he would abandon the call to his new religion. This shows definitively, at least in the beginning, that the aim of the Prophet was to promulgate the new religion, not to set up a state or gain a leadership. There is nothing in the Qur'ān which clearly indicates that the Islamic mission was one to establish a state, a kingship or an empire.

On the other hand, there are two other indisputable facts: One, the Qur'ān includes rulings which Muslims are ordered to abide by, and some of those require an authority to represent the community in executing those judgments, such as the punishment of theft by amputation of the hand. Two, the execution of these rulings, which cover *jihād* and campaigning in the cause of Islam, had led to the development of the Islamic call into an organized state with institutions that expanded along with the expansion of the Muslim world – geographically, culturally and intellectually.

In addition to these four comparable facts which do not render a decisive conclusion on the subject, there is the Islamic historical experience and the jurisprudential thought as its theoretical basis.

It is historically known that the first serious argument that broke out among the Muslims is their disagreement, immediately after the death of the Prophet, about the appointment of his successor. Both the Muhājirūn [immigrants from Mecca] and the Anṣār [native inhabitants of Medina and 'helpers'] thought they had the right to provide a successor, namely the caliph, and that he should be one chosen from among them. Judging from historical analects, it seems that the theoretical and legitimate arguments of both parties were equally tenable. What settled the matter in the end was the reminder by the Muhājirūn to the Anṣār that 'the Arabs will not follow except this quarter of Quraysh'. This meant that the only tribe qualified to lead was Quraysh, so it tipped the balance of power that decided the matter in the end. Hence, 'From us one prince, from you another' was an idea defeated, and all power was left in the hands of the Muhājirūn as they swore the *bay'ah* to Abū Bakr as a caliph after the Prophet. So Abū Bakr declared, 'We are the princes, you the ministers', addressing the Anṣār.

The meeting of the immigrants and Anṣār in the bower of Banī Sāʿidah to choose the caliph was the main frame of reference, if not the only one, on which the Sunni *fuqahā'* relied in formulating their theory of the caliphate. Although the *fuqahā'* did their best to lend Islamic legitimacy to all the rulers known in the history of Islam, they remained committed to the proceedings of the meeting at the bower of Banī Sāʿidah. They considered those proceedings and their results as Islamic precedents which have the force of law or a 'source' (*aṣl*) on which can be based new rules. This origin comprised three main elements, the first of which was reducing the entire issue down to 'who will succeed the Prophet'.

So, who would be chosen to manage the affairs of the Muslims? The Sunni theory of the caliphate does not pose the state as an institution; it is only concerned with the person who will be chosen to rule the people by the Book of Allāh and the *sunnah* of His Messenger, for an indefinite period of time, and without any conditions as to institutions, channels or the machinery through which he will exercise the absolute power he was given. This is because the Islamic community delegates the rule completely to the caliph including the executive means, the build up of the government system, the choice of ministers and assistants, etc. Moreover, that community does not reserve the right to monitor the actions of the ruler, because, as soon as homage is paid to him and he is elected caliph, he becomes responsible before God and not before the people who elected him. Hence, the people have only to obey, as long as the orders and the rules of the caliph do not fall under the Islamic principle which says 'There is no obedience of the created in disobedience to the Creator'.

The second element in the Sunni theory of the caliphate is the oneness of the caliph; that is, a single caliph in all the countries of Islam. This one caliph, though, may delegate someone to rule in his name, from among the ministers or governors. Yet, on the theoretical, jurisprudential level, the caliph of the Muslims remains one, and it is not possible to recognize the legitimacy of more than one caliph. When the Umayyad caliphate was established in al-Andalus, and the Fatimid in Cairo, in addition to the ʿAbbāsid caliphate in Baghdad, each one of those considered itself, and was considered by its followers, to be the only legitimate caliphate. Naturally, this is the theoretical and jurisprudential view. But in reality, the Muslim countries have witnessed several contemporaneous states, competitive and sometimes fighting with each other. Yet, all of them were or have been Islamic states.

The third element is that the caliphate, according to the Sunnis, is by 'choice' (*al-ikhtiyār*) and not by 'textual specification' (*al-naṣṣ*). This principle is contrary to the Shīʿites' opinions. The supporting argument to this principle is that since the Companions exchanged opinions after the death of the Prophet and disagreed, then they agreed to pay homage to Abū Bakr, it means that the Messenger did not assign anyone to the caliphate after him. But 'choice' in the Sunni theory did not go beyond saying the Prophet did not specify anyone to succeed him. As for the manner of choosing the caliph, it was to be decided by the balance of powers. The caliph who claims the caliphate for himself wins by virtue of his might and rallies the people around him, regardless of their will for or against it. It is true that the majority in early Islamic times specified the caliph be from Quraysh. But this condition was challenged by other parties because it lacked a clearly legitimate basis in *al-sharīʿah*. Whatever the case, the decisive factor was power, not lineage. This is precisely the sort of homage which usually followed the victory of pretenders to the caliphate, which renders the *bayʿah* a kind of acceptance of a fait accompli.

Therefore, the Sunni theory of the caliphate is generally an attempt to legalize an accomplished fact. Consequently there was no great difference between the theories of *fuqahā'* on the caliphate and the actual forms of rule in Islam. The only invariable point in the traditional authority is that there are judgments specified in the Qur'ān that need for their execution 'one in charge' as a representative of the Islamic community. The concept of one in charge in Islam is so wide that it can mean the head of the family, the tribal chieftain, the *faqīh* or the Muslim ruler in *dār al-Islām* (the territories of Islam), whether he be a governor, a prince or a caliph. It is worthy of note in this connection that the term occurs in the plural in the Qur'ān: 'O you who believe! Obey Allāh and obey the Messenger, and those given authority among you' (4, al-Nisā', 59). This indicates that it is not necessary according to *al-sharīʿah* to have only one person in charge.

Therefore, since the Prophet had left the matter to his Companions to decide after him what they and what the caliphs did after them, what the *fuqahāʾ* said about the caliphate is all a matter of *ijtihād* (consultative opinion). The results of *ijtihād* concerning any matter left for Muslims to decide will certainly vary with times and circumstances. Again, the only certain thing in *al-sharīʿah* is that there are rulings that require 'someone in charge' to execute. As for the Islamic state, it was, since the meeting at the bower of Banī Sāʿidah, a state where the Muslims decided matters according to what was dictated to them by the balance of power, morals and material. And, since they were all Muslims, or at least they behaved as such, the issue of the relation between 'state' and 'religion' was never posed for discussion, nor could it ever be. It was not a viable question, because Islam was embodied in everything in Muslim society, except what was proscribed by the Qurʾān or forbidden by the Messenger. There is no text which commits the Muslims to a certain type of rule, nor one that prohibits them from another type. This is what led some sectarian leaders to argue about the possibility of doing without a caliph completely, and ultimately the state, so long as everyone performs his religious duties, which would eliminate the need for a ruler.

## The Caliphate: Constitutional Flaws

It is noticeable that authors and writers on 'contemporary Islamic thought', whether moderates or zealots, do not elaborate on the basic needs of our age, and occupy themselves with what is less significant compared with the challenges that face us today. There are those categorized under what is termed the 'Islamic Trend', who raise the banner of 'Islam is the solution'. This is posing something of a moot issue when declaimed in the face of Muslims, as a person cannot be Muslim if he does not believe that Islam suits every time and place, and it is always the solution, in the same manner that a Christian, a Jew or a Buddhist feels about his own religion. Yet, those who raise such a slogan intend to use it as a political ideology in the face of other ideologies. In this case, discussion should deal with the content of this ideology in connection with certain situations and concerning certain issues.

The question which is raised here is: What are the implications of this political slogan, 'Islam is the solution', intended by those who proclaim it? Here, everyone interested in this issue is lost in a vacuum. One wonders: What is the political system that permits a description as Islamic and remains, at the same time, in harmony with our times and responsive to the needs and development of history? It does not suffice to say that government in Islam is based on consultation (*al-shūrā*), justice (*al-ʿadl*) and brotherhood (*al-ikhāʾ*), as all religions and all political and social ideologies profess such maxims, because they express eternal human values and ideals to which all human beings aspire, in all times.

Since neither the Qur'ān nor the *sunnah* include a legislative text which regulates the issue of government, and since the Prophet died without assigning a successor or the way of choosing a successor, nor did he define the particular qualities of one or specify the duration of his rule, the entire issue remained within those affairs connoted by the Prophet's own words: 'You are better informed about your worldly affairs.'[1] The issue, then, is left for 'wisdom' and '*ijtihād*'. Consequently, when 'Islam is the solution' is proclaimed as a political motto, it remains void of meaning, unless those who subscribe to it advance certain clear and detailed ideas about the political issue, especially that of government.

*Ijtihād* in Islam, and in all religions and schools of thought, does not arise in a vacuum, since nothing comes out of nothing. Furthermore, *ijtihād* in Islam can either be exercised in matters which may fall under the rubric of a ruling of *al-sharī'ah* based on a text, or in matters which lack a textual basis. In the latter case, the public good (*al-maṣlaḥah*) dictated by the times becomes the authoritative referent, the Islamic morality becomes the guide, and the historical experience of the *ummah* is the focus of consideration.

To begin with the last point, we may ask: What is the basic lesson learned from the historical experience of the Arab nation in the area of government? An answer on which no one can disagree may be put as follows: The major political incident in Arab-Islamic history is the conversion of the caliphate into kingship. The inevitable question here is: Why was the caliphate converted into a kingship? Why was the political crisis, which developed towards the end of 'Uthmān's caliphate, not handled in a political and constitutional manner, to put an end to the deterioration of the situation and save the *ummah* the seditions and the civil wars which ended with the 'conversion of the caliphate into kingship'?

If we wanted to derive political lessons from the events of the 'great *fitnah*', during the last six years of 'Uthmān's term, it is inevitable to conclude that what happened was caused by a large constitutional vacuum in the system of government which was established after the death of the Prophet. Present-day observers such as ourselves perceive this void as the result of three main issues:

(i) The absence of one specific manner for the appointment of the Caliph: Abū Bakr was appointed under exceptional and hasty circumstances. It was a 'slip of the tongue', as 'Umar put it, meaning that it was done without prior arrangement. However, the hurried meeting of Anṣār at the bower of Banī

Sā'idah to choose a caliph from among them, joined later by the immigrants, the heated arguments, and the conflicting opinions in that meeting (which could have ended in an open confrontation), led to 'Umar's initiative to declare the *bay'ah* to Abū Bakr, followed by both the immigrants and the Anṣār. That was a better settlement of the matter than if there had been no haste.

Abū Bakr was the first among the Companions to gain the people's approval of his choice. He avoided a recurrence of the previous slip-up by appointing 'Umar after consulting the people and securing their approval. And 'Umar was equally wary when he appointed six of the Companions to choose one from among them to succeed him in the caliphate, when 'Uthmān was their choice. Hence, there was no one way to appoint the Caliph, and the issue was open to all forms of *ijtihād* and all possibilities, too. If it were possible to relate the roots of the revolt against 'Uthmān to the contention between his supporters and those who supported 'Alī, during the days of 'consultation' that ended with appointing 'Uthmān as Caliph, it would be safe to say that the political ambiguity and the bloody *fitnah*, which ended in the murder of 'Uthmān, would have been avoided had there not been a constitutional vacuum. (This is obvious, in addition to what is asserted in the next two points.)

(ii) The absence of a text specifying the term of office for the Caliph: This is understandable when we remember that the basic duty of the Caliph, at that time, was to be a 'commander' (*amīr*) over the Muslims, leading their struggle in the 'wars against apostasy' first, and later in the campaigns to propagate Islam. In the old Arabic sense, the 'commander' was the leader of the army in the battle. Since no one could predict how long the war would continue, it was not conceivable to determine the period of the 'rule' of that commander. His term would last as long as there was a war, except if he were deposed or killed, then another person would be appointed to replace him. But his duty would certainly come to an end with the end of the war, then he would lose the title of 'commander' and resume his former place. Since there was no legislative text, either in the Qur'ān or the Sunnah, to regulate the question of rule, and since the Arabs had no established traditions in the fields of government and state, the model that was present in the conception of the Muslims after the death of the Prophet was that of the 'commander of the army'. That was the dominant model in the Arab political mind at the time. Thus, when the Companions chose Abū Bakr as a caliph to succeed the Prophet, they did that so he would succeed him in managing the affairs of the nascent state, foremost among which was fighting the apostates. Therefore, they chose him as a Commander General of the Muslim armies. It is not conceivable that they would specify the length of his term of office. When Abū Bakr died, only two years after his appointment, and 'Umar was chosen to succeed him, people started to call him 'Caliph, or Caliph of the Messenger of Allāh'. 'Umar did not savour that title and preferred 'commander of the faithful', which was used by someone who addressed him. 'Umar liked the title because he felt it expressed the essence of his duties, which were to command the Muslim armies in the wars they were fighting against the apostates, first, and later against the Persians in Iraq and the Byzantines in Syria. Therefore, 'Umar was a commanding general of the Muslim armies, and a supreme commander over the army commanders. It was not conceivable that his term of office would be specified while the Muslims were fighting their major wars of conquest. 'Umar was assassinated while the war was ongoing, and 'Uthmān was chosen to succeed him for the same duties, and, again, it was not conceivable to specify his term of office, for the same reason.

The new phenomenon that occurred with the tenure of 'Uthmān is that his term extended until 'people were bored with him'. He was in his seventies when he was chosen. In his later years, many problems developed, and the contention led to a constitutional crisis. The Caliph was very old and was surrounded by relatives and people with selfish interests to serve. They made the decisions for him and were not always doing the right thing. Advice did not help to improve the situation, as the 'pressure groups' and the 'decision makers' around the Caliph knew how to make him retract his promises of renege. So the rebels had no choice but to demand his resignation. But how? And who would manage the affairs after him? By what 'law' or precedent would he be asked to resign? It was a serious constitutional crisis which could not be solved except by blood: 'In the absence of the law, the sword has the word.'

(iii) The absence of a definition of caliphal authority: This was the case when Abū Bakr 'Umar and 'Uthmān were chosen for the caliphate. The reason is that the model of the 'commander of the army', which dominated the Arab political mind at the time, did not allow for the discussion of the issue of authority. This issue was not among 'the thought of issues' at the time of the conquests, war booty and expansion in the world. But with the growth of affluence and the emergence of some objectionable phenomena, the question of authority asserted itself. It was zealously argued when the rebels against 'Uthmān registered objections, which can be reduced to one issue, namely that he had overstepped his authority, by nepotism and disposing of one-fifth of the war booty, etc. When the revolt erupted against him, he addressed the people, saying, 'What have you lost of your dues? I have not done what my predecessor did not do (meaning 'Umar) and you did not, then, object. There was a surplus of funds, so why should I not dispose of it the way I see fit? Why am I a leader then?' When they said to him, 'Dismiss your corrupt

> governors and appoint others under whom we feel safe about our lives and property, and amend the wrong that was done to us', ʿUthmān said, 'I find myself stripped of power if I were to appoint the people you approve, and dismiss the ones you do not. The power will be yours, then!'

Thus, the third constitutional flaw was revealed through the words of the Caliph himself. He rejected the criticism and the demands of the rebels because he felt that it was his prerogative to dispense with the 'surplus of funds' the way he saw fit; and it was his prerogative alone to choose governors and officials; and that the *amr* (power and authority) would lose its constituency and significance if it were stripped of these prerogatives. The rebels were supported by major Companions such as 'Ammar ibn Yasir, Ṭalḥah, al-Zubair and 'Alī ibn Abi-Talib himself. They could not accept unlimited powers for the Caliph, so they said to ʿUthmān, 'By Allāh, you have to do [what we advise] otherwise, step down or you will be killed. So, choose for yourself.' He refused, and insisted on staying in power, saying, 'By God, I will not discard a mantle bestowed on me by God.' So they besieged him for 40 days, then a group climbed up the walls of his residence, led by Muḥammad ibn Abī Bakr. ʿUthmān was killed while he was reading the Qur'ān in his hands.

Thus, there is no system of government legislated by Islam. A system was developed with the *da'wah* of Muḥammad, based in the beginning, after the death of the Prophet, on the model of the commander of war, which was dictated by the times and circumstances. When the Islamic Arab state developed with conquests, booty and the expansion of Islam, the model of a commander of war was no longer capable of subsuming and integrating the new developments. So, a constitutional vacuum appeared as a result of the three flaws described above. Since the issue was not handled peacefully and jurisprudentially, the decisive word was left to the sword, and 'the caliphate was converted into kingship'.

## The Ideology of Power and Islamic Ethics

The constitutional flaws that appeared towards the end of ʿUthmān's rule and which led to 'the conversion of the caliphate into kingship' did not connote the only political lessons to be learned from the historical experience of the Arab-Islamic nation. There are other aspects that ought to be highlighted, especially the manner adopted by the rulers in Islam to lend legitimacy to their rule, starting with Muʿāwiyah, the first 'king' in Islam.

Muʿāwiyah knew only too well that he had usurped rule by the sword; therefore he lacked the legitimacy on which rule in Islam had been built since Abū Bakr, namely the Islamic legitimacy of by *al-shūrā* (consultation). So he tried to seek that legitimacy in 'predestination and fate' (*al-qaḍā' wa al-qadr*) on the one hand and, on the other, in trying to gain the people to his side by hinting at bestowing on them a share of the fruits of rule, especially the material ones. We find him reiterating in his speeches that the war between himself and 'Alī, his victory and seizure of power were all 'predestined by God'. Thus, it was God who predestined, through 'His prior knowledge', that the Umayyads should assume the rule, because they were equipped for it and more experienced than others. His governors reiterated this claim, including Ziyād bin Abīhi, who said in his famous speech *al-khutbah al-Batra* (the 'truncated speech'), 'O people! We have become your masters and defenders. We rule you by the authority which God has invested in us, and protect you by the power which He has bestowed on us.' Mu'āwiyah addressed the opponents to the appointment of his son Yazid as his heir apparent, saying, 'The matter of Yazid was a divine preordination (*qaḍā'*), and human beings have no choice in that.'

On the other hand, Mu'āwiyah followed a 'realist' policy, doing his best to make people look at the question of rule in the manner of 'political realism', which is based on accepting the *fait accompli*. He delivered a speech in Medina when the '*bay'ah*' was accorded to him in the 'year of consensus'. He said, 'I was installed not through your love of me or pleasure at my installation, but I fought you for it with my sword.' Then he added that he tried to bring himself to follow in the course of Abū Bakr, 'Umar, or 'Uthmān, but he could not do it: 'So, I betook myself to follow a way that is beneficial to you and me: good food and fine drink. If you do not find me the best among you, then I am, nevertheless, the best fit to rule you.' The Umayyad 'caliphs' followed in his steps, and adopted 'predestination as an ideology, and gifts as a political exercise, making of both the basis of legitimacy on which they built their rule'.

When the 'Abbāsid revolution succeeded in establishing its state, the Umayyad ideology of predestination *al-jabr* could no longer be relied upon since the 'Abbāsid leaders opposed and fought the Umayyads, proclaiming the opposing ideological slogan of *al-qadr*, meaning the freedom of the human and being able to choose, and, consequently, his bearing responsibility for his actions. Thus, the 'Abbāsids attempted to find legitimacy for their rule not in predestination – *al-qaḍā' wa al-qadr* – as the Umayyads had done, but in the 'divine will' (min irādat allāh wa mashī'atihi). So, they said it was God who willed it that they should rule, and that they rule by His will, and act according to His wish. Abu-Ja'far al-Mansur, the actual founder of the 'Abbāsid state, addressed the people, saying, 'O people! I am but the power of God in His land. I rule you by

His guidance and support. I am His guardian over His property. I dispense with it according to His wish and grant of it by His permission.' Thus the Caliph who was at the time of the Rāshidūn, a caliph of the Prophet (Abū Bakr), or a caliph of his caliph ('Umar) became now a 'Caliph of God' and 'His authority in His land'. That was the basis of the 'Abbāsid legitimacy, a basis absolutely incompatible with Islam. It was established through what Ibn al-Muqaffa' and others of the 'Sultanate authors' copied from the Persian Sultanate ideologies and similar sources, which compare the despotic ruler to a god. Sometimes the correlation between the two is so close, the ruler attains to 'divinity'.

'Political jurisprudence' did not appear until rather late, with al-Mawārdī, in particular. Before that, it was merely 'a discourse on the *imāmah'*, the religious leadership, on which the Sunni *muhājirūn* disagreed with the Shī'ites, especially the *Rawāfiḍ* (rejectors), who refused to recognize the caliphate of Abū Bakr, 'Umar and 'Uthmān, claiming that the Prophet had specified 'Alī to be imām after him. The Sunni muhājirūn refuted their claim and validated the caliphate of the four Rāshidūn, supporting their argument with historical evidence. Then, they based on that what they considered to be the conditions and prerequisites of *imāmah* and the method for appointing the *imām*. They tried to elevate the way issues were run in the time of Rāshidūn Caliphs to the level of 'precedent' in legislation. All this was done in order to disprove the Bāṭinis and Rawāfiḍ of the Shī'ites. So, the political jurisprudence was, in essence, a legislation of the past rule in Islam, especially in the Rāshidūn period. It was not a legislation for the present or the future. It is true that al-Mawārdī tried to lend a kind of legitimacy to that part of the rule, in his time, dealing with governmental offices such as administrative positions and 'religious assignments' such as judicature. But that 'legislation' of his was no more than a description of a reality, and an attempt to lend it a type of jurisprudential legitimacy. The political jurisprudence after al-Mawārdī developed through a series of concessions and omissions of conditions, to end in a recognition that rule is taken by might and subjugation (as according to al-Ghazālī and followers). Finally, the *fuqahā'* formulated a 'comprehensive principle' which eliminated the political jurisprudence altogether. It is the principle of 'Obedience is obligatory to the mighty' or in the parlance of the average person in Morocco 'Allāh helps whoever is'.

These are the political lessons learned from the historical experience of the Arab-Islamic nations. They are derived from the applied policies, first, before the conversion of the caliphate into kingship (the constitutional flaws which appeared towards the end of 'Uthmān's rule), then after the caliphate turned into a system of rule that sought legitimacy in ideological distortion and political ingratiation, and by the principle of 'might is right' all the way through. But the historical experience of the Arab-Islamic *ummah* is not the applied policy alone. It is also what I call here Islamic ethics in rule. It is the ethics which continued to inspire the free thought and revive the hopes for reform and change. The basic elements in those ethics to be found in the age of the Prophet are:

(i) *Al-shūrā* (consultation): The Qur'ān has made consultation one of the praiseworthy traits, together with the belief in the One God, the reliance on Him, the avoidance of major sins and the performance of *al-ṣalāt* (prayer). 'Whatever you are given [here] is [but] a convenience of this life; but that which is with Allāh is better and more lasting: [It is] for those who believe and put their trust in their Lord. Those who avoid the greater sins and shameful deeds, and when they are angry, even then forgive. Those who hearken to their Lord, and establish regular prayers, who [conduct] their affairs by mutual consultation; who spend out of what We bestow on them for sustenance. And those who, when an oppressive wrong is inflicted on them [are not cowed but] help and defend themselves' (42, al-Shūrā, 36–39). The Qur'ān stresses the same meaning, as it addresses the Prophet, to make consultation one of the good qualities that serve as a basis for his relations with his Companions: 'It is part of the mercy of Allāh that you deal gently with them. Were you to have been severe or harsh-hearted, they would have broken away from about you: so pass over [their faults] and ask for [Allāh's] forgiveness for them, and consult them in the matter' (3, Āl 'Imrān, 159).

(ii) Responsibility (*mas'ūlīyah*), shared by all members of society. The political thought in the ancient eastern civilizations, whether pharaonic, Babylonian, Jewish or Persian was based on the model of the 'shepherd' and his flock of sheep. The ruler is a 'shepherd', and the people are the 'flock'. This model is based on a comparison between the 'shepherd of the universe' (God) and the shepherd of the 'flock' of human beings. In Islam during the Prophet's time, not in the time of the sultanate ideology, 'shepherd' assumed another significance through the famous *ḥadīth* of the Prophet: 'Each of you is a shepherd, and each is responsible for his flock. The leader (*imām*) of the people is a shepherd, and he is responsible for his flock; the husband is the shepherd of his household, and he is responsible for his flock; the wife is the shepherdess of the household of her husband and the children, and she is responsible for them; the slave is a shepherd of the property of his master, and he is responsible for it; each and everyone of you is a shepherd and is responsible for his flock.' It is quite obvious that 'shepherding' here means worthiness of trust and shouldering responsibility. It is not the special concern of one individual, but is distributed among all members of society, from the highest to the lowest. The political significance of this principle is in its insistence on sharing responsibility, without monopoly or despotism.[m47]

(iii) The third element of Islamic ethics in the fields of rule, politics and other worldly affairs for which there is no text is the one expressed in the *ḥadīth* of the Prophet which said: 'You know better in your worldly affairs.' It is reported the Prophet was passing by some people who were pollinating their date palms. When he asked them what they were doing and they said, 'We are pollinating the palm trees so they will bear fruit', he said, 'Could you not leave them alone?', which they did. When the trees did not bear fruit, the men went to the Prophet and told him of what had happened, so he said, 'You are better informed of your worldly affairs.' As the Prophet died without assigning a successor, the way of appointing one or the type of powers of such a successor or any other of the rule or political affairs, it becomes inevitable to consider all these affairs as being subsumable under the content of the *ḥadīth* above. Abū Bakr stressed that when he made his inauguration speech: 'O people! I was appointed to lead you and I am not the best among you. If you find me on the right track, support me. If you find me on the wrong track, set me right.'

These, as I see them, are the bases of Islamic ethics in the affairs of rule and politics. I use the word 'ethics' because the texts which specify those principles are not legislative texts, or at least they were not considered so. Therefore, the field of *ijtihād* in the affairs of rule expands beyond all limitations, except for those set by the Islamic ideals. Hence, it becomes clear that a rebuilding of the political thought in Islam should start not by returning to the ideas of al-Mawārdī or others, because they are not binding upon us, as they were dictated by the circumstances of their times. Such a process must begin with a revival of the three principles explained above, in a manner compatible with the needs and demands of our age. It is paramount to specify the manner of conducting consultation (*al-shūrā*) through free democratic elections; to specify the term of office of the president in the republican system and to entrust the executive power to a government answerable to a parliament, in both republican and monarchist systems; and to specify the powers of the head of state, the government and the parliament in a manner that makes the latter the only source of power. Those are all principles indispensable in any consultation process in modern times, and they alone can remedy the three constitutional flaws that appeared towards the end of 'Uthmān's rule and led to 'the conversion of the caliphate into a ferocious kingship'.

Hence, I do not see any justification for the wariness of some 'Islamic' political movements concerning modern democracy. Justifications which claim that the caliph in Islam may be appointed by one individual or a certain number of individuals; that his term of office cannot be specified on the assumption that the pledge of *al-bay'ah* is like a sale contract in that neither can be retracted; that the appointment of the caliph requires entrusting the rule to him without specifying his powers are all justifications which have no bases in the revelation or in reason. They are all reiterations of opinions of political jurisprudents such as al-Mawārdī and others. But I have already demonstrated that those opinions were in response to needs dictated by their own times, either as refutations of the Shī'ite and Rāfiḍī arguments or as an endorsement of a *fait accompli* imposed by the rulers of their times, by might and subjugation.

## Note

1. Among the incidents which relate to this *ḥadīth* is one transmitted by Muslim (2361), wherein the Prophet, newly immigrated to Medina, observed some of the locals grafting a date palm. He asked them if it weren't better to proceed according to a different technique than the one they were using so they followed his advice. When the yield was deficient, they asked him about it and he is reported to have replied: 'When I command you in something about your religion, then do it; but when I command you something that is my opinion, then I am only human.'

CHAPTER 2

# Religion and State in the Renaissance Authoritative Referent

## The Necessity of Avoiding Provincial Problems

> Since our people cannot see the difference between religions which must be about the relation between man and his Creator, and civic matters, which must be about the relation between man and his countrymen, or between him and his government, which are the basis of social situations and political associations; and since they do not see the difference between these two domains, both in nature and purpose, there is obviously no hope that our people will achieve success in either field, let alone in both of them, together.

Hence:

> The necessity of distinguishing the presidency (*al-riyāsah*), which is the spiritual power, from polity (*al-sulṭah al-madinīyah*), which is the civil power. This is because presidency, by its very nature, is connected with constant inner convictions, which do not change with times and situations, while polity is connected with external affairs, unstable and open to change and reform, according to place, time, and situations. Therefore, mixing these two powers which are so different in nature and so contradictory in their spheres of interest, will lead to disagreement among us, and will definitely affect both judgments and religions. And it may not be an exaggeration to say that, in such a plight, civilization and growth will be impossible to achieve.

Butrus al-Bustani wrote this on the sectarian strife which flared up in Lebanon and Syria in 1860 in *Nafir Suriyya* (*The Bugle of Syria*), the newspaper he edited. Like most texts, this one is defined by its purport, the situation of the author and the occasion on which it was issued. When these three aspects are examined here, they will be found to be the same elements which define the issue of religion and state in the referential authority of the modern Arab renaissance.

The purport of the text is quite clear; it is an open call to separate religion from the state, to draw a line between religions and civil affairs; i.e.

between the spiritual power and the civil power, or, in the words of Christ, 'to render to God what is God's, and to Caesar what is Caesar's'. That is a prerequisite for progress and rebirth.

It is clear that this call would be meaningful to a trend of thought that differentiates between God and Caesar, and finds, in its store of basic and vital mental images, one image or more where God stands on one side and Caesar on the other, either as rivals or as allies. Such a situation is found in the experience of Christian Europe, in several forms, perhaps most significant of which are the following three.

The first situation dominated at the advent of Christianity. On one side there was the state ruled by Caesar, the Roman Emperor, following no particular religion as a state. On the other side there was Christ, the son of Mary, and after him the Fathers of the Church, who propagated the Christian faith across the Roman Empire. The relationship between the religion and the state, then, was one of rivalry. The state fought and persecuted Christianity, considering it a subversive activity.

The second example appeared with Caesar Constantine I, or the Great, who, after one of his victories in AD 312, decided to recognize Christianity as the religion of the Roman Empire. This opened the door for the Catholic Church to become a state within a state. It even became, during long periods of European history, an institution above the state, with control over spiritual life and domination of social, economic and political life.

The third type of situation was that connected with the European Renaissance and the developments which led to the separation between religion and state, i.e. to 'secularism'. The term does not signify opposing or fighting religion, but it means separating what is worldly from what is 'otherworldly'. That puts the political power, education and other facilities in the hands of men religiously neutral and keeps all these out of the hands of the priests, the clergy and all representatives of the Church.

In all these cases there is the religion and there is the state: either antagonistic towards, intertwined with or independent of each other. Religion is an institution represented by the Church and its branches, the state is an institution represented by its departments, and both religion and state are embedded in society. Thus the referential authority adopted by al-Bustani is the experience known to Europe as the issue of the relation between religion and state.

Butrus al-Bustani was a Christian Arab from Lebanon and one of the pioneers of the modern Arab renaissance (*al-nahḍah*). He lived in the nineteenth century when Lebanon, like most Arab countries, was an Ottoman governorate. The Ottoman Empire, as it is well known, ruled in the guise of a caliphate, and, at the same time, exercised despotism and tyranny over the Arabs, both Muslims and Christians, in the name of Islam. Hence, in the mind of al-Bustani, as in the minds of other Arab intellectuals, especially the Christians among them, the concept of renaissance and revival became closely connected with the separation of the religion from the state: first, because the renaissance model they had in mind was that of Europe; second, because the despotism of the Ottomans, their caliphate and the history of their relations with the Arabs appeared to the Arab intellectuals as a source of backwardness. Consequently, it meant that progress cannot be achieved without independence from the Ottomans and what they stand for, and it also meant the separation from the 'caliphate', leading to a separation of religion from the state.

The occasion of the essay was the sedition of 1860 which flared in Lebanon between the Christians and the Druze. Al-Bustani devoted his efforts to alleviate the consequences of religious hatred caused by that sedition. He thought, as we have seen, that the solution to the sectarian problem in Lebanon would be a separation between religion and state.

It is clear from the above discussion that the basic elements which define the dichotomy of religion and state in the authoritative reference of the Arab renaissance are three: adopting the European religious experience; solving the problem of religious sectarianism; and connecting progress with the separation between religion and state, i.e. adopting the principles of the European Renaissance. These three elements are completely different from those which define the relation between religion and state in the traditional Islamic authoritative referent. This is what makes mutual understanding difficult, if not impossible, between those who subscribe to this referent as authoritative and those who subscribe to the Renaissance as the authoritative referent, defined by the above-mentioned elements, especially when the issue of renaissance [itself] (*al-nahḍah*) is linked to the separation of religion and state. Here, the traditional thinker finds matters conflicting with the claims of the secular thinker. The Arab-Islamic historical experience provides the former with an indisputable historical fact: the Arabs were able to rise only with the help of Islam. It is by Islam that they were able to establish a state, conquer kingdoms and build up a civilization. This ingrained an indelible image in the mind of the traditionalist, an image which links adherence to religion with renaissance and revival, as a relation between cause and effect, exactly as the Arab secularist links the separation between religion and state with renaissance and revival, as a relation between cause and effect.

Here lies the falsehood in this dichotomy, the dichotomy of religion and state in contemporary Arab thought. It is represented in the adherence of each party to his own authoritative referent as the only eternal truth. But the conditions of progress are not always the same. They are multiple, intricate and changeable with times and circumstances. The same element which may be a prerequisite for progress in a certain historical experience may be either neutral or even an impediment to progress in another. The dichotomy of religion and state in the contemporary Arab thought is a false one, because it masks the problems of the present and jumps over them, only to pose alternative problems, making their solution a prerequisite for progress and a necessity for the future.

I believe that eliminating the falsehood created by this dichotomy lies, above all, in separating the issue of the relation between religion and state from the issue of revival and progress. We have to look at each as an independent issue subject to several variables, at the top of which are probably the type of social structure, the dominant social economic relations, and the type and nature of the political authority. In short, the issue of the relation between religion and state must be addressed in the light of the special, real facts in each Arab country independently.

It is indispensable, then, to start from the present fact of reality that the Arab homeland is not one country and not one society, but a number of countries and societies. I only hope that they will unite, one day, into one country and one society and the Arab people must work towards that end. But in the present historical situation, each of these societies and countries has its own special characteristics which colour a number of questions, including the relation between religion and state. Therefore, we have to look at this issue in the light of the realities of each Arab country separately. We have to avoid generalizing the provincial and local problems in a manner which makes them look like national problems, and make the call for Arab unity a call to transfer the problems from the special to the general field.

The issue of the relation between religion and state in the Arab homeland is not a national problem but a provincial one. How can we address it, then, in a manner that can serve the national cause?

## Sectarianism and Democracy

The foregoing analysis of the religion-state dichotomy in modern and contemporary Arab thought reaches the following conclusion: the traditional authoritative referent, entertained by large sectors of old and young Arabs, does not savour this dichotomy. This is because it is nonexistent in the traditional authoritative referent, nor, as a result, in the minds of those who subscribe to that authority. However, when that dichotomy is addressed according to the modern Arab renaissance authoritative referent, it does not actually reflect a national problem, common to the entire Arab homeland, but it reflects a social and political situation, related to certain Arab countries in varying degrees, and it is described as religious sectarianism. So, I have come to this general conclusion that the relation between religion and state should be addressed in the light of the facts in each Arab country separately, and that we should avoid generalizing provincial problems in a manner which makes them sound like national problems.

How do we address the problem, then, on the provincial level, in a manner that may serve the national interest? The following remarks may help us to think of the matter seriously.

A quick look at the present situation in the Arab countries would show that the relation between religion and state does not present a problem for thought, society or the ruling authority, except in countries where religious sectarianism is one of the basic components of society. These countries are Lebanon, Syria, Egypt and the Sudan. The rest of the Arab countries, such as Morocco, Mauritania, Algeria, Tunis, Libya, Jordan, Saudi Arabia, Yemen, the Gulf countries and Iraq, have no problems of religious sectarianism, or the religious minorities there do not form a percentage which makes religious sectarianism a social and consequently a political problem.

Religious sectarianism is not of the same type and weight in all the Arab countries which have suffered from that problem: in Lebanon it is different from that of Syria. In Egypt, sectarianism has a historical peculiarity which made it a plurality inside unity; the unity of the country, nay, the unity of national sentiment. In the Sudan, the problem is connected with language, religion and ethnic affiliation. This means naturally that the solution that suits Lebanon does not necessarily suit either Egypt or Syria nor the Sudan. Hence, a suitable solution cannot be one and the same for all these countries, nor can a solution be dictated to this country or that. The people of the country themselves must find their own suitable solution.

It is not my right or responsibility, therefore, nor the right or responsibility of any other Arab intellectual, to represent the people of this Arab country or that in solving their own provincial problems. This attitude is not an evasion on my part. It is an objective attitude required by the national interest. Any other attitude would be harmful to that interest. This is because any Arab intellectual, no matter what his intensions, or how loyal he is, will be committing a grave mistake if he posits himself as a speaker on behalf of Arab intellectuals from other provinces and starts to think of solutions to their problems. This mistake might not only be on the level of cognizance or the correctness of the solution, but it will definitely be a mistake on the national level.

What happens most of the time is that an Arab intellectual may think of a provincial problem in a country other than his own, and from a national perspective, which leads him to make generalizations. He may conceive of the entire Arab homeland through the perspective of the special situation of Lebanon, Syria or Egypt. He may proclaim, as has happened repeatedly, that secularism is the only solution for the problems of the Arab homeland. Most probably, the Lebanese would find this a sound idea and they would adopt it as a symbol of progress. But a Moroccan, a Mauritanian or an Algerian would, in all probability, say, 'But what is "secularism"?' or 'Why "secularism"?' Such queries indicate that such a solution does not mean a great deal to them.

All the above has been about the 'special' aspect of the question. But there is no such thing as a purely and absolutely special aspect. In every 'special' there is always something of the general. Similarly, the general is nothing but the quintessence of what is common in the elements of every aspect of the special. Therefore, we should not ignore the general aspect underlying the 'special' in the sectarian question in any country.

If we look from the 'general' perspective at the problem of religious sectarianism in the Arab homeland, we shall find it, undoubtedly, a social and historical reality. But this sectarian reality does not emerge as a problem except when the social reality as a whole is suffering from a general problem. The general problem plaguing the entire Arab reality from 'the Gulf to the Ocean' is the problem of democracy in its political and social dimensions. If we take this problem into consideration, the sectarian problem and the problem of religion-state relations appear as some of the results.

I shall take Lebanon as an example, where the relationship between sectarianism and polity was arranged, in the 1940s, in a manner that reflected the Lebanese reality at the time, to a great extent. The balance of sectarian power was tipped to the side of the Maronites, because they were more developed and more widely prevalent in modern Lebanese society, for historical reasons known to everybody. It was natural that the relations would be 'democratically' organized on the basis of this reality. So, the Maronites got the lion's share of the political scene, which reflected their actual, or at least apparent, power among the other sects (whether this was legitimate is not the issue here). Despite all the injustices done to the other sects, Lebanon remained a relatively democratic country, at least on political, intellectual and journalistic levels.

But Lebanese 'democracy' did not develop along the Lebanese reality itself; instead, it remained imprisoned in the same order and structure with which it started. The Maronites remained powerful, politically and economically, and became more so under the auspices of the Lebanese 'democracy' itself. At the same time, other sects developed, demographically, economically and politically, and the disparity between the Maronites and the rest of the Lebanese narrowed down to almost zero, at least at the level of awareness. Then Lebanese democracy began to exercise a thinly-veiled despotism, politically and economically, in an atmosphere of secularism and freedom of thought and expression. Naturally, secularism and freedom of thought and expression do not make up for discrimination in other spheres. They cannot alleviate forever the injustice perpetrated by one sect monopolizing the greater part of the political and economic power. The Lebanese body grew too large for the 'shirt' of democracy in which it was dressed in the 1940s. Therefore, it was inevitable for the shirt to burst open and for the body to emerge in its reality: a body diseased with sectarianism which assumes a special form, namely, the exploitation by one sect of other sects, directly or indirectly. Since the Lebanese have not yet been able to weave a new democratic shirt, large enough for the development achieved by other sects, the civil war can have no end.[1]

Lebanon is an Arab sectarian example that, in the absence of democracy, screams through roaring cannons. In the Arab homeland there are other voices expressing the same phenomenon differently, for example in the Sudan. In other Arab countries which do not suffer from religious sectarianism, people express their need for democracy and social justice through different means. Some proclaim democracy, others call for the application of *al-sharī'ah*; some demand minority rights, and others call for a rebellion against feudalism, etc.

The religion-state dichotomy in modern Arab thought is a false one. It is false because it masks sectarianism, which, though a real problem in some Arab countries, is not common to the whole of the Arab homeland. It is a dichotomy intended to replace a common, real problem, which is the absence of social and political democracy from the Gulf to the Ocean.

## Democracy and Rationality: Substitute for 'Secularism'

It can be said, generally, that there is no motto adopted by modern Arab thought which has been a cause of ambiguity and misunderstanding like the slogan '*al-'ilmānīyah*' (secularism). The Arabic word is an erroneous translation of the French *lacisme*, because *lac* or *laque* in French has no connection with 'science', Arabic *'ilm*. The origin of the word is the Latin *lacus*, which means 'what belongs to the laymen', in contrast to the Latin *clericus*, the 'clergy', i.e. men of the Christian Church. *Laque* then is anyone who is not a cleric, or a man of the Church.

This is the original meaning of the word, but it was misused in French, to indicate enmity towards religion and the clergy. As religious teaching was the responsibility of the Church and took place in monasteries and convents, the public teaching set up by the state was mainly limited to the sciences: mathematical, natural and human. Hence, *lacisme* in France was identified with teaching, 'the teaching of sciences in schools and the instruction of religion in the Church'. Jean de la Croix has said, 'The idea of lacisme is not the opposite of the idea of religion, but it suggests, at least, the distinction between the worldly and the holy. It supposes that one aspect of human life is not subject to religious instruction, or at least it falls outside the power of the clergy.' Hence, *lacisme* was a trend insistent on keeping public life outside the power of religion and the authority of the clergy. (Religion here means the teachings of the Church as an institution at rivalry with the state in exercising authority over the people: the state owns their bodies, the Church their souls.)

It is clear, therefore, that *lacisme* is an idea basically related to a special situation; namely, that of a society where the Church assumes the spiritual power, and in which religion is not based on the direct relation between man and God, but on a relation mediated by a 'man of religion', a man for whom religion is a profession and a living; a man who is connected with a supreme religious organization which considers itself the only legislator in the field of spiritual life. It is also quite obvious that this idea is completely foreign to Islam and its followers. Islam is based on a direct relation between man and God. It does not recognize any intermediary, as it gives no party a spiritual authority and another a temporal authority. Briefly speaking, posing the slogan of *lacisme*, which was translated as '*al-'ilmānīyah*' (secularism), in a society where people are Muslims, is neither justified nor legitimate, nor does it have any significance. Why was this slogan raised, then, in the Arab world? What were the needs that it was supposed to answer?

The slogan of secularism was first raised in the Arab world in the mid-nineteenth century, by Christian intellectuals from Syria. The Syrian region, like most of the eastern Arab countries, was under the Turkish Ottoman rule which governed a vast empire in the name of the 'Islamic caliphate', explicitly or by implication. The Christian Arabs who proclaimed secularism, at the time, wanted to express, in a modest and shy manner, what other Arab intellectuals expressed openly and strongly, when they raised the banner of 'independence from the Turks'. Then the two slogans and trends converged into one, called at first the trend of 'Arabism', and later 'Arab Nationalism'. Secularism, then, was posed in the Arab world in an organic connection with the theme of independence from the Turks. Since the independence from the Turks meant, at the same time, the rise of one Arab state (uniting, at least, the Arab Ottoman governorates in the East), the three concepts of secularism, independence and unity became organically linked to mean one thing: the establishment of an Arab state in the East, not subject to Ottoman authority. This is how Arab nationalistic thought adopted secularism, a concept confused with that of independence and unity at the time. Then, a rival movement emerged under the name of 'The Islamic League', which was mainly a kind of opposition to the independence of the Arab countries from the Turks, encouraged by the Ottoman authorities, themselves. Thus the opposition was set in two directions: one calling for an Islamic League under the leadership of the Turks, and another for an Arab state or an Arab Union. The supporters of 'Arabism' did not intend to set aside either Islam or religion. It is well known that the slogan of 'Arabism' was originally raised to oppose 'Ottomanization'.

This, in brief, is the original framework within which secularism was proclaimed in Greater Syria. It should be mentioned that this slogan was never proclaimed in the Western Arab countries, or in the Arabian peninsular countries. It was probably not so boldly proclaimed in Egypt itself, where there is a sizable Coptic minority. When the Arab countries became independent, and theoreticians became concerned with the idea of Arabism and Arab Nationalism, the issue of secularism was raised once more, especially in the Arab countries where there are religious minorities (Christian in particular). This proclamation was justified by the feeling of these minorities that the one Arab state sought by Arab Nationalism would have a Muslim majority, which may again create a situation similar to that which was current during the Ottoman rule. The real significance of this issue in the new context of theorizing for the one state, then, was organically linked to the rights of the religious minorities, especially their right not to be governed by the religion of the majority. Consequently, secularism came to mean building a state on a democratic, rational basis, not on the basis of religious domination. In the heat of the political-ideological controversy among parties and intellectual trends, secularism was posed to mean the separation of religion from the state, which is a completely objectionable idea in an Islamic society, as there is no contradiction between religion and the state in Islam. This contradiction exists only where the religious affairs are managed by an organization which claims for itself the right to exercise spiritual authority over the people, in return for a temporal authority exercised by the body politic, which is the state.

Therefore, the question of secularism in the Arab world is a false one, because it indicates needs that do not correspond with that term. The need for independence under one national identity, the need for democracy which respects the minority rights and the need for a rational exercise of politics, are all objective needs. Indeed, they are all reasonable and urgent needs in our Arab world. But they lose their rationality and urgency, even their legitimacy, when they are described as 'secularism', itself an ambiguous term.

The conclusion I want to reach is that Arab thought is required to review and scrutinize its concepts, in order to make them expressive of the real needs under discussion. In my opinion, we should remove the term 'secularism' from the dictionary of Arab thought and replace it with two words: 'democracy' and 'rationality'. Only these two terms express the real needs of Arab society, as 'democracy' means protecting the rights of individuals and groups, while 'rationality' means exercising politics according to reason and its logical and moral criteria, and not in accordance with whims, fanaticism and capricious moods.

On the other hand, neither democracy nor rationality implies, in any way, the exclusion of Islam. Judging by objective facts alone will lead us to say if the Arabs are really the 'substance of Islam', then Islam is the soul of the Arabs. Hence, Islam should be considered a basic element of Arab existence: spiritual Islam for the Muslim Arabs, and cultural Islam for all the Arabs, Muslims and non-Muslims alike.

The Arab nationalistic thought that raises the banner of 'Arab Unity' and the 'One Arab Homeland' from the Ocean to the Gulf should be rebuilt on the dual principles of democracy and rationality, not secularism, as well as on observing the rightful position of Islam, both in theory and practice.

## Note

1. This text was written and published in 1985.

CHAPTER 3

# Religion, Politics and Civil War

To conclude this discussion of the religion-state issue in contemporary Arab thought, I shall present a brief analysis of a phenomenon that marks the current Arab political reality, namely the political exploitation of religion and its consequences of civil war, open or covert.

To avoid any misunderstanding, if I fail to highlight the various levels in the same phenomenon, it is necessary to point out, once more, that I distinguish between secularism, which separates religion from the state, on the one hand, and the presence of Islam as *al-sharīʿah* and ethics in a society where the majority are Muslims, on the other hand. Secularism in the latter case is a meaningless term, because it does not correspond with reality or perform a positive function, except where there is an organization which represents religion and speaks for it, and, at the same time, competes with the state as an authority. The result will be a state within a state or one state against another, in the same society. It is clear in such a case that the solution lies in separating one from the other, and specifying the jurisdiction of each, so each authority will exercise its powers without impinging on the other. Such separation took place in Europe, where the Church took charge of spiritual authority and the state temporal (political) authority.

What a Muslim society needs, in the absence of a religious organization, is to separate religion from politics, namely, to avoid the exploitation of religion for political purposes, as religion represents what is constant and absolute, while politics represents what is relative and changeable. Politics is motivated by personal or group interests, while religion must be above all this; otherwise it will lose its essence and spirit.

The essence and spirit of religion is to unify, not to separate. The Islamic religion is a religion of absolute 'unification', on the level of faith (one God); on the level of society (one *ummah*, nation); and on the level of understanding and exercising religion ('As for those who divide their religion and break up into sects, you have no part in them in the least'

(6, al-An'ām, 159). But the essence and spirit of politics is to separate. Politics thrives on disagreement, wherever it may arise. Hence, politics is nearest to the art of managing disagreement more than anything else. Management or administration here means managing the existing disagreement or trying to create a new one. Hence, connecting religion with politics, on any level, will necessarily introduce the germ of disagreement into religion. When the disagreement in religion has a political base, it will necessarily lead to sectarianism, then to civil war. Present and past history are witness to that. From the time of 'Uthmān, when religion began to be used politically in Islamic society, disagreement has been ongoing and civil wars have ceased only to flare up again, but always through the exploitation of religion in politics, in one way or another.

How does the exploitation of religion in politics lead to civil war? This is a basic question which demands a clear answer; since to say that using religion in politics leads to civil war sounds contradictory with the essence of religion, especially its unifying character. Logic dictates that religion, as a unifying factor, should lead to a type of unity in politics, at least to prevent disagreement and slipping into civil war.

But the actual situation is different. What happens is that the 'political mind' of the group resorts to the exploitation of religion in politics when the group finds it is not in their interest to express their social-economic issue in a politically direct and accurate manner, because that would expose the materialistic and exploitative nature of that issue; or when the group cannot do that due to a weakness of awareness, caused by the failure to reach a level of development enabling it to present its social-economic issue clearly and openly. In both cases, using religion in politics assumes a 'sectarian' or 'ideological' aspect, informed by a revival of an old dispute, its symbols and ideological implications, all of which are necessary to make of that group a 'spiritual tribe', as the conditions of the social existence of that group do not elevate it to the level of a 'social class'.

What happened in Lebanon provides the best example that explains my view. The Maronite group uses religion in politics as they adhere to sectarianism (meaning the distribution of public offices and material benefit on the same unjust sectarian principle, the basis on which the Lebanese state was first established), as it is not in the interest of that group to present its issue, the protection of their economic privileges, in an overt political manner. Since politics is the power which protects those privileges, the group resorts to linking that power with religion to make of politics a fundamental reality that cannot be changed. Therefore, they link politics to religion by making the right to differ in religion include the differences existing in politics, i.e. class differences. On the other hand, the poor masses in Lebanon, the hardest hit by the Maronite monopoly of political and economic authority, are unable to protest against this 'harm' in an overt political manner, because the conditions of their social and economic existence have not reached the level that makes of those masses a social class powerful enough to pose their issue in their capacity as a class. When we add to this the fact that the basic rivals of those masses (the Maronites, who exercise the political and economic exploitation) present themselves as a religious sect, and not as a social class, we realize how the awareness of that exploitation on the part of the poor and weak masses in Lebanon would take, in its turn, a sectarian form (Shī'ites, Druze and Sunnis). Inevitably, the struggle would soon slip into a sectarian civil war, even if it assumes, at first, the appearance of a class struggle.

What happened in Lebanon is an example of what could happen in any other country where the use of religion in politics forms a political exigency. Generally speaking, the Arab countries are liable to suffer such exigency in one way or another. Therefore, the responsibility of what is nowadays called 'Islamic Orientation', 'Fundamentalism' or 'Political Islam' is a very serious one as there is nothing easier than making a religious call transform into a call for separation. Religion would then turn into a factor of separation and destruction instead of one for integration and unification. What may justify the rise of 'political Islam' today, on the historical level, is the despotism and oppression which characterize the conduct of the state and the elite holding the reins of power. Oppression is suffered materially and psychologically by the poor masses and their spiritual leadership in cities and in the countryside. Modern ideological trends – in the Arab countries – could not check that despotism and oppression and enforce a democratic alternative in their place. If we look at the question from this viewpoint, we shall see that 'political Islam' today represents a struggle of one 'sect' against another. One sect, at least theoretically, is the overwhelming majority of the nation, who are generally the exploited weak. The other is the elite, which is theoretically and practically the ruling group and their cronies. The first sect is basically not sectarian because it practically represents the overwhelming majority; yet it is constantly in imminent danger of turning into a fertile ground for sectarianism because it is not possible to avoid disagreement in politics, whether concerning interests or ways of confronting rivals. Hence, the chronic malady suffered by the groups which exploit religion in politics: the malady of division into factions and sects that accuse each other of infidelity. This renders those factions oblivious to the real enemy, because they are overwhelmed by internal strife.

Therefore, political Islam cannot succeed in achieving its historical objectives which give it its raison d'être, unless it could rise up to the level of those objectives, unless it could pose the question of despotism, oppression and related political, social and economic issues in an overt political manner and in open political discourse, and until it enters politics through its wide, contemporary, recognized door. But to reduce Islam in its entirety to the issue of 'veiling' (*hijāb*), 'amputating the hand of the thief' and the like is an escape, or a failure to address the real political problems. This would consequently lead to the situation of 'those who divide their religion and break up into sects', and into sectarianism and civil war. We have to beware, then, of letting politics turn religion into a factor of division, instead of keeping it, as it is in essence, a factor of integration and unification.

# Part Two

# The Question of Applying *al-Sharīʿah*

CHAPTER 4

# Awakening and Renewal

The term 'Islamic Awakening' has become popularized in contemporary Arab-Islamic discourse in recent years. This term is connected with certain events, especially the 'Iranian Revolution', and with the appearance of some trends and organizations which adopt 'the call' for application of the 'Islamic System' in the various aspects of political, economic and social life. Yet the word 'awakening' *(al-ṣaḥwah)* remains, in my view, alien to the Islamic lexicon, or, at least, it does not sound compatible with reality or with how things should be.

To describe what happened in Iran, or in some Arab or Islamic countries where certain movements and trends adopted a call to apply the Islamic System, as an 'Islamic Awakening' would suggest that, before that time, Islam was 'asleep' or 'absent'. As a faith, a legal system (*sharī'ah*), or as the ultimate ideal for life, Islam was never 'dormant' or absent, neither in the conscience of Muslims, nor in the conduct of most of them.

On the other hand, I do not find the word 'awakening' fully expressive of what is expected of Muslims these days, when they are challenged by modern life, in all its aspects and complexities. The word 'awakening' denotes a reaction, not an action. Muslims need and are even required to take action and not merely react, even when such reaction is an expression of their innermost feelings. It is not unlikely that the Arabic word '*al-ṣaḥwah*' was a translation of a European term, since the Western press had actually described certain movements in the name of Islam in some Arab and other Islamic countries as an 'Islamic Awakening'.

Whatever the case, I believe that the word, whether devised by some Muslim Arab authors or translated from some foreign language, does not belong to the Islamic lexicon in any way. By the 'Islamic lexicon' I mean the concepts which abound in our Arab-Islamic tradition and which express best what *al-ṣaḥwah* is expected to denote. The most salient of such concepts of an Islamic origin is the concept of 'renewal' (*al-tajdīd*).

I prefer the word 'renewal' to that of 'awakening' not simply because the first is original in Islamic thought and tradition, while the other may be translated from another language and consequently may belong to a different tradition but because of the connotations of the two terms are not unitary. 'Awakening' refers to a circumstantial and transient phenomenon, which was, most probably, in the minds of foreigners who used the term 'Islamic awakening'. As such, this phenomenon remains on the surface of history, not in its depths, while 'renewal', which is a deeply-rooted activity, brings its full weight to bear on the future. Thus, innovation lies deep in the core of history, accompanying its development, directing it and aspiring to gain full control of it.

What Muslims need today is a 'renewal' and not a mere 'awakening'. The challenges which face the Arab and Islamic world today require action, and not merely reaction. Action in the present age is first and foremost the action of the rational mind. The action of the tongue (speeches, sermons, guiding words) and that of the hand or the muscles (of whatever form or force) are no longer of any use today. In the present age, everything depends on rational action: on discipline, organization, calculated steps, limiting expectations, and reducing hazards and keeping surprises to the minimum. In the face of this new reality, awakening alone is useless, even if it were an 'intellectual awakening'. Renewal, alone, is the answer.

From the Islamic perspective, renewal is part of life itself, as indicated by a famous *ḥadīth*: 'Once every hundred years, Allāh sends to this *ummah* someone to renew (*yujadid*) its religion' (or 'the affairs of its religion'). Since Islam does not separate religion from worldly affairs, but, on the contrary, links prosperity in religious affairs with prosperity in worldly affairs, it follows that renewal in one is, at the same time, renewal in the other. But as worldly affairs change from time to time, so should the understanding of 'renewal' and its requirements in accordance with conditions and times.

Some of the ancient *fuqahā'* defined 'renewal' as a 'breaker of innovation' (*kasr li-l-bid'ah*) and a returning of Muslims to the conduct of the righteous predecessors (*al-salaf*). But we should not remain within the confines of this traditional meaning and mimic the early jurisprudents and the definition they gave to 'innovation' which derived from the circumstances of their age and the givens of their reality.

Moreover, 'innovation' (*al-bid'ah*) in Islamic terminology is not always disparaged or absolutely proscribed. The ancients themselves distinguished good innovations that are beneficial to people and corrective to their behaviour from bad ones that are harmful to people and apt to cause deviation from righteous behaviour. But many jurisprudents from the age of stagnation and decline went to extremes completely unacceptable in

Islam, branding as 'innovation', in its blameworthy sense, many new inventions that were not only useful but quite urgently needed and even necessary. Among the *fuqahā'* of the period of stagnation and decline were some who considered building schools a blameworthy innovation, on the pretext that knowledge had been obtained in mosques at the time of the righteous ancestors. Similarly, there were others among them who considered building bridges a devious innovation as the Companions were not known to have built them.

The response of the Andalusian faqīh *and mujtahid* Imām al-Shatibi (d. 790 AH/1388 AD) to such *fuqahā'* was, in my view, an excellent historical, rational Islamic reply. He called them to look upon 'renewal' not as something that was not known at the time of the Companions, or not practised by them, but to consider whether innovation could be beneficial. He said:

> If they consider every new custom to be a [heretical] innovation, then they should consider as such everything which [the Companions] did not know in the way of food, drink, clothing, speech or matters which had no precedent in this first period of time. This is a distortion. Some customs may change with times, places and nations. Otherwise, everything which is different from what the Arabs knew or did, at the time of the Companions, should be considered a novelty and a heresy, a notion, highly censurable.

Al-Shatibi marks the distinction between innovations in matters of worship (*al-'ibādāt*) and religion and those concerned with customs required by social life and its development. Anything that does not lead to the abandonment of a form of worship specified by Islam, and neither introduces a form of worship not specified by Islam, is not an 'innovation' in the blameworthy connotation of the word.

This clarifies the inadequacy of the old definition of 'renewal'. If we restrict that definition to a 'harmful innovation' as asserted by some of the *fuqahā'*, then we have narrowed its scope to the degree that it has become limited to fighting against deviation in acts of worship, either through augmentation [of them] or abandonment. Even if this were at all sufficient in previous ages, it can no longer answer the requirements of renewal at present. This could be called an 'awakening'. In this case, 'Islamic Awakening' will denote what we witness nowadays of people's keen observance of religious rites and their abiding by some perfunctory aspects of religious ethics. The other worldly affairs will therefore be waiting for innovation, and we have so many such affairs.

It is true that one aspect of what nowadays is called the 'Islamic Awakening' is a call for the application of the 'Islamic system' in life in all its aspects, which has always been the demand of every Muslim. This is because there is no Islamic system, ready-made and well-defined to cover life in all its aspects. In addition to the concerns of worship, personal statutes and some transactions specified by texts, there are only some general ethical principles in fields such as economics and politics. Consequently, the Islamic system in these and other fields is left to *ijtihād*. The real awakening needed, then, or the real renewal required, is to find practical solutions to the issues facing us in our present age which were unknown in our past. We want these to be solutions informed by Islamic ethics, but also to be capable of putting us on the path of progress, so that we can pursue our age's achievements and participate in enhancing them.

Looking at the question from this perspective is not an easy task. It requires not a mere awakening or a 'good innovation', but a root-level renewal, in depth and from the deepest level. The contemporary civilization in which we live, whether we like it or not, is not the same type as that known to our forefathers. It is not a direct extension of that former civilization, just as it is not of our own making but of the making of the others. We are only followers in it and after it, in the various fields of science, technology, economics, customs, thought and ideology. Consequently, the challenges facing us are not of a nature that may be branded as 'innovation' so that we might connect 'renewal' with 'harmful innovation'. Nor are they of a sort that could be adequately addressed by an 'awakening'. These are the challenges of a totally new civilization which need to be faced by a totally new philosophy and totally new approaches. This is much greater and far deeper than a mere 'awakening'.

The matter would have been somewhat easier if we were only facing a gap caused by the stagnation and decline we suffered before modernity woke us up. But the gulf is growing wider every day between us and the products of contemporary civilization, in the fields of science and technology, even in the period since we have been 'woken up'. The question, then, is not one of 'awakening', because the sleeper who sleeps the night and wakes in the morning can resume his normal course of life. But [sleepers like] the 'people of the cave' [*sūrat* al-Kahf], or those like them, need more than an 'awakening' to resume the course of life. They need first and foremost to renew their minds, so they can see the new life in its reality. Even if we have not suffered the experience of the cave sleepers, like the other so-called 'primitive' peoples, for instance, we have been suffering the experience of Plato's cave, where those hurled into it were forced to turn their faces to the wall, so that they do not see the light of day but only the shades and shadows cast on that wall by the daylight.

## CHAPTER 5

# Traditionalism (*al-salafīyah*)...or The Historical Experience of the Nation?

In the 1940s and the early 1950s, when I was in my youth, I remember that the salient characteristics of the image of the *salafī* [person adhering to the traditions of the pious ancestors] were: enmity to foreign occupation, fighting religious charlatanism, denouncing tomb visitation and many other 'popular' social customs and traditions nowadays generally regarded as folklore, in addition to piety and the observance of religious duties. Briefly, in the social and cultural atmosphere of the 1940s and 1950s, the traditionalist was a person of renewal (*rajulan mujaddidan*), opposed to the current situation, whether the one represented by foreign rule (colonialism) or that represented by the backward national situation, inherited from the pre-colonial period.

There was no title more honouring to a man than that of a 'traditionalist' – *salafī*. People considered it a higher title than that of the 'patriot [or nationalist]' (*waṭanī*), as nationalism was only a component part of traditionalism (*al-salafīyah*). But traditionalism, at least as social and religious conduct, was not necessarily a component of nationalism. In other words, the traditionalist was a nationalist and *more* than that. When I was young, I used to look at the *salafī* as a patriot in this world and in the hereafter. He was faithful to both and sincere in serving them both.

This was the situation in the Maghrib in my childhood and youth in the 1940s and 1950s. It was also the same in the two decades before that. Undoubtedly, the situation was similar in some other Arab countries in that period, or a little before, but with one basic difference: the *al-salafīyah* movement in Maghrib tended to merge with the national movement, adopting its modernistic objectives and finally identifying with it, especially when the colonialists recruited members of Sufi orders (*al-ṭuruqīyah*) and the retrograde forces working with them, against the nationalists and the *al-salafīyah* together. It may even be said that the national struggle issued from the belly of the *al-salafīyah*, exactly as the latter permeated the society and defeated its rivals and religious adversaries by merging with the national movement, and leading the struggle against colonialists and their supporters and agents.

Undoubtedly, traditionalism in the eastern Arab countries must have followed a somewhat different course of development due to certain situations that were non-existent in Maghrib, but here is not the place to discuss them. Yet, traditionalism, in the eyes of its followers and in the eyes of the majority of the Muslim Arab masses, meant: righteousness of conduct, renewal in religion and working for the future through a call to return to the 'conduct of the righteous predecessors'. *Al-salafīyah* in this sense was not a product of the twentieth or the nineteenth century, as all reform movements in Islam, among the Sunnis, are traditionalist in this sense.

Indeed, all those movements viewed the future through a certain era of Islamic history, namely the era of the 'righteous predecessors', which some authors limit to the age of the Companions and the Followers, the Rāshidūn Caliphs, in particular. Others extend that era to cover all the kings and rulers who followed in the steps of the Rāshidūn Caliphs, such as 'Umar bin 'Abd al-Azīz, or the *fuqahā'* and *'ulamā'* who followed in the steps of the Companions, irrespective of their era or age. This attraction to the conduct of the righteous predecessors is the meaning given to traditionalism by all who adopt it as a code of conduct, thought or reform.

To present the image of *al-salafīyah* in such a bright and realistic manner at the same time is to define its position in Islamic history. It is not to call for another traditionalism, old or new, but to highlight the historical and religious significance of a belief system which has come to be associated with backwardness and reactionism, avoidance of modernization and modernity, and resisting the ideas and methods of our modern time.

A discussion of traditionalism will remain incomplete and non-historical if I only deal with its bright and realistic image at the expense of 'the rest'. That 'rest' does not involve any negative aspects or any shortcomings that traditionalism may have suffered in the past or the present. What I mean to establish here is that traditionalism, as an intellectual, social and political movement, or as a certain approach to faith and religious conduct, was never alien to Arab-Islamic history. It was rather one aspect of the historical experience of the *ummah*: one of its aspects of reform.

If we look at all the traditionalist movements in Islamic history, in the context of the Arab-Islamic civilization, which was the world civilization at the time, we shall find that all those movements were a restoration of self-balance to the course of Arab history since the rise of Islam. In other words, traditionalism was always that part of the historical experience of Sunni Islam, by which that experience regained what preserved its existence and continuity, when its internal development produced what threatened that existence. It is, therefore, a type of self-resistance to maladies of inner origin. That resistance was sufficient when the Arab-Islamic civilization suffered no competition or threat from another contemporary civilization.

It is known that the civilization in which we live today imposes itself on us and on all peoples, in thought, technology, goods and weaponry, as a civilization for the entire age. It is totally different, falling outside Arab-Islamic civilization, which is plagued with backwardness and is now threatened from inside and out.

Consequently, the historical experience of the Arab-Islamic nation, in dealing with the contemporary civilization, cannot thrive on inspiration derived from 'the righteous predecessors' alone. That model was sufficient for us when history was of our own making, and the entire world was contained within our own precincts. But nowadays we have to be convinced, if some of us still need to be persuaded, that we no longer stand on our own, and certainly we will not be standing on our own in the future; the foreseeable future, at least. Therefore, the model to be followed in order to rebuild ourselves, and safeguard against obliteration, is not that of the 'predecessors', which poses as a self-sufficient world. It should encompass the entire historical experience of our nation, and it should learn from the historical experience of other nations who are, like us, struggling to protect their existence. And why not? We should also learn from the experiences of the nations that have imposed their civilization today as one for the entire world.

Recourse to identity as *al-salafiyah* was sufficient and effective when we were alone in our own home. But now that we have become a part of a whole, the only way to assert our existence and identity within that whole is to deal with it on its own logical terms, but from our own premises, not the premises of others. The logic of the whole to which we belong, i.e. the logic of contemporary civilization, can be summed up in two principles: rationality and critical outlook. Rationality should reign in economics, politics and social relations; and critical outlook should deal with everything else in life: nature, history, society, thought, culture and ideology. The logic of the conduct of the righteous predecessors representing Utopia in the historical experience of the Islamic nation was something else: it was a logic based on the concept that this world is merely a bridge to the other world. This logic was functional when the age was purely one of faith, and not an age of science, technology and ideologies.

True, this logic of faith is good for all time and places, for all people in general and Muslims in particular, because it stems from their own tradition. But, in the present age, it is good only as a moral principle, a guide for human behaviour towards God, and in his otherworldly aspirations. 'Conduct' here should remain a 'moral conduct', a source of virtue and piety, etc. But outside morality and ethics, we have to look for another logic in life itself, in its law of development, its direction and balance of powers.

Certainly, Islam is not merely the 'conduct of the ancestors', which is a thing of the past. It is, as every Muslim believes, good for all time and place. But to put this in words is one thing, to carry it out in deeds is another. Moreover, followers of all religions consider their religions good for all time and places. Therefore, they adhere to their religions and consider them the ultimate truth. If the Buddhists, Jews or Christians believed that the validity of their religions was limited to a certain time and place, or that it was temporary or relative, they would not have been religious or considered so. To follow any religion starts with the absolute faith in the validity of that religion for all time and places.

The question, then, is not whether Islam is good and valid for all time and places. No Muslim would remain Muslim if they doubted that religious postulate for a moment. But the question which should always be asked is whether the Muslims of today are good enough for their own time, able to live in their own age, to inaugurate a new 'conduct', compatible with the old 'conduct of the forefathers', making it a living reality, suitable to be followed by future generations in building their own code of conduct.

The historical experience of the nation has to be revived, by starting a new chapter, which will enable it to adapt to the present age, the age where each and everyone of its components asserts that it is the age of posterity, not of 'ancestry'.

## CHAPTER 6

# Extremism: Right and Left

When 'Islam' or 'Islamists' are mentioned in contemporary journalistic and political discourse, what mostly comes to mind are the extremist groups which raise the banner of Islam in one way or another. This is one of the common mistakes caused by the inaccurate usage of words. The Islamic trend, or what is sometimes called 'Political Islam', covers a large sector of contemporary Arab public opinion, spreading from the centre left to the extreme right, i.e. the extremist religious groups. Similarly, the modernist trend in the intellectual Arab arena extends from the centre right to the extreme left, i.e. the extremist leftist groups.

When I use the duality of right/left, I am using it functionally, as a means of classification only. The ideological implication of right/left in the West associates the 'right' with capitalism, liberalism and reactionism, while 'left' is associated with socialism and progress. But this is not my concern here, as it does not correspond with the current situation in the Arab world, where not everyone associated with modernity is considered a socialist or progressive, nor anyone associated with the Islamic trend considered a capitalist or a reactionary. I am using the terms only to indicate the positions of the two extremist groups. One is placed at an extreme end, the 'left', the other is placed at the opposite extreme, the 'right'.

The question to be asked here is: Against whom stands the extremism of the extreme left, and against whom stands the extremism of the extreme right? If we do not deal with this question, the impact of the terms may mislead us to think that the extremism of the left opposes those who stand at the extreme right. But this notion is refuted by the history of the rise of extremism on either side, as well as by the attitudes and arguments of both parties.

In fact, the left extremism is directed against the left itself, as much as the right extremism is directed against the right. The most bitter enemies of the extremist on either side are most often the 'people' nearest to him. In the present age, extremism of the left appeared in the second half of the 1960s in Europe, reaching its peak there and in many parts of the world in the late 1960s and the early 1970s. The leftist groups presented themselves as the alternative, not to the right, but to the left itself. Consequently, the immediate rivals to those new groups were the typical Communist parties, and the socialist parties in general. The leftist groups were not 'struggling' against the right, or the far right, but they were directing all their powers against the left itself, which they placed to their right.

Similarly the extremism of the right rose to object and protest against the right itself and not against the left. The extremist Islamist groups directed their objections and opposition against the 'central' or 'moderate' Islamic trends, as in the case of al-Khawārij [lit., those who go out] in the early stages of Islam. At the time, 'Alī bin Abī Ṭālib represented the religious trend, while Mu'āwiyah represented the worldly tendency inside Islam, not outside it. The extremism which appeared among the ranks of 'Alī whom his companions termed 'al-Khawārij', was basically against 'Alī himself; and they were so-called because they went out against him. It is true that they were also opposed to Mu'āwiyah, but their dissent did not harm Mu'āwiyah in aught; on the contrary, it was to his benefit. Moreover, when they dissented from 'Alī because he accepted arbitration, they did not go to fight Mu'āwiyah first, but they fought 'Alī and his followers. Furthermore, they did not conspire to assassinate Mu'āwiyah only, but both of them. As it happened, they succeeded in killing 'Alī but could not reach Mu'āwiyah. Had they thought carefully before carrying out their conspiracy, they would have realized that it was quite possible to assassinate 'Alī, because he did not surround himself with guards and sentries, while their chances with Mu'āwiyah were slim, as he was heavily guarded and quite wary. Extremism blinds the person and veils the objective facts, making him see the world through enchanted eyes.

The various contemporary extremist groups are similar to the Khawārij. They tend to 'dissent' or 'revolt' mostly against the leniency or the moderation of their own group towards the rival group. (The leftists revolt against the left and protest against its dialogue with the right. The extremists on the right revolt against their own group for their moderate tendencies.) Nonetheless, the result, in the majority of cases, is a blow against the party out of which the dissent has issued, and proves a benefit to the other party. In the end, this leads to the isolation of the extremist groups, whether right or left. They become marginalized as they repeat the same experience of extremism against themselves, separating into rival groups, accusing each other of 'heresy' in the manner of the Khawārij. The first opponent will always be the nearest neighbour, and thus extremist movements are fragmented and dispersed.

What should be emphasized here is that it has never happened, nor do I think it will ever happen, that an extremist group has ever changed a situation or made history. In most cases history is made by the struggling groups in the centre. Even when extremists take part, revolutions end in the same way: power is held by the 'moderates' who are in the 'centre' or near it. This is a fact known by the extremists, which is why their aim, in most cases, is not to assume power, but to die for the 'cause'. Of what type is this cause? How is it to be realized? What are the means of serving the cause practically and historically? These are questions the extremist does not and cannot consider. Extremism, in this case, becomes a kind of enchanted view of the world, assuming the form of escaping forward. Therefore, it is not surprising to see the extremist leaping from the extreme right to the extreme left, or the other way round. The escape forward may take the form of 'emigration' to other countries which were previous opponents, where the extremist assumes the role of peon or lackey mercenary for 'no cause'. (This reminds one of a verse by al-Mutanabbi: 'When the coward is alone in the arena he calls for jousting and fencing'.) This is the type of false awareness, where the individual forgets his real identity, and sees only what he is not.

Extremism is of various types and forms. The type which is active inside the traditionalist trend in contemporary Arab thought may undoubtedly find some justification in the absence of social and political democracy. Other justifications lie in the failure of the traditionalist trend, to date, to introduce the required innovation in Islamic thought, a type of innovation which keeps up with development and relates to reality. This is similar to the case of leftist extremism, which reached its peak in the late 1960s and the early 1970s, and found its justification in the absence of democracy on the one hand, and in the intellectual stagnation which plagued the 'left' in general on the other hand.

Finally, I have to point out that extremism in religion always follows politics. When politics is exercised in religion in matters of creed, extremism affects creed; when in matters of *al-sharī'ah*, it is seen in that field. This will be detailed in the next chapter.

# CHAPTER 7

# Extremism Between Creed and *al-Sharīʿah*

Islamic history has seen various types of extremism since the early decades of Islam. Some of these are still present in contemporary Arab religious thought one way or another. A review of the extremist movements in Islam, since the Great Fitnah ['strife' pursuant to the assassination of 'ʿUthmān bin 'Affān in 656CE], will show that they were all, without exception, connected to politics, directly or indirectly. This is so obvious that it is possible to say that extremism in Islam has always been an expression of a certain political position. This is easy to understand when we take into consideration the connection between religion and politics, or vice versa in the experience of Islamic civilization. Politics was exercised in the name of religion, seeking legitimacy from it and working under its umbrella.

There is no need, here, to be reminded of the political aspect of the extremist movements in Islam, such as the Khawārij, the extremist [Shīʿite] Ghulū, the movements of the Bāṭinīyah, etc. But I would like to demonstrate what makes the contemporary extremist Islamic movements different from those of the past. The old ones practised extremism at the level of creed (*al-ʿaqīdah*), whereas the contemporary ones practise [extremism] at the level of *al-sharīʿah*. None of the trends of the Khawārij or Bāṭinis posed the question of 'applying *sharīʿah*', nor did they take that as a slogan, rather all of their slogans pertained to 'creed', such as the relation between the essence of God and His attributes, between predestination and free will, as well as divine justice, the process of creation, etc. It is true that the central issue that gave rise to *al-kalām* (Islamic theology) in creed was that of *al-imāmah* [leadership of the imām/'imamate'] or the caliphate, which sparked disagreement in Islam, but it is also true that this issue was addressed at the level of creed not of *al-sharīʿah*. This means that politics was practised at the level of creed (*al-ʿaqīdah*) and not at the level of *al-sharīʿah*.

Today the situation is completely different. As the extremist Islamic movements disagree among themselves on matters connected with *al-*

*sharī'ah*, it follows that politics is exercised today in the sphere of *al-sharī'ah*, not of creed. It is enough to remember that the slogan of these movements is 'application of *al-sharī'ah*' for us to realize that the field where they practise is politics. So, instead of questions such as predestination and free will, belief and unbelief, inimitability and semblance, etc., which were the issues of contention in the past, on the basis of which the *muhājirūn* (theologians and rhetoricians of *al-kalām*) were divided into moderates and extremists, we find today other issues connected with *al-sharī'ah* and its application, such as amputating the hand of a thief; usury; the *hijāb* (veil for women), etc. In other words, politics today is exercised in Islam in the sphere of *al-sharī'ah*, and not that of creed as was the case in the past.

What is the cause of this shift? Why did Muslims in the past exercise politics in the sphere of creed and have no political disagreement on matters of *al-sharī'ah*? Why do they disagree today, politically, on matters of *al-sharī'ah* and not on those of creed? The answer to this question lies in history; that is in politics, and not in the religion itself.

History tells us that disagreement on matters of creed in Islam passed through two stages. The initial one, where the central issue was the *Imāmah*, is basically an internal matter. The second one was the stage of consolidation and standardization; the latter stage began when Islam collided with the creeds and religions of peoples who converted to Islam. A disagreement began, assuming a political-social aspect at first (the Mawalis, *ahl al-taswīyah*, *al-shu'ūbiyah* [all groups of non-Arabs integrating into Islam and to the Arab tribe, *al-qabīlah*, to varying degrees]), developing later into a 'purely' intellectual contention. There was disagreement on the level of creed because there was a multiplicity of religious and intellectual systems; whereas, socially speaking, there was but one social system, at the same level of development. This could not have caused disagreement about matters of *al-sharī'ah* (except on minor issues such as the disagreement between the Hanafis of Iraq and the Malikis of Medina, whose development differed only in degree, not in kind).

Similarly it may be said, and this is actually what happened, that the contemporary *salafī* (traditionalist) trend had started internally. Its central issue at first was the innovations which developed inside the Islamic society itself (visitation of tombs, the Sufi orders). Then that trend was standardized and this was the second, contemporary stage which developed from a clash between Muslim society and the economic, political and social systems of modern European civilization. Here again, the confrontation at first had a political aspect (resisting the European colonial expansion, on the one hand, and the relation with, or against, the

Ottoman caliphate, on the other). Then the matter developed into a disagreement of principles, concerning the social system (the Islamic system and Islamic *sharīʿah* against capitalism and Communism, etc.).

As extremism in creed expressed itself in the past against moderate doctrines, it expresses itself in *al-sharīʿah* against moderate doctrines as well. Issues of *al-sharīʿah* in the past were of lesser importance (differences between the schools of *fiqh* did not rise to the level of extremism). Today, differences between creeds (Sunni, Shīʿī, al-Ash ʿarī, Ḥanbalī) are side issues where focus is placed on *al-sharīʿah* and the slogan of its application is raised.

The conclusion we can draw from these comparisons is that from the historical perspective the phenomenon of disagreement in Islam, extremism included, is a process of acclimatization and adjustment to the incoming intellectual systems. The extremist tendencies were fragmented when the al-Ashʿarī doctrine arose in the midst of the Sunni doctrine (as the 'Twelver' doctrine arose in the midst of the Shīʿite doctrine), and led to a reconstruction of credo/theology (*ʿilm al-kalām*) by introducing the methods of logic and the philosophical concepts known at the time. So *al-kalām* was nourished on creed that began to rely on the 'abstract' rational intellect rather than practical thought, i.e. politics, as was the case at first. Nowadays it seems that comparing the 'future' with the 'past' will be something akin to 'comparing water to water' as it is said. That is to say that extremist trends will withdraw from the field when the moderates of the *salafī* orientation take upon themselves the task of rebuilding the principles of *al-sharīʿah* (*al-fiqh*, jurisprudence) by using, in a really practical manner, the contemporary methods and concepts of economics, sociology and politics, all of which are a product of the development of knowledge and society together. The superficial processes of 'reconciliation' are a thing of the past; they are just like those known in *al-kalām* in its early stages. What is needed today, in the field of *al-sharīʿah*, is to do what was done by the Ash ʿarite philosophers in the field of creed (Fakhr al-Dīn al-Rāzī, for instance); namely, a reconstruction of a methodology of thought in *al-sharīʿah*, starting with new premises and contemporary 'intents'. In other words, what is needed today is a renewal (*tajdīd*), emanating not from a mere resumption of *ijtihād* in the branches, but from re-rooting the origins. The starting point in our present age is to rehabilitate the mind of the *mujtahid*, renewing its construction. As without new minds there can be no new *ijtihād*.

## CHAPTER 8

# For the Procession of *Ijtihād*

Since the beginning of the modern Arab Awakening, towards the end of the nineteenth century, in particular, the slogan of 'opening the door of *ijtihād*' has been reiterated by those who reject 'Westernization'. They called for 'renewal' (*al-tajdīd*) in Arab-Islamic thought, as a solution for the contemporary problems and challenges facing Islam, both as a system of life and a framework for public and private social relations. There were some attempts in that regard made by certain Islamists, but they were mostly marked by ideological controversy, coupled with superficiality and overlooking the essence of problems. Other than that, the call for *ijtihād* has remained merely a call, raised under the pressure of occasional challenges, soon to be overlooked. At the same time, life resumes its usual course, while problems multiply and become more complex, widening the gulf between the jurisprudents of the past and the reality and complex problems of present life.

Needless to say, the reason for this situation is the lack of *mujtahidūn* qualified methodologically and conceptually to exercise *ijtihād* that rises to the level of the problems and challenges of the age. *Ijtihād* was originally resorted to for the sake of legislation in Islam, but it is not a text like the Qur'ān or the *sunnah*. It has no precedents of religious credibility and legitimacy like those grouped under the 'Consensus (*ijma*') of the Companions' or the 'Conduct of the Madinans', in the words of Imām Malik. *Ijtihād* is a method (*manhaj*) before anything else, and the *uṣūlīyūn* considered it the utmost exertion of the *mujtahid* to deduce the legal rulings of *al-sharī'ah* on the basis of the indicators [of the cases]. The exertion (*al-juhd*) meant here is, of course, the mental/conceptual effort (*al-juhd al-fikrī*). The basic evidence of judgments comes from the Qur'ān, the *sunnah* and what was affirmed by consensus.

*Ijtihād*, then, is first and foremost a mental/conceptual effort. It goes without saying that the necessary mental effort which must be expended, in whatever field, varies in type as well as style and means – that is, method, according to the variations in the problems which must be solved and the matters which the researcher – or the *mujtahid* – intends to treat. Since the problems of our age differ categorically from those of the past, it follows that the mental effort expected by present day *mujtahidūn* should be different in kind from what was expected of them in the past. To be more specific, we must take a quick look at the type of mental effort which was necessary and sufficient in the old *ijtihād*, in order to discern the type of intellectual effort needed today.

We must notice first that, until the end of the nineteenth and the early twentieth centuries, the lives of the Arabs and Muslims had run along the same lines since the rise of Islam. Their lives were defined by the same cultural, economic, social, political and institutional guidelines, all of which remained the same in nature and essence. True, there were many new events which faced the Muslims and were the drive behind the activity in *ijtihād*, and the rise of the so-called 'theoretical jurisprudence' (*al-fiqh al-naẓarī)*, which went far beyond the practical jurisprudence or the Islamic solutions for practical problems. But these 'new' problems which developed within the Arab-Islamic culture across the ages, previous to our exposure to contemporary Western culture and most of its products and institutions, were all of the type of the 'old' problems addressed in the time of the Prophet and the Companions. Therefore, the method adopted in *ijtihād* was based on analogy (*al-qiyās*): comparing particulars to particulars; comparing what is not directly provided by a text to the ruling of a text; comparing new situations and circumstances and problems 'similar precedents'; or relying for support on a text, a consensus or the *ijtihād* of previous *mujtahidūn*.

With the passage of time and the increasing number of *mujtahidūn*, it was natural that the possibilities provided by this kind of analogy would be exhausted. The particulars of the past, which are similar in nature, were restricted, or can be restricted. The *sharī'ah* texts are limited, and the efforts made to understand the meanings and significance of their wording were exhausted, too. The inevitable result was that the door of *ijtihād* 'closed up' (*inghilāq*) of its own accord and was not 'closed', as it was claimed.

The truth is that no one in Islam has the authority to 'close' the door of *ijtihād*, neither the rulers, nor the *fuqahā'* nor any other. There is no Church or any other institution in Islam empowered to 'close' or 'open' the door of *ijtihād*. *Ijtihād* is an essential source (*uṣūl*) of [Islamic] legislation (*al-tashrī'*), and it is, as we have mentioned, a mental effort to attain knowledge in rulings (*aḥkām*) of *al-sharī'ah*. It is the right of every Muslim possessed of the necessary knowledge and prerequisites of such endeavour.

The door of *ijtihād* closed on its own when there remained no room for more *ijtihād* within the scope of the cultural framework of the Muslims. When all the problems at hand were covered within that framework, when all the possibilities of the relation between words and meanings were exploited, when all precedents that could be used for analogy were exhausted, it was inevitable that the door of *ijtihād* should close up on its own, and that the people should resort to 'imitation' (*al-taqlīd*). The schools of jurisprudence became limited to four main ones, and people began to imitate the leaders of those schools, setting up a kind of argumentative 'competition' among them: an activity known as 'argumentation and discrepancies'.

Despite all this, it cannot be said that *ijtihād* has ceased completely. Every now and then *'ulamā'* would come to call for the abandonment of imitation to save the jurisprudential thought from the stagnation caused by the vicious circle of discrepancies. There is no doubt that these calls, and the attempts which accompanied them, stemmed from a realization of the disparity between past and current realities and their different natures. Such sentiment began to emerge in al-Andalus (Moorish Spain), especially when several historical, intellectual and political factors developed there to make the difference between the 'precedents' of the past and the later developments wider and deeper than what was experienced in the eastern Arab countries. That is why the need arose in al-Andalus for a methodology of *ijtihād* based not on 'analogy' and the relation of particulars, but one more capable of responding to new issues emerging from the development of civilization. Al-Shatibi was the most eminent renewer (*mujaddid*) in this field of *ijtihād* methodology.

Al-Shatibi was deeply aware that *ijtihād* by the old method had exhausted all its possibilities and, for the door of *ijtihād* 'to reopen', a 're-rooting of the roots' was needed by adopting the universals (*kulliyāt*) and *intent* (*maqāṣid*) of the *sharīʿah*, rather than being restricted to comprehending the meaning of the utterances (*alfāẓ*) in the texts and deducing the judgments from these, or using analogy by comparing one event to another where there is no supporting text.

Thus, if we undertake a comprehensive reading of the particulars transmitted in the *sharīʿah* rulings and infer general universal rules based on this survey, we shall have a foundation of comprehensive rules applicable to any particular eventuality that may emerge. Similarly, if we begin from the standpoint that the [legal] intent (*maqāṣid*) of *al-sharīʿah* is ultimately, in the final analysis, in consideration of the public good (*al-maṣlaḥah al-'āmah*), and that the *sharīʿah* texts themselves aim at such consideration, then the public good becomes the guiding principle, superior to any other.

Some followers of al-Shatibi went as far as saying that, when a *sharīʿah* text conflicts with the public good, the latter is preferred, as the text had originally come to safeguard it. Whatever the case, there can be no doubt that the public good is coloured by conditions, cultural givens, and historical developments; moreover, *ijtihād* that is based on and proceeding from the public good will lose its significance and effectiveness if it is not a dynamic and innovative *ijtihād* emanating from a dynamic and innovative mind.

Hence, it becomes clear that calling for *ijtihād* and opening its door will remain meaningless without 'opening' the mind entrusted with the task of *ijtihād*. That is because the door of *ijtihād* was never 'closed', but it 'closed up' of its own accord when the mind that was practising it became closed, within the framework of a culture and civilization that had itself stopped moving and growing. It is indispensable, then, for there to be an opening up (*infitāḥ*) of the Arab-Islamic mind, in order to face the opening up in [world] civilization that has recently taken place. Without this, there can be no *ijtihād* commensurate with the level of contemporary events.

The opening up of the mind must begin with opening up to life itself, to the new givens that carry with them the laws governing its development. It was sufficient for the *mujtahid,* in the past, to be knowledgeable in the Arabic language, its grammar and rhetoric and in religion, the *ḥadīth*, Qur'ānic commentary (*tafsīr*), and *al-fiqh*. But the economic and political aspects of life did not differ in the age of the *ijtihād* from prior ages nor did the 'public interest'; its points of similarity were the like of the particulars of the past upon which the reasoning by analogy (*al-qiyās*) depended and of the same kind and nature; therefore, daily experience was enough to deal with them. But, today the situation is different.

The tremendous change brought about by the industrial civilization that persists today along with the 'scientific revolution' in astronautics, atomic science, biology, economics and sociology, makes opening up to these disciplines, their epistemological principles and their impact on the human race a necessary prerequisite for the qualification of the *mujtahid*. Such knowledge is no less important than being competent in language and religion. This is the only way for *ijtihād* to catch up with life and its development. The majority of Muslim *'ulamā'* today lack the ability to exercise *ijtihād* that can keep abreast of life. Their *ijtihād* lags behind, so it does not benefit the present, and the past has no need for it.

The need is urgent, then, for the inauguration of a 'new age of codification' in a field of *ijtihād* that can keep abreast of contemporary life, which is first and foremost a question of method...a matter of rational behaviour.

CHAPTER 9

# The Rationality of the Rulings of *al-Sharīʿah*

I have so far been stressing the necessity of rebuilding Islamic thought on the assumption that the rebuilding of a conceptual methodology in *al-sharīʿah*, based on new premises and contemporary [legal] 'intent', is necessary. In other words, what is needed is a renewal, stemming not from a mere resumption of *ijtihād* in the branches, but from a 're-rooting of the sources (*taʾṣīl al-uṣūl*)'.

'Re-rooting the *uṣūl*' was the project of Imām al-Shāṭibī, the Andalusian Maliki faqīh (d. AH 790/AC 1388). In his book *The Correspondences* (*al-muwafaqāt*), he tried to restructure a methodology of jurisprudence based on a consideration of the [legal] intent of *al-sharīʿah*, which had remained since the times of al-Shāfiʿī dependent on 'exploiting the utterances (*istithmār al-alfāẓ*)' and 'discerning the causes (*istinbāṭ al-ʿillal*)', by using analogy. The consideration of [legal] intent is an old idea, as old as Islamic legislation itself. Yet, there are those who base their thought and *ijtihād* on analogy, comparing a branch to a root, because they have a common factor which is the 'cause'. Such thinkers do not pay any heed to the intent of *al-sharīʿah* or the [public] good except when there is no 'cause' to be found, so the [public] good will be considered, at that point, a suitable cause (*ʿillah*) (which is what al-Ghazālī did, for instance). Yet, there are those who base their thinking and *ijtihād* on a consideration of [legal] intent, using the causes and the exploitation of utterances as auxiliary sources.

In the final analysis, the starting point is the same; namely, the *sharīʿah* rulings, the commandments and prohibitions mentioned in the Qurʾān and *sunnah* are not arbitrary or lacking a logical basis; rather, they are judgments based on rationality and wisdom. The Legislator has not specified in an explicit text the rationale or wisdom behind most of the rulings (if He did not, for example, textually specify the reason for the prohibition of wine or the prohibition of adultery). The rulings mentioned in the

Qur'ān and *sunnah* do not cover all particulars, circumstances and incidents and the cases which appear or which emerge as a result of development. Therefore, the 'application of *al-sharī'ah*' requires the *mujtahid* to set the principles to be observed in this application, the function of which is to establish the rationality of the rulings which he promulgates in response to events and developments. It is clear that the rationality required here is not the abstract rationality alone such as that which belongs to human positive law, but it must be the rationality behind the *sharī'ah* rulings mentioned in the Qur'ān and *sunnah*. And since the latter is not specified by text, mostly, the *mujtahid* has to build it up and establish its origins, by setting principles and premises as a frame of reference.

And here the two methods part company: one adopts analogy, causation and the exploitation of utterances; the other calls for a consideration of [legal] intent as a basis and starting point.

The first method takes each ruling apart, looking for the presumed cause that the Legislator is thought to have considered in promulgating it. Next, the judgment is generalized to include every case where that cause may exist. The simple and well-known example in this connection is the proscription of wine. The Qur'ānic text proscribes wine without giving the cause for that proscription. The *mujtahid* would posit the rationality of this proscription on the cause which he believes was causally associated with the ruling, namely that of intoxication. (Intoxication inactivates the mind, and impinges upon culpability.) Then, the ruling is generalized to include wine and all other alcoholic beverages for the same cause of intoxication. This is an example of analogy where wine is compared to all alcoholic beverages: comparing the branch to the origin (which is textually specified). This is an easy and useful way because it is applicable, but only when there are subdivisions of the same type, with a ruling concerning one of them. But when there are subdivisions of a different nature, or developments that fit under no [precedent] ruling, the process becomes complicated. The 'causation' becomes far-fetched and weak, and the *mujtahid* may give up and resort to imitation, because the circle of causation, analogy and exploitation of utterances narrows down to a degree that does not allow a continuation of uninterrupted *ijtihād*.

The second method proposes to start with the intent of *al-sharī'ah* in the process of establishing the rationality of judgments, without which *al-sharī'ah* cannot be applied to the new developments or the various dissimilar cases and circumstances. Since the good of the people is the foremost intent of the Legislator ('Allāh is not in need of any of His creatures'; 3, Āl 'Imrān, 97), the consideration of [public] good should establish the rationality of *sharī'ah* judgments, hence that interest is the origin of all origins (*uṣūl*). Obviously, this method has an unlimited scope of movement, which makes *ijtihād* viable in every case.

To delineate the limited nature of the first method and the unlimited of the second, it is sufficient to point out that, in the first method, the search is for the 'cause' of the ruling, by trying to deduce what is thought to have been in the consideration of the Legislator when He issued his ruling. To put this in inappropriate fashion, we might say that the *mujtahid* in this case looks at the Legislator (God) the way he looks at a human judge, trying to discern his intentions: Why did he judge this way and not that way? And to explore intentions is a matter of surmise, completely void of certainty. The limits of surmise are so narrow that they leave no room for preferring one opinion over another. In regard to the second method, the starting point is basically rational: there is a primary 'cause' at the base of all *sharīʿah* rulings, which must also be the basis of applying *al-sharīʿah* in every time and place, and that is in consideration of public good. In addition to this basic general principle, we have the task of defining the interest in every case and judgment, which is a manageable task, because the search here is carried out within a human field, namely the tangible field of life, not the field of 'intentions', which are not known with certainty except by the party who entertained them. Moreover, this method opens the door to perpetual renewal and *ijtihād*, because the consideration of [public] good develops in accordance with the development of those interests, with the developing situations and changing times.

There is another difference to be considered here, i.e. the method of analogy and causation binds the *mujtahid* to the language (i.e. the text of the ruling). So, the language becomes a participating factor in legislation. This is because 'discovering' (*iktishāf*) the cause (*ʿillah*) is mostly dependent upon a type of relationship which the *mujtahid* establishes between words and meaning. If the text proscribes wine, for instance, the method of causation and analogy would force us to define the word 'wine' in the language of the Arabs at the time of the Prophet and to determine whether the imperative mood of the verb 'avoid it' is binding or not. [There are some verbs in the imperative mood in the Qurʾān and *sunnah* which are not binding, or at least they do not carry legislative force, such as 'go about your ways' (after the communal prayers) or 'eat and drink'.] This method also demands that the *mujtahid* should make decisions about unusually abstruse questions: were the words intended to legislate for one particular case or for a number of cases, in general or vice versa? A decision in such cases is difficult, as it depends on surmise, not on certainty. Hence all jurisprudence (*fiqh*) based on this method is entirely presumptive. To get out of this state of 'presumption', and to base judgments on 'decisiveness' (*al-qaṭʿ*) (which in *al-sharīʿah* is equivalent to certitude in rational disciplines), there is no way other than that of considering the intent and the [public] good as bases in legislation. It is because in this case the *mujtahid's* concern is not the utterance – the reality, the metaphor (*al-majāz*), the similarity, the particulars (*al-khuṣūṣ*), or the generalities (*al-'umum*) – but the 'occasions of revelation' (*asbāb al-nuzūl*). This is a very wide field which permits the conferral of rationality upon rulings in a manner that facilitates their application by the *mujtahid* in the different cases and circumstances.

To save the reader from getting lost in generalities which are commonplace to the specialist, I will use the example of the judgment of 'amputating the hand of the thief', which is a textually-specified ruling in the Qur'ān. How can this judgment be rationalized?

The first method, which depends on analogy and the exploration of the meanings of words, is completely incapable of building a rationale for this judgment. It can only say that proscription of robbery was in consideration of the public good (protection of property). In other words it makes the public good and the [legal] intent the 'causes of the ruling'. But since all the effort in this method is geared towards finding the 'cause', the method ends with the conclusion that: 'Protection of property is a necessity of human social life. Therefore, proscription of robbery is mandated in accordance with [public] good, which is also the cause of the ruling.' But someone may ask: 'Why is the penalty of theft the "amputation of the thief's hand" and not imprisonment or lashing, for instance?' The followers of analogy and causation will be at a loss for an answer. If they try, they will be lost in hypotheses which may lead to conjectures completely negating rationality. For example, some may justify the amputation by saying that the thief used his hand in stealing, so the hand must be amputated. Since this method depends on analogy, one may say, 'Why should not the punishment of adultery be penalized by amputating the organ that affected the crime, or at least to resort to castration?' Thus, the follower of analogy will get lost in a world of conjectures and hypotheses, and get farther and farther from the rationality of the rulings of *al-sharīʿah*.

The second method does not fall into such labyrinths, because its starting point is [legal] intent, that is to say that a ruling must be justified and rational in connection with a certain situation. So, if we liberate ourselves from the impact of analogy and diction, and turn our attention more seriously to the 'occasions of revelation' (*asbāb al-nuzūl*), which, in this case, is the social situation that apprehended a certain kind of [public] good and a certain method in considering it, we shall find that amputating the hand of the thief was a justified and rational measure within the context of that situation. Looking back to the time of the mission of Muḥammad, and considering the rulings of *al-sharī'ah* applied in those days, the following facts emerge.

Amputating the hand of the thief was in force in Arabia before Islam. Also, in a Bedouin society, where the people move about with their tents and camels in search of pasture, it was not possible to penalize the thief by imprisonment. There are no walls or prisons in the desert, and no authorities to guard the prisoner and provide him with food, drink and clothing. Therefore, the only alternative was corporal punishment. Since the spread of robbery in such a society would definitely lead to its destruction, for lack of walls and safes, it was necessary to make the corporal penalty serve two purposes: to obviate against the possibility of perpetual recidivist theft; and to put a mark on the thief so as to warn people against him. Amputation certainly fulfils both aims. Therefore, amputating the hand of the thief is quite a reasonable measure in a desert Bedouin society, where people are nomadic.

With the advent of Islam, the civic and social situation was no different from what it used to be. The amputation penalty for theft was among the measures, traditions and rites that were transferred from the Arab society before Islam, to be incorporated within the Islamic ethics, as a *sharī'ah* ruling and not a mere convention. (The same thing may be said about the conditions laid down by the jurisprudents to prove incidence of adultery [i.e. the requirement of four witnesses to the act of penetration]. Those conditions were mandated because they could obtain in a Bedouin atmosphere where there are no walls, or rooms or fences. So, the details of the action could be seen easily by the witnesses. But is it reasonable to stipulate the same conditions in a modern city? That renders the crime impossible to prove.)

To build the rationality of a *sharī'ah* ruling on the 'occasions of revelation' within the scope of considerations of [public] good would open the way for the construction of another rationality concerning other occasions of revelation, or new situations. This would renew the life of jurisprudence and *ijtihād*, and *al-sharī'ah* would be able to cope with development and be suitable for application in every time and place. All this raises an important jurisprudential question: Does the *sharī'ah* ruling conform to the 'cause' (*al-'illah*) or to the [public] good?

CHAPTER 10

# Rulings and Dependence

Some time ago, a serious argument flared up in Egypt about a *fatwa* (Islamic legal opinion) issued by the Mufti of Egypt (official interpreter of *al-sharī'ah*), which permitted acceptance of interest in certain financial transactions such as investment certificates and bank shares, on the assumption that there is no exploitation in this kind of transaction. It is known that the prevention of exploitation is the significance of proscribing usury (*al-ribā*). One of the responses I had the chance to read was by an eminent legal authority in Egypt, considered to have an Islamic orientation. He opposed that *fatwa* on various grounds, one of which was that *sharī'ah* rulings follow the underlying causes (*al-'illal*) and not their [legal] consequence(s)/significance [lit., 'wisdom' – *al-ḥikmah*].[1]

The difference between 'cause' (*al-'illah*) and 'consequence' (*al-ḥikmah*) in the terminology of the *fuqahā'* is that 'cause' (*al-'illah*) is a characteristic of the thing about which a ruling was promulgated. Intoxication is a characteristic of wine, and by it the prohibition is known, so it then is the 'cause' of its proscription. The increase or 'interest' (*al-fā'idah*) imposed in usury is the quality that caused the proscription of this kind of sale. Travelling and sickness are two causes for dispensation from fasting in Ramadan, etc. The [legal] 'consequence' (*al-ḥikmah*) is the motive behind the promulgation of the ruling, namely providing a benefit or warding off harm. The consequence of proscribing wine is to ward off its stupefying of the mind. The consequence of proscribing usury is to ward off the harm of exploitation. The consequence of the dispensation from fasting in Ramadan for the travellers or the sick is to ward off harm of hardship and warding off harm is in itself a benefit. Therefore, the significance, in the final analysis, is the benefit sought from promulgating the ruling.

The *fuqahā'*, in general, specify that the *sharī'ah* ruling should depend on its *cause*, not its consequence.[2] They argue that consequence may be implied and not defined, while the cause must be stated and well-defined. They add that the consequence may be a benefit left for the people to evaluate, and they inevitably differ in their assessment of it. The consequence of dispensation from fasting in Ramadan for the traveller and the sick, as shown above, is to ward off hardship. So if we connect the ruling with the hardship [itself], whether it exists or not, we will disagree about the assessment of the hardship that allows for this dispensation. This may also lead to allowing dispensation from fasting under other types of hardship, like that experienced with work in factories. To avoid all this, they hold firmly to the cause in their rulings and not to the consequence, as they believe that this way the [wisdom inherent in the] consequence will also be realized.

Undoubtedly, this kind of reasoning is quite sensible and justifiable within an epistemological system based on the jurisprudential principles laid down by the ancient *fuqahāʾ*, including those principles of causation, analogy, dependence and the like. But these jurisprudential principles were not prescribed by *al-sharīʿah*, neither by the Qurʾān nor by the *sunnah*. They are the work of the jurisprudents themselves. They are principles of thought and methodology. There is nothing against the adoption of other principles of methodology if they can realize the aim(s) of legislation at a certain time, in a better way. The *mujtahidūn* are distinguished from others because they have the ability to derive principles to be followed, though they may differ in one way or another with different *mujtahidūn*. The schools of jurisprudence (*al-madhāhib*) – the Hanafis, Shafiʿis, Malikis, Ḥanbalīs, Ẓāhiris and others – differ in their methodological principles. Some adopt causation (*al-taʿlīl*), others reject it. Some use analogical reasoning (*al-qiyās*), others avoid it. Some believe in the dependence (*dawrān*)[3] of rulings on their causes, others (like the Hanafis) reject that. Some (the Muʿtazilites) think that dependence/variance leads to certitude (*al-yaqīn*), others say it leads to supposition (the Ash'aris in general). Still, there are those who believe that this dependence is a condition for the correctness of the cause (*al-ʿillah*), but it is not a proof of its soundness.

Therefore, to say that rulings depend on/vary with their causes and not on their consequences makes no sense except to those who believe in causation and dependence. But those who follow neither this nor that opinion are not in need of such a claim. When we put this matter forward, here, in the scope of the call for a rebuilding of the sources (*al-uṣūl*) and for a re-rooting of them, we want to direct the thinking of the *mujtahidūn* who desire genuine renewal and those who are actually legislating it, to the foundation principles of the *uṣūl* themselves. We want them to rebuild these [principles] and come out with a new methodology fit to cope with the development taking place whether in methodology or in trends of thought and induction, or in social life and its current activities imposed by the requisites and needs of the age.

The foundations of the *uṣūl* (the jurisprudential principles) which have informed the Islamic *fiqh* up to the present time go back to the 'Age of Historical Record and Standardization', which is at the beginning of the 'Abbāsid Age [ca. 750CE], and some belong to a later era. Before the Age of Recording, there were no standardized principles to inform *ijtihād* thought. The *fuqahā'* who laid down those principles were following the epistemological system current in their time, and the needs and interests which imposed themselves in that age. Since our age is different from the 'Age of Historical Record', whether in methods or [public] good, it becomes necessary to consider this difference and respond to its needs.

'Umar bin al-Khaṭṭāb acted according to his own *ijtihād*, and that of the Companions whom he consulted, in a matter covered by a text. He imposed the land tax (*al-kharāj*) on the conquered territories instead of dividing them among the warriors, out of regard for the present and future welfare. He also opted not to divide the war booty equally, as was the practice of the Prophet and Abū Bakr, saying that 'justice' (*al-'adl*) demands division on the basis of precedence in Islam and the degree of kinship to the Messenger. If 'Umar bin al-Khaṭṭāb, the first legislator in Islam after the Qur'ān and *sunnah*, put the interest and intents of *al-sharī'ah* above any other consideration, why do not the present day *mujtahidūn* and renovators (*mujaddidun*) follow in his footsteps, rather than follow the *fuqahā'* of the 'Age of Recording and Standardization'? Why do we make things difficult for ourselves and confine our *ijtihād* to principles that once responded to [public] good and [legal] intent, in one way or another, in past times, when they can no longer serve the same purpose satisfactorily at the present? Moreover, those principles were based on assumptions by the *mujtahidūn* and they contain nothing decisive or certain, as testified by those *mujtahidūn* themselves.

The dependence of rulings on [public] good is a self-evident principle, so long as we decide that [public] good is the original basis of legislation, which I think was the principle adopted by the Caliph 'Umar bin al-Khaṭṭāb. *Ijtihād*, then, should not be about accepting or rejecting a principle, but about removing the mechanical feature from the concept of 'dependence', and in rising with the concept of the good to the level of the real public interest, as defined by Islamic ethics. Without this kind of renewal, every *ijtihād* within the confines of the old jurisprudential principles will be an imitation and not a renewal, even if it proffers 'new' *fatwas*, or interpretations termed by the old jurisprudents as 'jurisprudential tricks'. The development that marks our age has no use for those tricks, whatever they may be. It is a development in social, economic and political life, on national and international levels, which cannot be embraced except by a mind that can rise with *ijtihād* and renewal to the level of that development. The Islamic trend in contemporary Arab thought is required to rebuild in this context, and on these bases, if they want to relinquish ambiguous slogans such as 'Islam is the solution', and move on to practical solutions for practical problems posed by contemporary life: real Islamic solutions, but contemporary ones as well.

## Notes

1. The term for 'ruling' or 'judgment' is *ḥukm* (pl. *aḥkām*) and it is from this same root (ḥ-k-m) which the term for 'wisdom' – *hikmah* – derives and, in this case, may be translated as 'significance' or 'consequence' of a given law. That is, legal penalties, for example, have legal significance or consequences for the society such as maintaining the social order or deterring theft or other crimes.

2. The distinctions in *al-fiqh* are best illustrated by an example such as provided by the author in the case of wine (*al-khamr*). Wine has numerous 'characteristics' or 'qualities' which describe it including taste, odour, colour, as well as its intoxicating properties. *Al-khamr* is also made of fermented grapes as opposed to *al-nabīdh*, which is made from fermented dates. The *fuqahā'*, in deliberating the legal implications of its prohibition, considered the characteristics of wine in aggregate in order to attempt to determine which of the characteristics was 'causative' or constituted the *'illah* for its proscription, and this was, almost uniformly, agreed to be the intoxicating properties of the drink. That is, *al-khamr* was prohibited on the basis of its intoxicating effects and the 'wisdom' (*al-ḥikmah*) or legal consequence of this was that it prevented the impairment of human faculties of judgment and impinged upon 'culpability' (*al-taklīf*), which prevented the performance of one's prayers, for example, or which were apt to cause social disturbances. In brief then, the *'illah* is the 'cause' and the *ḥikmah* is the principle corresponding to the [intended] effect of the ruling. As the author has stated, there is a hazard, bordering on the sacrilege, in attempting to surmise the 'legal intent[s]' or *maqāṣid* of *al-sharī'ah*, as the 'legislator' (*al-shāri'*)is assumed to be *divine* and it is not moot for the human to speculate in such matters. For some of the *fuqahā'*, the matter of positing an *'illah* for the purpose of analogical reasoning (*al-qiyās*) was already a transgression of bounds given that *al-sharī'ah* could potentially be anything that God commanded, whether or not it was in accordance with human reason (*al-'aql*) or suppositions about 'public good' (*al-maṣlaḥah*) or not. The most famous exponent of this approach was the Andalusian jurist Ibn Ḥazm (d.1064) – the textualist *par excellance* who rejected analogy and, for example, in the case of wine restricted the ruling only to *al-khamr* as it was this beverage alone which was *textually* specified and not other.

3. The term '*al-dawrān*', which can literally mean 'rotation' or 'going around' and here has been rendered as 'dependence', is used in a number of contexts by the *fuqahā'* and is susceptible to multiple definitions. It may be referred to in a connotation of being a 'probable cause', but it may also refer to the fact that legal status can change or 'turn'. For example, grape juice is legal to drink; once this juice ferments to become wine, it becomes prohibited; if this juice ferments further to become vinegar, it is again legal.

## Chapter 11

# Every Age has its Special Needs

It goes without saying that the most prominent feature of contemporary life is change and exchange, whether people consider this change as a sign of progress and ascent in civilization or as entailing much deviation and a retrograde decline in 'noble human values'. There is no denial that developments in every field of life are accelerating by the day and the hour. This makes it essential for civilized people who keep pace with development to review the laws they make for themselves, to regulate their individual and communal conduct. While revision does not necessarily mean the removal or the suspension of one law or another, or of one rule of conduct or the other, a revision sometimes necessitates a rearrangement of priorities and needs, which may entail the addition of supplementary statutes here and there.

In the Arab-Islamic world, we live in the midst of this change, yet we are steeped in the colourful and vital heritage of a deep past. We are often oblivious to this situation and we go on seeking renewal, wondering what we should take from our heritage and from the laws of our age, namely the laws of the countries that are the builders of the present civilization. In our so wondering, we forget or ignore the fact that in order to deal with the situation of which we are in the midst, as a result of the ceaseless, fundamental and expansive change that affects our life, we need a thorough revision of our norms and the basic principles of our conduct. It is not enough to wonder what we should pick and choose, as if life were still and frozen in one state, as it used to be in the past, or as if the train of development is waiting for us to pick and choose.

Needless to say, it is no longer possible for us to be selective. I believe that human life across the ages has not been based on such an act of selection. While it is not fair to strip men of their power to control events, neither is it fair to ignore the relative nature of this power, which gives men the ability to choose from the alternatives in which they imagine they are at liberty to exercise their choice. But in reality, all men can do, with or without success, is to adjust to developments, whether those in which they take part, or others that may overtake them unawares. Adjustment means to adapt/accommodate oneself or the collective self to the new developments; not to succumb to them, but to somehow regain the power to control them. The deeper the awareness of the type of development, the wider the possibilities before the self to protect its independent authenticity and to ensure the continuation of its origins and [cultural] referents during the required process of adjustment/accommodation, which will then assume deep dimensions and combine rebuilding reality with re-rooting the original sources (*uṣūl*).[1]

I am not alone in these thoughts. There are many others who think that it is possible to overcome many problems facing us in present day life by establishing a kind of coordination and integration between the modern demands of renewal and our traditional values and codes, which are a part of our identity and culture. I want to emphasize in this context that the call to realize original authenticity (*al-aṣālah*) and contemporaneousness, which has been uselessly reiterated in our speeches and writings for more than a century, will remain a mere call beaten about by the waves of change imposed on present life, unless that call could rise to a level which makes it a call for conscious adjustment to the new developments in order to control them, by focusing on a new re-rooting of the original sources. Here are some ideas that may help in deepening the awareness of some aspects of the problem in question.

Some of the *uṣūlīyūn* and *fuqahāʾ* who tended towards renewal when the door of *ijtihād* closed up began to think of re-rooting the origins of *fiqh* in accordance with the [legal] intent(s) of *al-sharīʿah*, rather than limiting *ijtihād* to analogy; namely, comparing sub-divisions supported by a text with others not so supported. They began with this 'original' premise: '*al-sharīʿah* was laid down for the benefit of human beings in the present and the future'. The intents of *al-sharīʿah*, therefore, fall into three categories: necessities, needs and improvements. The necessities they specified as five: religion (*al-dīn*), self (*al-nafs*), mind (*al-ʿaql*), offspring (*al-nasl*) and wealth (*al-māl*) (some placed self before religion). The needs are all that require the removal of hardship and distress, such as the dispensation from the fast in Ramadan for the sick and for travellers, and the enjoyment of innocent pleasures. The improvements cover the adoption of what the mind discerns as good among customs and new developments, and the avoidance of what is bad, whether among necessities or needs. Then those jurisprudents added a complement to each of those five parts, provided they do not annul one of the source principles of the *uṣūl*. They considered the necessary intents to be an origin each of the needs, improvements and accoutrements, considering that 'both the interests of religion and those of worldly life are based on the five points mentioned above' – i.e. the preservation of religion, self, mind, offspring and wealth. Moreover, they insisted that these five points were not deduced from the Islamic religion alone, but also from 'looking into reality, and the customs and laws of nations'.

However, our main concern here is not details that belong to the field of jurisprudence; we may still look into these five intents of *al-sharīʿah* from a historical point of view.

Our ancient *fuqahāʾ* defined those intents by induction, i.e. by considering the givens of their civilization at the time, and by referring to the commandments and prohibitions of *al-sharīʿah*. They deduced the five necessities mostly from within Islamic society of the time, which was a world of its own, independent from other societies, which were of little importance compared with the Arab-Islamic society whose civilization dominated the whole world. But today we live in a different world, one in which we follow, and are not followed, a world of different situations, rights, duties, contentions, threats, etc. Any serious thinker of renewal and of opening the door of *ijtihād*, and of realizing original [cultural] authenticity and contemporaneousness together, must take into consideration the new changes, which are both deep and numerous.

True it is that the five areas denoted by our ancient *fuqahāʾ* as necessities have always been, and will always be, indispensable. They are the basic intents of any legislation aiming completely at serving the 'welfare of the people'. But those interests are no longer limited to those five areas. We must also include the right to freedom of expression, the right to political affiliation, the right to choose and change rulers, the right to employment, food, residence and clothing, the right to education and health-care, and all the other basic rights of a citizen in present day society. In addition to the needs mentioned by our ancient *fuqahāʾ*, there are now many new needs, like the need to provide for health and the prevention of disease by establishing sufficient hospitals and other health services, and the need for taking necessary measures to encourage intellectual activities in various scientific, artistic and theoretical fields, in order to acquire sound knowledge about reality and events. As for the improvements to be decided by our age, they are simply innumerable.

But all the above is only one aspect of the requisites of life on an acceptable level in present day society, namely, the rights and the needs of the citizens as individuals. The other aspect is related to what is necessary, required, beneficial and fulfilling for the nation as a whole. I do not believe that there is anyone in the Arab nation today who would argue that in order to defend our national existence it is indispensable to realize a minimum unity among the Arab countries, based on joint planning, actual cooperation and real solidarity, in the hope of reaching a comprehensive unity or federation. I have no doubt that all Arabs today believe that among the necessities of stability in the Arab world, and the realization of a minimum degree of the sought after unity, is the liberation of Palestine and securing the right of its people to self-determination. Nor do I believe that there is anyone among the Arabs who does not think that in order to realize development and progress in the Arab world of today it is essential to build authority on real democratic bases and to establish social justice. The needs are innumerable, but the most essential are the needs for development, liberation, power and sovereignty. The improvements demanded, on every level, are also innumerable. None of the accoutrements deserve mention here more than the protection of the nation's fame by avoiding whatever may impair its values and ethics, and the necessity of promulgating its values and gaining supporters and allies for its causes on every level.

These are only some of the necessities, needs and improvements demanded by our age. Undoubtedly they do not abolish or substitute for those specified by our ancient *fuqahāʾ* in their jurisprudential efforts. On the contrary, they complement them and provide the conditions for their protection in present day life.

To conclude, I may say that while there are general, eternal necessities such as those defined by our ancient *fuqahāʾ*, it must be stressed that each and every age has its own special necessities, needs and accoutrements. So, when we succeed in making the necessities of our age part of the intents of our *al-sharīʿah*, we will have not only opened the door of *ijtihād* to the developing and renewing events of our age, but will have also begun to re-root the original sources of our *sharīʿah* itself in a manner that enables it to respond flexibly to any new development or change that may occur.

## Note

1. Here, again, the author is discussing the concept of *ta'ṣil al-uṣūl*, which literally means re-rooting the roots. The term *asl* (pl. *uṣūl*) means 'source', 'root', or 'origin'. Thus the term *al-aṣālah* connotes an original cultural authenticity that is rooted in the ancient sources of Arab-Islamic civilization. It bears mentioning that the term *uṣūli* derives from the same root and refers to a scholar of the *uṣūl al-dīn* (root-sources of the religion).

CHAPTER 12

# 'Avoid the *Ḥudūd* Penalties when in Doubt'[1]

Since the modern Arab Awakening, which soon swept across the entire Muslim world, with the efforts of Jamal al-Din al-Afghani (d. 1897CE) and Muḥammad 'Abduh (d. 1905CE), the Muslim masses have used the slogan of 'application of Islamic *sharī'ah*' to propound to the masses, the alternative which they hoped would take them to the enjoyment of a free and honourable life. Every member of the Muslim masses, all over the world, aspires to the day when Islamic *sharī'ah* will be applied in a manner that can remove political and social injustice, realize freedom and dignity for the human being, and pave the way to good deeds and noble conduct in order for these principles to become the bases of life in Islamic society, nay, in the whole of human society.

The Muslim *ummah*, and many Muslim intellectuals, have consciously realized that the ideal Islamic life cannot be achieved except under exceptional situations, and probably not before the end of human life on earth. Therefore, the perfect application of *sharī'ah* and justice is linked to the advent of the 'awaited mahdī' (*al-mahdī al-muntaẓar*).

This idea of the awaited mahdī has a profound significance. It indicates that the application of Islamic *sharī'ah*, namely, the realization of the Islamic Utopia, will remain relative in worldly time, the time of human systems of government, and that it will not be complete until the advent of the awaited mahdī, who will realize, directly and comprehensively, the divine will on earth.

I believe this is the idea which guided the people of authority in Islam, since the time of the Prophet, whether they were caliphs, kings, jurisprudents or any other personage who had a say in the application of *al-sharī'ah*. I am also of the opinion that they all believed that applying the divine *sharī'ah* by humans over humans, who are inherently imperfect, cannot be done except in a relative manner. This relativity gives Islamic life its meaning, because if perfection is reached, neither life nor laws would have any meaning.

Relativity, then, is the feature that marked the application of Islamic *sharīʿah* across the ages, since the rise of Islam. The Qurʾān, which includes the principles and rulings of this *sharīʿah*, was not revealed all at once. It was revealed in portions and stages, over a period of 23 years. Consequently, the application of *sharīʿah* rulings was relative, in that sense, even at the time of the Prophet. It was gradual and in stages; as a ruling would be textually specified, another one would come to complete or adjust that ruling, as if the first were a precursor to a final ruling.

Such has been the relativity, from the death of the Messenger up to our present day, characterizing the application of Islamic *sharīʿah*. Naturally, there were degrees in that relativity. At the time of the four Rāshidūn (Orthodox) Caliphs, the application of *sharīʿah* was probably between 80 and 90 per cent [complete], but that fell markedly in later ages. After the first century of Islam, people felt that *al-sharīʿah* was no longer in effect, so there was a public outcry for its application. The people in charge, who had genuine religious sentiment and noble character, became aware of the necessity of applying *al-sharīʿah* gradually, step by step, as if Islam were in the beginning of its [first] appearance.

This is what was on the mind of the 'fifth' righteous Caliph, ʿUmar ibn ʿAbd al-ʿAziz, when his son, ʿAbd al-Malik, inquired of him one day, 'Why don't you apply the rulings, in full? By God, it does not concern me if rage were to boil over against you and me in the application of what is right.' That is, in simple terms: 'why do you not apply *sharīʿah* fully, come what may?' ʿUmar replied, 'Do not be in a hurry, my son! Allāh condemned wine twice in the Qurʾān, before He prohibited it the third time. I fear if I were to confront people with what is right all at once, they might reject it all at once. That would be disastrous.'

This is one view. Another aspect is that the application of Islamic *sharīʿah* does not mean applying penalties only, such as amputating the hand of the thief, for instance. There are other principles and judgments that must be applied too, like the principle of 'consultation' (*shūrā*) in political life; the principle 'poverty is almost tantamount to blasphemy' in social and economic life; the principle 'are those equal, those who know and those who do not know' (39, 'al-Zumar', 9) in intellectual life; and the principle 'people are equal, like the teeth of a comb' in the various fields of life, etc. I believe that the application of these principles must come before the application of certain *ḥudūd* penalties of *al-sharīʿah*, especially the penalty of theft. The removal of objective reasons which prompt theft is a necessary condition to ascribe the responsibility to subjective reasons alone. It is well known that penalties are not an end in themselves, but a means to deter destructive, selfish, subjective tendencies; those which undermine the interest of the community and the nation.

Moreover, the application of penalties is systematized and governed by a Prophetic *ḥadīth* which says, 'Avoid *ḥudūd* penalties when in doubt'. This has become a basic principle in Islamic legislation. Another Prophetic *ḥadīth* which is even stronger and more indicative states: 'Avoid penalizing Muslims as much as you can. If you can find a way out for the Muslim, let him go free. It is better for the Imām to commit a mistake in issuing a pardon than to make one in decreeing a penalty.' The *fuqahā'*, realizing the significance of this *ḥadīth*, enlarged the scope of doubt wherein a *ḥudūd* penalty is dropped to the point of saying, 'The mere assertion of doubt in a case where the criminal deserves the *ḥadd* penalty is enough to drop that penalty without the need for confirmation.'

The matter does not end at this point. Our *fuqahā'*, especially the four major ones, made active endeavours in *ijtihād* in the question of *ḥudūd* penalties, of which I shall mention a few in regard to theft.

They stipulated that the stolen object should be of a certain value before the hand of the thief is amputated. Some put the threshold at the value to three *dirhams* (Imām Malik and the *fuqahā'* of the Hijaz). Others restricted the value to ten *dirhams* (the *fuqahā'* of Iraq). The difference is a matter of exchange rates, as each party assessed the value in his own country, in accordance with the value of the theft that led to amputation at the time of the Prophet. It was also said that if a group of people stole property, where each person's theft was up to the limit of penalty, then no one of the group is to be penalized by amputation, in reference to the principle of 'numerous hands may not be amputated where *al-sharī'ah* specifies the amputation of *one* hand'. They also stipulated that stolen property should have been protected by the owner, in a manner that makes it difficult to steal. In that they relied upon a *ḥadīth* which says, 'No amputation applies to a [theft] from suspended fruit or a flock by a mountain side.' This means that a person is not penalized if he only helps himself to some fruit from an orchard that belongs to someone else or from a flock of sheep grazing by a mountain side, in an open area, because protection is not provided here. The *fuqahā'* disagree about the means of protection, though they agree that a locked door to a house constitutes protection. They also agree that a person who steals from a house which is not of joint occupancy should not have his hand amputated until he leaves the house. They disagree about the house of joint occupancy. Some say that a thief's hand is amputated if he is one of the inhabitants, provided he exits the house, whereas others say there is no amputation unless he leaves the house [without intent to return]. Imām Malik believes no amputation is due when one takes away any jewellery or clothing from a child, because a child is unable to protect what he has.

All the eponymous founders of the four major *madhabs* and their followers applied the principle of 'Avoid when in doubt'. They said that a king's strong suspicion suspends the *ḥadd* penalty. A slave who steals his master's property is not to have his hand amputated. Neither is the spouse who steals the other's property nor a father who steals his son's property, according to Imām Malik. Al-Shāfi'ī says neither the major nor minor line of progeny is to be severed – that is to say there is no hand-amputation for one who steals from his father's, grandfather's or great grandfather's property or from his son's, grandson's or great grandson's property. Abū Hanīfah extended that to the maternal relatives and the next of kin: mother, sister and all relatives among whom marriage is not permitted in Islam. The *fuqahā'* disagree about the case of stealing from the public treasury (*bayt al-māl*), or from war booty. But they agree that when one steals something for which his hand is amputated, and he repeats the theft, he is not penalized similarly on the second occasion. They also specify the testimony of two just witnesses to prove the theft, or the confession of the thief if he is a free man. If he is a slave, they disagree about the acceptability of his confession.

Naturally, the removal of the amputation penalty due to the emergence of doubt does not automatically acquit the accused. The dropping of punishment, whether in the case of theft, adultery, wine-drinking or defamation, means dropping the special type of penalty textually prescribed (amputation of the hand, lashing, etc.) which is called the 'Right of God'. Yet, there is the public right (*ḥaqq al-'ām*) which entails other penalties, such as imprisonment, when the accused is not proven innocent, as a form of chastisement. This means that all the rulings issued by *fuqahā'* in the past, and by the courts of Islamic states at present, are Islamic rulings, where *al-sharī'ah'* was applied as a corrective or means of chastisement, i.e. a relative application. But the full application of the ruling by the execution of the textually prescribed penalty would serve as a reminder to 'avoid *ḥudūd* penalties when in doubt', and would make an impartial judge think long before making a decision. The judge may be compelled to find imprisonment a sufficient punishment, especially in the case of theft, since the equitable Islamic society in which there is no excuse for stealing, under pressure of need, is non-existent. It is well known that 'Umar bin al-Khaṭṭāb suspended the *ḥadd* penalty of theft in the year of famine.

If we add to this that suspicions and doubts in our age are so numerous and so many-sided, as a result of the complexity of modern life with its multiple drives and motives, it would be possible to say that resorting to punitive measures such as imprisonment and fining may become a necessity. But when we add to this the 'political' doubts, the penalties would be confounded with political motives and objectives; and that constitutes doubt beyond all doubt!

## Note

1. The term *ḥadd* connotes 'boundary' or 'limit' and the *ḥudūd* penalties of Islamic *sharīʿah* are the most severe and reserved for grievous sins and crimes such as the amputation of the hand for theft. The title of the chapter is taken from Prophetic *ḥadīth* which commend the suspension of the *ḥudūd* penalties when there is doubt about a case and the avoidance of their application to the extent possible as their severity correlates to their deterrent value. It is worth noting that according to the Qurʾān and the *ḥadīth*, Muslims are obliged to uphold the law and to apply the *ḥudūd* penalties as a facet of the implementation of *al-sharīʿah*. This consideration led numerous Arab and Muslim countries to hesitate or refrain from signing Western initiatives such as 'The Universal Declaration of Human Rights' – not because there was a lack of concern for human rights, but because certain of the *ḥudūd* penalties were proscribed by these declarations.

CHAPTER 13

# Concerning 'Complete Application of *al-Sharīʿah*'

In Egypt, early in the summer of 1987, a vehement controversy flared up about how far Islamic *sharīʿah* was applied in the various epochs of Islamic history. In his daily column in *al-Ahram*, the well-known Arab journalist Ahmad Baha'uddin wrote that Islamic *sharīʿah* was not applied in all stages of Islamic history. This instigated a number of negative reactions by various writers and intellectuals interested in Islam and Islamic thought, in different newspapers. Baha'uddin had to reply, quoting the opinions of several Azhar authorities and scholars, to prove that Islamic *sharīʿah* was never fully applied in all stages of Islamic history, with the exception of the era of the Messenger and the Rāshidūn Caliphs. Undoubtedly, the author must have felt relief to find that the Azhar authorities support his opinion.

Ever since that polemic, my conviction has been that this is one of those 'spurious' problems which have no basis and yield no benefit. The seriousness with which the subject was surrounded cannot be justified except in a feverish, even poisonous, atmosphere where emotions overwhelm reason, and attitudes are honed to 'confront' the rival before they have a chance to express their opinions and complaints.

I humbly confess that I am, thank God, largely free from that state of consciousness which puts one on the defensive even when there is no need for that feeling of weakness. I do not hesitate for an instant to state that Islamic *sharīʿah* was never *fully* applied at any time. I emphasize the word 'fully' because I think it is the essence of what I call the question rather than the problem, because the whole matter is quite straightforward.

The Islamic *sharīʿah* was not applied 'in full' at the time of the Messenger for a very simple reason evident to all those familiar with the life of the Prophet, namely that *al-sharīʿah* was not revealed all at the same time, but it extended from the moment the Message was revealed to the Prophet in the last days of his life. This is because the Qur'ān, which is the primary source of *al-sharīʿah*, was not concluded until the famous verse was revealed: 'This day I have perfected your religion for you, completed my favour upon you, and have chosen for you Islam as your religion' (5, 'al-Mā'idah', 3). It is said that the Messenger did not live more than 81 days after that (and other verses may have been revealed during those days, but the matter of what was actually the last to be revealed in the Qur'ān is a matter of debate, as is well known). The second source of *al-sharīʿah*, which clarifies and details the first source, is the *sunnah* of the Prophet, his words and deeds and what he approved of other people's words and deeds. It is obvious that the *sunnah* did not come to an end until the death of the Messenger. Therefore, before the conclusion of the revelation and the death of the Messenger, the *al-sharīʿah* was not fully applied, simply because it was incomplete until then. It follows that what was applied in any of the stages of the revelation was only that part of *al-sharīʿah* known then, and not the whole of it.

The Islamic *sharīʿah* was not fully applied at the time of the Rāshidūn Caliphs either for the simple reason, this time, that the Companions were faced with events and developments that had no precedent in the time of the Prophet. So, they resorted to *ijtihād* and mutual consultation, which inevitably led to discussions, agreements and disagreements. In all cases, they had to act either according to their *ijtihād* or by consensus (*ijmaʿ*), which are the third and fourth sources of legislation in Islam. It is clear that *sharīʿah* is complete by the completion of its sources. (And there is no point in arguing about the authority of consensus and *ijtihād*, because all except the Shīʿites are in unison about the validity of the consensus and *ijtihād* of the Companions. The disagreement is only about the Followers concerning these two points.) Therefore, in principle, there could be no application of *sharīʿah* in full except when the four sources were all established, and this happened only after the period of the Companions, the time of the Rāshidūn Caliphs.

The Islamic *sharīʿah* does not comprise only the texts of Qur'ān and *sunnah*, the consensus and *ijtihād* of the Companions. It also includes what was established by the *mujtahidūn* among the *fuqahā'* of all succeeding ages and in the ages yet to come. Therefore, it is senseless to claim that the Islamic *sharīʿah* has always been fully applied since its general principles and basic elements were laid down (by the Qur'ān and *sunnah*) with the mission of Muḥammad. Many of its aspects have been clarified and enriched, first by the *ijtihād* of the Companions, then by the *ijtihād* of the *fuqahā'* of the past and present; and they will continue to be enriched in the future. Since the Islamic *sharīʿah* is for all times and ages, the *mujtahidūn* have to find solutions and formulations for new developments all the time. Thus, it is more sensible to say that *al-sharīʿah* is or should be in a state of constant growth. Yet, it may be said that 'in full' refers to what was known of *al-sharīʿah* at the time of the Messenger and the Rāshidūn Caliphs. This opinion may be addressed by the following argument.

The *sharīʿah* at the time of the Messenger, at the level of the Qur'ānic text or the Prophetic and *sunnah*, had gone through a development which made it viable, not a static *sharīʿah*. This development is clearly reflected in the 'abrogating and abrogated' (*al-nāsikh wa-mansūkh*) verses. The questions that may be asked here are: Would the judgments that were in force, then later abrogated by 'something better or similar' (2, 'al-Baqarah', 106), enter into the locus of 'full' application of *al-sharīʿah* or not? Is not 'in full' here ascribed to the abrogating (*nāsikh*), and not the abrogated (*mansūkh*), rulings?[1] Did all the people who embraced Islam at the time of the Prophet start to practise what was prescribed by the rulings, such as performing *al-salat* (prayer), paying *al-zakah* (alms), stoning or lashing the adulterer, or amputating the hand of a thief as soon as they declared their Islam? Was not the Prophet in the practice of receiving the delegates of the tribes, who were accepted by their mere declaration of embracing Islam, then later came the stage of 'teaching them the affairs of their religion' through emissaries sent for the purpose? Moreover, were not many desert Arabs who embraced Islam, when 'not yet has faith entered' their hearts (49, al-Hujurat, 14), who were negligent in applying what was known of *sharīʿah*, a laxity not unknown to the Messenger? Taking all these facts into consideration, is it acceptable to say that *sharīʿah*, or what was known of it, was applied in full among all people who declared their Islam at the time of the Prophet?

The same remark may be made about the age of the Companions and the Conquests. The people who embraced Islam at the time of the conquests, in the times of Abū Bakr, ʿUmar, ʿUthmān and later ages, did not apply *sharīʿah* completely and fully as soon as they declared their Islam, by choice or force. It was necessary to give them enough time to learn the affairs of religion, and to have enough stability for judges and advisors to be appointed. This means that some time must have passed after their conversion without fully applying *al-sharīʿah* among them.

And what can be said about the *ijtihād* of the Rāshidūn Caliphs, which includes resembling abrogating and abrogated rulings? It is known that Abū Bakr followed certain ways, styles and apportionment in distributing war booty. When ʿUmar bin al-Khaṭṭāb assumed the caliphate, he followed a different style and [system of] apportionment. Subsequently, ʿUthmān bin ʿAffān is known to have differed significantly in many matters from his predecessors, let alone the objections made against his conduct in his later years. Which one of those forms of conduct may be considered a 'full' application of *al-sharī'ah* – that of Abū Bakr, which was 'abrogated' by 'Umar's conduct, or 'Uthmān's conduct? Here, we must quote a saying by the *fuqahā'*: 'They made their own *ijtihād*, and each *mujtahid* is in the right.' But does every *ijtihād* come under the rubric of 'full' application of *al-sharī'ah?*

Now, let us come to our times and the times to come. When the Muslims travel to the moon, or walk in space, or take a stand on fertility treatment, is not the application of Islamic *sharī'ah* going to be on a much wider scale than was the case in the past or is at present? Isn't its tendency to fullness and perfection in this case much stronger than what it was like at any time in the past?

I conclude these dialectical arguments with the following simple fact: Fullness and perfection in the application of laws, as in any other field, is only relative, whether in the time of prophets, their disciples or companions, or in the times that came after them. There is no perfection in this world, either in the field of applying *al-sharī'ah* or in any other field.

And finally, do you not see with me, dear reader, that there are many issues which occupy our minds and keep us apart and lead us to contention, and sometimes to name-calling? These issues are in fact of no value. They keep us away from what is important, let alone what is most important. Both the important and most important issues are related to the present and the future. Let us look at our entire past from a historical perspective, with the 'occasions of revelation' in mind, taking our past in its entirety as a history of Islam and the Muslims, the history of their strengths and weaknesses, their successes and failures. Let us look at the future in the same historical fashion, which sees perfection as an act of 'becoming', not a ready-made, rigid act.

## Note

1. The question of *al-naskh* or abrogation is a complicated one, both in terms of Qur'ānic commentary (*al-tafsīr*) and jurisprudence (*al-fiqh*); and there has not been historical consensus on either the sum total of the instances of its occurrence or even on the tenability of it with regard to the Qur'ān itself, although the majority has affirmed its possibility. (Modern scholars such as Muḥammad Asad have argued that it was intended only with regard to preceding religions and not to Islam itself, while still others such as the Shī'ite scholar Abu al-Qasim al-Khoei have argued that what is in effect 'specification' or '*al-takhṣīṣ*' rather than 'abrogation'. Classical lexicons define the operation of '*naskh*' as a kind of 'replacement' – just as 'sunlight replaces shade'; and therefore in order for an occurrence to be established among the source materials, there must be a clear 'replacement' of one thing (or ruling) by another. For this reason, Ibn Ḥazm argued that increasing censure of wine-drinking in the Qur'ān, ending ultimately with its prohibition, did not represent an occurrence of *naskh* as it

was never promoted in the first instance. Similarly, many of the advocates of *al-naskh* cite the first instance of its occurrence as being in relation to the change of the *qiblah* (orientation of prayer) from *masjid al-aqṣā* in Jerusalem to the *kaʿbah* in Mecca 16 or 17 months after the *hijrah* (migration) to Medina as described in *sūrat al-baqarah*, 2:143. The salient point with regard to the author's discussion is that one does not 'operate according to' verses or rulings which are considered abrogated (*mansūkh*); therefore, facing Jerusalem in prayer would be invalid after the change to Mecca approximately 13 years after the Prophet Muḥammad began his message. It is from this standpoint that the author is arguing that *al-sharīʿah* was not 'complete' or not completely implemented even during a major portion of the Prophet's mission.

VOLUME II

# DEMOCRACY AND HUMAN RIGHTS

# Introduction

It is common practice for the author to write an introduction to a book after having completed it, so that the introduction is congruent with the book's prevalent spirit, paves the way for the issues it will pose and directs the reader towards its theme and domain. If an author were to set about writing an introduction before having commenced writing the body of the book – a rare occurrence indeed – he or she would not be able to do so without having adequately and conclusively envisioned the entire book in his or her mind, thereby defining its theme, structure, issues and findings. In other words, a book's introduction and conclusion are logically and chronologically delayed.

This practice is a circumstance imposed by logic and time. However, the text that is incorporated here as an introduction to this book is a different matter altogether. It was written and published as an independent essay three decades ago, at a time when I had no inkling of this present book, nor did I even have the ambition to write one. Now that 30 years have elapsed since I wrote this essay, I have retrieved it in order to elevate it to another plane, that of an introduction. It could have been used as a conclusion as well, for it can function as either. It may even be useful for the reader to read it as an introduction and then, after completing the body of the book, to read it anew as a conclusion: a text that summarizes the book and opens up new horizons.

What is the secret here? What makes this text appear as if it transcends time? Is it because our times are rigidly static, or is it because this text deals with issues from the metaphysical world which, by definition, transcend the bounds of time?

Neither is the case! The 30 years that separate us from the time in which this text was written have witnessed events and developments of such magnitude in every Arab country, and indeed in the entire world, that time has rushed by with unprecedented velocity, disruptions and convulsions. The text in question is part and parcel of this era, as it addresses issues closely related to reality and attempts to put its pieces back together again and find a way for them to keep abreast of the times as well as history.

Hence, this text neither transcends time nor outstrips history; it adjoins them both and is subject to their consequences, so much so that if I were to publish it today as a 'new', independent text – without indicating its date or circumstances of authorship – numerous readers would attack me for 'dropping behind' the contemporary intellectual procession and 'cleaving' to unpopular stands. And who bothers to speak these days of 'social democracy', 'the working class' or 'nationalization', etc., all of which are issues addressed in this text? But every 'why' has a 'wherefore', and the why of the body of this book justifies, nay, calls for this essay. Let the reader be the judge.

My aim in this foreword to the text, which I am incorporating here into the introduction, is to highlight two points: first, that I sincerely believe that this text is indeed appropriate as an introduction (as well as a conclusion) to the chapters of this book, even though it preceded them by 30 years. This means that I still believe that the issue posed in this text is valid and worthy of being revived anew. I even emphatically assert that the valid, future-oriented view of the issue of democracy is that which is posed in this introduction/conclusion, and that the questions that are not posed in the chapters of the book are aired in this old (new) text.

Second, by re-publishing this text, I have proven to myself, let alone others, that my stand towards democracy has not changed. For during the time when numerous nationalist, progressive intellectuals throughout the Arab world were assailing, even lampooning and cursing political democracy, devoting themselves, heart and soul, to 'social democracy' (or Socialism) alone, I found it correct and necessary to express that which I consider right as forcefully as I could: that social democracy is unachievable without political democracy. And the latter, if it is a means to achieve the former, is also an end in itself. Moreover, one may not renege on political democracy on account of its flaws and because it can be manipulated and used as a tool to achieve goals that diverge from those of the people. Therefore, the body of this book, written within the past two years and featuring its insistence on the necessity of political democracy, does not contain a conversion in my thinking, as is the case with numerous intellectuals of my generation. Quite the contrary: the body of this book is written along the same lines of my earliest convictions, dating back to the 1950s and 1960s, which are part and parcel of the convictions of the Moroccan nationalist progressive movement, with which I have been affiliated since that time.

There is another, more subjective aspect in that I am pleasantly surprised when I read this text, published in November 1964,[1] while I was still in my early days of serious writing. I feel that what I have learned in the past three decades, even though it is a great deal indeed, was not necessary for the clarity of expression, the transparency of the idea or the profundity of the goals and objectives. This is not self-praise; it is rather a statement of fact in which I hope today's youth will believe: that maturity, sound ideas and opinions are not the exclusive province of older people alone, those of great age and wisdom. That about which youths write with veracity and suffering is mostly closer to the heart of the truth than that which is written by 'the adults', whose vision, speech and thoughts are muddled by blandishment, prevarication and an abundance of calculations and considerations.

This is why I wanted to introduce texts from my early sixties with a text I wrote in my thirties, the age of youth. And only youthfulness, when coupled with veracity, can lend truth its integrity. So here is the text from the youth of yesteryear to the youth of today.

## Democracy as a Means and an End

Some words and concepts acquire such widespread currency that they become 'clear', even familiar, but at the same time difficult to define! 'Democracy' is one such concept; for, when we use this word, we mean *something* by it, but, when we ask ourselves 'What exactly is it that we mean?', we abruptly lose our volubility. All we sense is that we are searching for something that we imagined we knew, only to discover that it is convoluted in the extreme, existing in a state of translucence, which allows one to see neither through it nor inside it.

In view of this, a survey of this word's history may aid us in understanding its precise meaning. However, even if we did this, we would still arrive at the same conclusion: that the concept of democracy changes and evolves continuously, deriving from the unstoppable movement of historical evolution. For in every era, perhaps even within one and the same era, there has been a concept of democracy which, if not opposed to the concept prevalent prior to it, was at least different from it to a great extent.

## The Evolution of the Meaning of Democracy

'Democracy' is a Greek word, and I believe that the person who used it first wanted to express an 'ideal', not reality, an experience in practice or an experience that can be practised.

I believe that 'people ruling themselves', the word's original Greek meaning, was never achieved, nor will it be, in any era: the notion of 'the people' calls forth the counterpart notion of 'the state'. For it is difficult to envisage a people without some system holding these people together. It is similarly difficult to envision a system without some coordinating, connecting machinery. And whatever the machinery, it can only be a state or an institution that closely resembles it. Besides, the word 'rule' itself cannot be defined unless there are two parties: those who rule and those who are ruled. There is also the tool, or the means, which symbolizes the necessary relationship between these two parties.

Thus, the definition of democracy as 'people ruling themselves' cannot be realized except in some utopia where, lost in the maze of 'the world of the intellect', some thinkers sought refuge as they could not find any possibility in the real world of putting their opinions and 'ideals' into practice.

In Roman times, as in the Middle Ages, it was not within any sane person's capacity to seek democracy in the sense mentioned above, i.e. 'people ruling themselves'. All that a 'lover' of, or a 'fighter' for, democracy could hope for at the time was a society in which individuals were not officially divided into masters and slaves, or noblemen and serfs.

As for modern times, the concept of democracy has been associated with the notion of election. Granting 'election rights' to all members of the nation, men and women alike, has come to symbolize the realistic meaning of the word!

## Political Democracy: Without Equality

However, democracy is not merely about election, although election is a kind of democracy. But for an election to be genuine, it must be built on democratic foundations! That is, on the basis of equality in potential, opportunity and means, otherwise the democracy which seeks to elect those who would rule the people can only lead to rulers of a single stratum or class: the perpetually ruling class which operates in a state of inequality.

Democracy in the Western world today means, first, political freedom – to enable citizens to fulfil their election 'duty'; and, second, economic (liberal) freedom, to enable every person, real or figurative, to carry out his or her economic activity according to his or her means and potential, without any restrictions imposed on freedom and conduct, and without any control on any aspect of this activity.

The inevitable outcome of such democracy is 'non-democracy', since 'political freedom' and 'economic freedom', although freedoms of course, are only freedoms for those who have access to them. And, since extreme disparity among the nation's individuals is the basic characteristic of today's society, only the 'upper crust' benefits from political and economic freedom. Thus, political election and liberal democracy only lead to non-democracy. Solely the capitalists are in a position to avail themselves of these freedoms, and are, therefore, single-handedly exercising 'the right' to rule the people and to hold sway over their resources and destiny.

The domination of a certain class was once one of 'legal' coercion, but now, by virtue of democracy, it has become one of 'choice' drawn from the election, 'enjoyed' by the whole nation.

## Election is Choice: Choice is Freedom and Will

What is this 'election' that constitutes the essence of political democracy? Election is about choice. To elect is to have several choices put before one. But is every individual able to choose? The answer is a definite 'No!' In order to choose, one must be free to will, to know what one wills and why, and to possess the capacity to achieve that which one wills.

This is where I place the relation between freedom and will, a relation that has occupied the minds of many a philosopher. I will not be swept away by metaphysical thinking in this regard. Suffice it to say that freedom becomes enslavement and exploitation if there is a disparity in the capacity to enjoy it. In other words, where there is no equality, the freedom of the people can only mean its domination and exploitation.

How can the poor be free alongside the rich? How can illiterate people be free alongside those who possess the weapon of knowledge and intellect? A hungry person cannot choose because he can only want one thing: bread! Similarly, an uneducated person cannot choose either, because even if that person knows enough to want, he will not know precisely what he wants or why he wants it, nor will he possess the ability to put the necessary will into practice.

We have seen how democracy boils down to equality. This may very well be the common meaning attached to it today, in our country and in others similar to it. If you were to ask a person in the street what democracy meant to him, he or she might give you an answer that could be subsumed under the term 'equality': equality in rights and responsibilities, in living conditions, before the court, in the corridors of power, at the school door and in every other aspect of life. In other words, people perceive democracy as that which has been termed 'social democracy'. They are therefore not concerned with the political democracy of elections and parties.

## Has Political Democracy Become Useless?

I find myself forced to pose the question: Has political democracy become useless, if not disastrous, to the people? Before answering this question one must point out that political democracy, 'the election of rulers', ostensibly at least, was and is meant to achieve conditions devoid of oppression, injustice and favouritism, hence, those of equality. When people, according to political democracy's supporters, choose their rulers, it is assumed that they will choose those who understand their wishes and goals. And it is assumed that these chosen rulers will operate according to these wishes and goals, otherwise they would lose the people's trust and be removed from government!

Has political democracy achieved this goal? Can it do so? Numerous experiences throughout history do not allow for an answer in the affirmative. For the issue, in essence, is all about the extent of the people's ability to choose as I mentioned above. That aside, there is another fact that must be of great concern to us. Every era had rulers and a people, and in every era the interests of the two sides were at odds with one another. Elections are a massive and complex process, shaped by the rulers themselves, and directed by those who own the media and excel in the art of manipulating public opinion however they wish. It is natural, therefore, that the result of the election is in the interest of both these groups, especially since they both belong to the same class and share common interests. On the other hand, no matter how aware and enraged the people may be, there always exist numerous methods to negate their will. And how many times have elections been rigged! Election and fraud have indeed become synonymous with one another in some countries, especially in those that have witnessed a conflict between the people and their rulers.

It would be naive to believe that the rulers in such countries stage elections with the intent of allowing people to choose who rules them. If they truly had that intent in mind, they would not require elections or anything at all. They would simply leave government and go on their way.

## The Issue is not One of Election, but of Conflict and Struggle

Returning to our previous question, Has democracy become pointless? Or, in other words, can political democracy be expected to realize the people's goals and aspirations only to be disavowed and fought against as a scheme of shamming and deceit? I find myself postponing the answer to this question yet again in order to pose another essential question: What are the goals and hopes of the people?

The peoples of every time and place have always sought a better life, a life free of social injustice. The fact that others have greater wealth and more opportunities will cause a person to feel deprived, even if he or she is not utterly impoverished. Such a person need not be alert to the reality and source of this social injustice; deprivation alone is enough to make him or her live in anxiety and misery.

The goals of the people, therefore, may be summed up in the desire to create conditions in which they can live free from anxiety or misery. It goes without saying that such conditions cannot be 'created' except from the remains of the oppressive situation from which the people suffer. These are the same conditions that allow a small circle of people to 'live the good life'. It is no wonder, then, that this group works and 'struggles' with all its might to maintain, if not consolidate, the status quo.

There is a conflict, then, between the vast majority, whose goals cannot be realized without changing the status quo, and the minority, who have found their happiness in keeping and maintaining the status quo. This is a conflict which, though fierce, often occurs unbeknown to this majority. This is due to various methods of trickery directed at it, and also due to myths and illusions that have been implanted in their minds, making them exist in a world of dreams, wishes and cravings, if not one of despair and surrender. If you were to ask any destitute peasant what his ultimate hope might be, he would tell you that he wishes he could own many hectares and cows and becomes like so-and-so, the owner of vast lands, huge villas, and numerous tractors and cars, etc. If you were to ask a factory worker, he would tell you that he wishes he could rest from this back-breaking labour by becoming the owner of his own factory, even if it be small, or at least run his own business, where others would come to work with him! If you were to ask a grocer or any shopkeeper, he would tell you that he wishes he had a bigger shop and more capital!

Ask any of these people how they would define 'democracy' and they would say 'equality', as mentioned above. Not 'downward', but 'upward' equality. They wish that all the poor could become wealthy, not the other way round.

This is certainly not the view of everyone within the deprived class, but it is the view of a huge majority, especially in the developing countries, where deprivation of the intellect reigns alongside material deprivation, and where the capitalist system and styles have become stamped on the minds of the people.

Let me go back to my previous question: Knowing all this, can political democracy realize the people's goals? I can now respond with an unequivocal 'No'. For political democracy is a democracy of the rulers and the wealthy. However, this does not mean that we are to renounce it and fight against it, not in the slightest. If we view it from another perspective, it is a means which, if used well, can aid in clarifying the reality of the social conflict described above.

In its emphasis on general freedoms, even though it is pro forma, political democracy offers many opportunities that enable one to open the people's eyes to this social conflict. In other words, it is a necessary means to raise the awareness of the masses.

Parliamentary life, multi-party systems, the 'freedom' of the press and campaign seasons are all opportunities provided by political democracy to raise the awareness of the masses and to direct them towards struggle. However, what do I mean by 'raising awareness', and who will carry it out?

The masses feel truly deprived, i.e. the destitute class of workers, peasants and similar small traders and artisans who seek refuge in the cities and shops, because they have neither lands to plough nor jobs in factories. Nevertheless, they are unable to fathom the true nature and causes of this deprivation. Their feeling is, therefore, one of negativity, their solutions are utopian and their hopes are marked by 'cravings', as explained above.

To raise the awareness of the masses, one must make them see that the only correct solution for the social crisis overwhelming them lies in changing the conditions under which they labour. The happiness of the peasants cannot be realized merely by moving them into the ranks of wealthy landowners, because this is not possible. And even if some of them managed to penetrate into this class, they would only be doing so at the expense of thousands of other peasants. There is no doubt that there must be 'donkeys' in order for there to be 'princes', or as the saying goes: 'If you are a prince and I am a prince, then who will drive the donkey?'

Nor can the well-being of the workers be achieved by moving them into the ranks of the capitalists, for they certainly will not become factory owners. After all, a factory has to have workers, and they are the workers! Moreover, the workers' conditions cannot improve sufficiently and permanently simply through an increase in their wages. For no matter what this improvement may amount, they will always remain exploited and deprived. The issue is not one of wages, but of a social state of affairs.

The proletariat must realize that genuine democracy, social justice and equality cannot be put into practice save through targeted, well-directed struggle. Raising the awareness of the masses is the responsibility of the enlightened avant-garde, the labour union leaders and the intellectuals alike. These are the intellectuals who moved upward from the deprived class but who are still a part of them and remain immersed in their suffering. In addition, there are those who moved beyond their own privileged class through their awareness and stood apart from it, joining the masses in their emotions, thoughts and behaviour.

The real mission of the avant-garde citizen is to guide the peasants' struggle for land and land reform and to do away with feudalism. It is to guide the workers' struggle, not only to increase their wages, but also, and this is the essence of the matter, to nationalize workshops, factories, mines and transportation.[2] This is the true path towards genuine democracy, i.e. social democracy.

This mission clearly cannot be accomplished except where civil liberties – political democracy – are guaranteed. This is where I place the relation between political and social democracy in a dialectical relation: neither can be achieved without the other. It would be utterly erroneous to frame the issue in paradoxical terms of 'Which came first, the chicken or the egg?'

The proletarian struggle must proceed along two fronts: one of political democracy as a means, and another of social democracy as an end. Wisdom dictates that we do not distinguish too sharply between means and ends in this instance for, when this objective is reached through these means, the means will become the aim, and vice versa.

## Notes

1. *Aqlam* magazine (Morocco), vol. 1, no. 6, November 1964.

2. I remind the reader again that this text was written in 1964, when nationalization was the primary demand of the nationalist progressive movement. The failure of various nationalization experiments in Eastern Europe and the so-called Third World can be traced back to mismanagement and the absence of political democracy. On the other hand, the countries of Western Europe, the governments of which are founded upon political democracy, did not fail in their nationalizations nor were their public sectors vulnerable (e.g. Scandinavia, Britain, France). Hence, demanding nationalization was justifiable, and it is still viable if it is proposed within the same context that I described, i.e. by connecting political and social democracy. Nationalization in the newly independent nations was a way to recover that which the colonial powers had monopolized, such as land and means of production, not so that a privileged few can in turn monopolize these resources, but so that these national treasures can be the starting point for an independent, national development. The motto of 'openness' and unrestrained, misdirected, wild liberalism has failed in achieving development; nay, it has exacerbated the social crisis by making the wealthy wealthier and the poor poorer. Is there, therefore, any solution but to combine political and social democracy so that a genuinely democratic state can be established to manage the economy democratically, limit class distinctions and realize social justice? And can this ever be accomplished while keeping the means of production in the hands of a few insatiable speculators who will not hesitate to smuggle 'their funds' out of the country, thereby leaving the nation in debt, as is the case with most Third World countries today?

PART ONE

# Democracy: Its Historical Role in the Arab World

CHAPTER 1

# A Demand in the Arab World

Unquestionably, the slogan of 'democracy' is the most popular of the 'popular demands' in the Arab world nowadays. It is a demand which gains consensus in the entire Arab world. Everyone is calling for democracy and proclaiming its vitality. Even those who are not enthusiastic about democracy, or do not expect much good from it, either praise it or, at least, refrain from voicing a contrary opinion. If you ask what democracy means in Arab public opinion, the answer will come in a list of political demands, at the top of which are freedom of thought, expression, political affiliation, formation of parties and the freedom of election, etc. In other words, what is demanded today is the same as was described in the same Arab arena a few decades ago as 'bourgeois democracy'; a democracy which, in the majority of Arab countries in the 1960s, was a target of criticism, vilification, satire, and even insult and epithet at times.

What does this reversal of attitude signify? Has democracy changed, or have the problems of the Arab citizen changed? Or is it that Arab thought itself has changed in its view of things?

I do not think that anything of the sort has happened. The democracy sought today is the same that was rejected yesterday; not only on the theoretical level, but also on the practical level. Many people, in this Arab country or that, do not hide their yearning for the 'good old days', for the press of the early 1950s, the parliaments and the cultural affiliations of those years. These institutions were viewed by many in the Arab world as the embodiment of sham and exploitation but are now described, without hesitation, as a thousand times better than the current state of affairs. If you were to ask these people about the current 'democratic experience' in some Arab countries they will express several reservations. They may even voice their dissatisfaction with the 'august opposition' in a certain country for being misled by the game of counterfeit democracy. But if you ask that opposition itself – though there is no need to ask questions as it is enough to follow their publications and the statements of their leaders and representatives in and outside parliament – you will come to one and the same conclusion: pressure on the voters, rigging elections and tampering with the will of the citizens have all become a hallmark of the 'democratic' experience in the Arab world. Yet, even in that form, democracy remains the quest of 'one and all'.

How can this phenomenon be understood? I do not think this is possible without analysing the components of this phenomenon, which I take to be three. There are, first, those who talk about democracy, demanding it and criticizing the way it is applied in the Arab homeland. These are covered by 'everybody' when we say 'everybody is calling for democracy today'. Secondly, there is the image of democracy which these people form for themselves, as 'the only way to salvation', the salvation of the present Arab situation from its pains and deprivation. Thirdly, there is the current situation itself in the Arab world.

To identify the first group, we have to ask: Who, indeed, calls for democracy today in the Arab world? The answer will certainly be something like: all those who are outside power; all those who do not exercise rule demand democracy. Such an answer implies the assertion that, since only a small minority of lucky, domineering and opportunist individuals benefit from power, all of the rest of the people call for democracy.

But is it true that everybody, except that minority, calls for democracy? Is it an overstatement to say 'everybody'? Is this not the type of generalization known as ideological generalization?

It is so indeed. Those who call for democracy as a necessary and urgent need are indeed a small minority of Arab citizens: members of that 'modern elite class' in the Arab world. They are those who have had contact with the liberal West on cultural and economic levels, or as political refugees, and have, as such, acquired a basic factor in their political and civilizational awareness. It is true that this modern elite class, like any other, has the right to 'legislate for the future' and speak in the name of everybody, or it would lose its identity as elite. Yet, we should remember that the elite class is not defined by the ideological aspect alone. There should be an organic relationship between the elite and the society it represents. The serious drawback suffered by this modern elite class in many Arab countries, not to say in all of them, is the absence of such a relationship, in all political, social and cultural fields, even in spiritual and religious fields, too. Therefore, when we say 'everybody calls for democracy' we have to realize that this 'everybody' is misleading, because it is not everybody as a reality, but only as a potentiality.

My aim from this remark is to stress that the overwhelming majority of the Arab masses, in the urban district or in the countryside, are not, or have not yet been, included in this 'everybody'. That is to say that there have been no channels, either in the past or the present, which connect these masses to the elite class which may, one day, draw those masses into the circle of 'everybody' indeed.

On the other hand, there is that party ignored by the 'modern elite', even though it is the party which is in actual existence everywhere on the popular level. It is the 'traditional elite', basically formed of those that are sometimes called the 'men of religion' or 'the *salafīs*', or 'the fundamentalists' and the like. In reality, and not only as a potentiality, these form an elite class, because, on the ideological level, they legislate for the future, even if by calling for a return to the past. On a purely social level, they are either organically connected with the masses or they are able to transform this connection into a reality in the shortest time possible and with the least amount of effort. Is it correct to say that these also call for democracy in their own name and in the name of the multitudes who are willing to follow them? It is true that this traditional elite class does not reject the 'general sense' of democracy; yet they prefer, and insist on using, the term '*al-shūrā*' (consultation) instead. Questions arise here: Is democracy the same as *al-shūrā*? Is there a correspondence between them? It is necessary to address these questions, otherwise, talk about democracy in Arab society will be futile. To reach a conclusion about this question, we must delineate the conceptions of *al-shūrā* and democracy in the minds of the traditional and modern elite classes in the Arab world.

The third factor in the call for democracy in the Arab world is the current Arab situation itself. The question to be posed here is not to what extent can the current Arab situation entertain democracy, nor to what extent can democracy solve the problems of that situation. The question should specifically be about the 'historic role' which democracy is expected to play in the Arab world in the present stage of its development. This means that the essence of the democracy needed in the Arab world today should not be sought in its essence and practice among the Greeks and the Romans, nor in modern Europe or America, nor even in the essence of *al-shūrā* as it was applied or should be applied in Islam. Its essence should be defined by the historic role it plays in the current Arab situation. How such a role should be defined is discussed in the following chapters.

CHAPTER 2

# *Al-Shūrā* and Democracy are not One and the Same

The words 'democracy', 'freedom' and 'unity' have become so popular in our contemporary Arab discourse that they no longer need to be defined, just like the word 'sky'. In referring to 'clear matters which need no definition', our forefathers used to say, 'this is like saying the sky is above us'. In the minds of Arabs, who call and struggle for democracy, its meaning is as clear as that of 'the sky above us'. Democracy, in this sense, is the opposite of injustice, just as the sky is in apposition to the earth. But is it enough, today, to be content with that equation, or with saying, 'it is what is up there'? In the past, and even more at present, the sky was and still is a multitude of intricate and unknown worlds. Each time a new expanse is discovered, man realizes there is still much more to be explored; it seems like an endless quest. The meaning of democracy in modern Arab thought, I fear, is similar in its clarity to that of the 'sky is above us'. This is because we take it as an alternative concept, defining it only passively, seeing it only as a situation where despotism is nearly or totally absent. But when we try to give a positive definition to that concept, pointing out its basic elements, the ambiguities begin to overwhelm our previous naive golden image of that concept. If you try to look for the model that inspires our intellectuals, let alone average people, in their writings about democracy, you will find that it is a concept, like other Renaissance concepts in our modern thought, defined by two completely different authoritative referents, neither of which represents the current Arab situation. These are the traditional and the Renaissance authoritative referents. The first reads democracy in the Arab-Islamic *shūrā*; the other derives it from the outcome of development achieved through the struggle for democracy in Europe, which persisted there for more than three centuries. Let us, then, define the image of 'democracy' in contemporary Arab thought as defined by these two authoritative referents, beginning with the traditional one.

In the nineteenth century, the Arabs began to have contact with the West and its liberal thought. Some, who came to be called the *salafīs*, began to look into European liberal concepts while trying to find parallels or approximations for them in 'old' Arab-Islamic thought. On the whole, they met with difficulties in their efforts, but not when they compared the European concept of democracy with the Islamic concept of *al-shūrā*. Since that point in time, the traditional intellectuals understood democracy to mean nothing but *al-shūrā*. A later development in *salafī* or *fundamentalist* thought would show the refusal to use the word 'democracy', and a finding of the word '*shūrā*' more expressive of the 'intended' meaning.

It should be pointed out that refraining from the use of 'foreign' words, and absolute loyalty to the 'authentic' Arab-Islamic words, reflects an ideological attitude which tended, more and more, to effect a cutting off from the European Renaissance authoritative referent. This is the attitude of the second generation of the *salafīs,* unlike pioneers such as Muḥammad 'Abduh and Jamāl al-Dīn al-Afghānī, who had an urgent desire to build bridges between the two cultures. It is useful to recall this desire when looking into the significance given to these Islamic concepts which they considered parallel to the European ones. Their aim in comparing democracy to *al-shūrā* was not because they saw them similar or because they did not realize the difference between the two. They rather did so with the intention of assuring the extremist, conservative *'ulamā'*, and probably the rulers too, that the call for democracy does not entail introducing an innovation (*bid'ah*) or an alien concept into the precincts of Islam, since democracy is nothing other than the name used by Westerners for what we call *al-shūrā*. This ideological attitude aims, on the other hand, to raise the concepts of our tradition and civilization to the standards of the times. This means that our problems can find their solutions in our own religious and intellectual tradition, and that the entire issue rests on the way we should understand that tradition. This is a well-known method of self-confirmation and self-defence.

This kind of ideological attitude aside, the image of *al-shūrā* as parallel to democracy, in the minds of the traditionalists, who see it as the better alternative to all types of rule, is not unlike the conduct of Caliph 'Umar bin al-Khaṭṭāb, traditionally described as despotism with justice. Hence, the ideal rule, in the minds of those operating from a traditional point of reference, is that exercised by a 'just despot'. *Al-shūrā*, then, in the Arab-Islamic tradition, is never an absolute substitute for despotism but only for the kind of despotism exercised by an unjust ruler, the kind of despotism predicated on injustice. The ruler can avoid oppression if he has the desire and is guided by God, so he adopts *al-shūrā*, as he resorts to the *fuqahā'* and the *'ulamā'* of religion before making any decision. *Al-shūrā*, however, is not binding upon the ruler. He simply consults, but the final decision is his own. He may choose to follow the advice of the people whom he consulted or take another course.

This is the significance of *al-shūrā* from the standpoint of the traditional, authoritative point of reference. It is without doubt that the thinker operating from this point of reference would depend for support on the Qur'ān and, in particular, the saying of the Almighty: 'so excuse them and ask for forgiveness for them, and consult them in the matter' (3, Āl 'Imrān, 159); and to '[they conduct] their affair in a mutual consultation (*shūrā*)' (42, al-Shūrā, 38). But the lexical meaning of '*shūrā*', like the context of the two verses, does not allow 'derivation' of an exact and detailed image of the rule as it should be in the Islamic perspective. The lexical meaning, also adopted by interpreters and commentators in Islam, denotes 'taking the object from its source'. *Al-shūrā* as consultation is an exchange of opinion, and seeking the opinion of whoever is capable of giving it. Again, 'taking the opinion' does not commit the 'taker', nor are the 'givers of opinion' specified. The latter are described as 'people capable of decision making', and those include anybody in the society with power, whether it is in the field of knowledge, economics or religious or social affairs, but without indication of quantity, quality, place or time.

The context of the two verses, on the other hand, does not indicate a sense of obligation. This is supported by the commentators on 'excuse them and ask for forgiveness for them, and consult them in the matter' (3, Āl 'Imrān, 159). The Prophet is addressed here, and the pronoun 'them' refers to the Muslims who were defeated in the battle of Uḥud. One commentary runs like this:

> 'So excuse them' refers to their conduct in the battle of Uhud, concerning their disregard of your advice [of not going down the hill so fast to collect the booty]. 'Ask for forgiveness for them', concerns the right of God, to have pity on them. And, 'consult them in the matter' means the matter of war and the like, where there is no relevant revelation, in order to calm their souls and hearts and elevate their morale.

The second verse, '[they conduct] their affairs by mutual consultation', talks about the good qualities of 'those who believed' in general, and not of the ruler in particular. This means that *al-shūrā* is a virtue in every believer. A believer consults his brother believer in every step he wants to take. But following the opinion given is not obligatory. Hence, all that the ruler is expected to do is to consult. But the decision is his own responsibility. The consulted parties are not responsible for the mistakes of the ruler, even when he follows their advice. Similarly, the ruler is not answerable to the party consulted.

This traditional and referentially authoritative concept of *al-shūrā* falls under 'good morals' and 'commendable behaviour', but not under 'obligations and duties'. Therefore, the 'fundamentalists' among the *fuqahā'* and others do not consider these two verses a source of legislation, but an indication of Islamic morality and religious virtue in general. Hence, despite the abundance of its topical headings, Islamic *fiqh* is devoid of a single chapter on *shūrā*. The theological writings on the caliphate do not even touch upon the question of *al-shūrā*. Anyhow, no Islamic traditionalist, whether *faqīh* or *mutakallim* (Islamic theologian), has considered *shūrā* a condition for the caliphate. Islamic jurisprudence views the caliph as responsible before God alone, and not before those who chose him, whether willingly or unwillingly. Therefore, the caliph is not bound before those who chose him, except to rule in accordance with the divine revelation. The divine revelation does not specify a commitment to the opinion of the people, neither to the elite nor the commoners. The caliph must apply *al-sharī'ah* according to his *ijtihād*. Hence, the provision that the caliph should have 'enough knowledge to enable him in *ijtihād* in eventualities and rulings'. Thus, the question of *al-shūrā* in Islam remains as a matter of advice, as a virtue in the ruler and never a question of obligation and duty. Therefore, '*al-shūrā* is one thing and democracy is another', as our elders would say. This difference will be seen more clearly with the analysis of democracy and its dimensions in its original European frame of reference.

## CHAPTER 3

# The Difficult Birth

One of the misconceptions ingrained in the way the Arab revival thinkers have dealt with modern European thought is the adoption of ideas and theories which appeared in Europe as a result of a long chain of development, over the centuries, as a pretext for the Arabs on which to build their future revival aspirations. In other words, what was an outcome there is taken here as a cause. I shall cite only two examples.

When Darwin's theory of evolution appeared in Europe, giving rise to philosophical and social theories that were ideological complements to it, both the theory and its complements were adopted in the Arab world. Political and social opinions were built on that theory to be presented as the 'scientific' basis which alone could secure progress for the Arabs. Democracy was adopted in the same manner, and it has been considered to be the main condition for any progress that the Arabs may achieve in any field.

In a situation that has extended over a century, we have been painfully mindful of the difference between the European Renaissance and our own. It is neither necessary nor possible to start from where Europe began its Renaissance, neither in the intellectual field, nor in the social, economic or industrial ones. But the logic of reason and the logic of the present age demand that we look for the shortest route possible to join the contemporary course of civilization as active producers, not merely as passive consumers. In the meantime we must keep an eye on what is happening in the rest of the world, as well as in our world. What is incumbent upon us, and upon every nation that intends to catch up with world progress, is not mere copying and imitation. This is useless, even harmful, especially because of the passive reactions among some parties at the receiving end. What we really need to do is to acclimatize ideas and theories, as well as institutions and systems that we borrow from the rest of the world. We have to adapt what we borrow to implant it in our own soil, in order to become an organic relation commensurate with the givens of our reality.

Without this, what we learn from others cannot turn into a dynamic for change, renewal or basis of progress.

Let us look then, in this light, at the issue of democracy. And, let me hasten to stress that I believe, not only emotionally but rationally, that democracy in the Arab homeland is, now more than at any time before, a necessity, not for progress alone, but for the sake of preserving the Arab entity as well. But this conviction should not stop us from looking at reality as it really is. And Arab reality, i.e. in its historical formation, has never experienced democracy at any stage of its development. It did not experience, throughout its extensive history, the same conditions and developments which distinguish democracy in Europe as an idea or as an institution. To the contrary, the Arab nation experienced, both in part or in toto from the beginning of its history – as far as is known, at least – particular conditions and circumstances that differ completely from those which led, in Europe, to democracy as a conceptual system and as a political and social system.

Historically, democracy is related to the disintegration of the tribal system and the breakdown of the tribal chieftain's power. Parallel to that, there was the rise of the 'city' phenomenon and the idea of the 'citizen' among the Greeks, then among the Romans. With the advent of Christianity in the midst of an empire, there soon began a long series of struggles between the Church and the State, represented by the Emperor. Each was trying to limit the other's power and to have the upper hand in the affairs of rule. A similar power struggle was rising between the feudal lords and the 'arch feudalist' – the king or emperor – who governed in their name, or at least exercised 'absolute' power based on what means the feudal lords provided him with, such as funds and fighters. Here, again, the struggle was going on to limit the power of the king or the emperor. This led to the formation of 'representative' councils, on local and general levels. Though these councils were not elected by all the people, but were formed either by appointment, inheritance or some kind of election by the 'elite', i.e. the feudalists, they still exercised some sort of control over the ruler's power, at least in financial matters. Thus, the ruler could not impose taxes which these councils did not endorse. This is how, even in Medieval, feudal Europe, there was a constant struggle, religious and civil, against the absolute despotism of the ruler. It may be significant to remember that Medieval Europe had devised the term 'tyrannicide', which means 'shedding the blood of the tyrannical ruler'. This was traditionally acceptable, and some of the clergy endorsed that openly. In modern times, especially from the seventeenth century onwards, the struggle against despotism accelerated and deepened with the rise of the cities and the classes of tradesmen and craftsmen as a social power. These were to develop, later on, into the class of bourgeoisie, who led the struggle for democracy in its modern sense, namely to build the rule on free elections to censor the rulers, and to separate the powers of the legislative, executive and judicial.

In the Arab homeland, matters took a totally different course. Setting aside the so-called Eastern despotism in the ancient pharaonic or Mesopotamian cultures, where the pharaoh or the king behaved not only as an absolute despot, but as a god, the rule in Arab-Islamic culture, to which we currently relate, remained an autocracy all the way through. Whether a caliph, a king or a prince, the ruler was always acting with unlimited power, whether he assumed the rule by 'consensus and homage', which was rare, or by force, which was more usual. This was deeply embedded in the Arab entity – at the levels of concept, conscience and religion to a degree ideal rule came to be seen as the one exercised by a 'just despot'. This is an absolute ruler who is just and who seeks consultation in matters of moment, though he is not committed to abide by any advice. In other words, Arab history has no record of any phenomenon where there was a struggle to limit or curtail the power of the absolute ruler, or exercise any supervision over him. The only 'fetter' that could encumber the ruler's excesses was his religious or moral sense. That is why political literature in Islam is not more than the type of recommendations found in the *'Advice for Kings'*. Counsel, then, and not supervision or restraint of power, is the main theme in the political thought of Islam. The ruler who accepts advice, and even acts in accordance with some of it, is the virtuous, ideal ruler. But how often do we find such a virtuous ruler? Were not the *fuqahā'* in every age forced to issue a *fatwa* (legal advice) to allow the appointment of the 'lesser' rather than the 'better' as ruler?! But could they do otherwise, when the choice was 'either this (acceptance) or that (the sword)'? The matter of 'Rising up against the imām' was not considered in the *fatwas* in order to 'avoid [civil] strife'. And from here, they endeavoured to consecrate the principle that 'an unjust ruler is better than no ruler'. This was a principle which followed from its effects which engendered the spirit of surrender and adopting the maxim of 'it is not possible to do better than what has been done' as a foundation for the political position.

My intention from this review of the history of Europe and of the Arab world is to stress the fact that when we call for democracy in the Arab nation we are, in fact, calling for a historical revolution the like of which our world has never seen – not conceptually, politically, socially, nor economically. Therefore, it is imperative to pursue that course with diligence and perseverance and the patience of Job. If the democratic experience in one Arab country or another happened to end unpleasantly or undemocratically, we should not undermine or condemn democracy per se. The mother who desires to have a child has to bear the travails of morning-sickness and the movements of the foetus in addition to various precautionary measures and the possibility of a difficult birth, which may require a Caesarean section. Democracy, in our Arab societies, is not an easy matter, not a mere transition from one stage to another. Rather, it is a new birth and a difficult one, indeed.

## CHAPTER 4

# Partnership in Human Governance

Some questions may sound superfluous when asked, as some people imagine that there is but one well-known, simple answer, and in addition, they assume that positing this 'well-known' answer as a question is to doubt what is unquestionably self-evident, such as the ultimate ideals of goodness, benevolence, beauty, etc. One such question spontaneously but persistently avoided, while we are 'all' calling for democracy and while we are all pledging to support this demand, is 'Why democracy?'. This is what is regarded as preposterous and unpalatable in our current situation. If someone were to insist on asking such a question and found another person patient enough to 'concede' an answer, it would mostly be a sort of rhetorical question, like, 'Why freedom? Why bread? Why air? or, Why water?', which means that democracy is as essential for life as any of these elements. Though true, this is a poetic answer. We Arabs admit, without reservation, that a poetic answer avoids the truth and resorts to metaphor. And, undoubtedly, metaphor is a feature of creative speech. But democracy, in our case and in all cases, belongs to the realm of truth, not to rhetoric.

Let us ask each other seriously, 'Why do we pursue democracy, and what do we expect from it?' The purpose of asking such a question must be to define the dimensions and the results of democracy, not merely to offer a definition of it. Some may imagine that its definition as 'the rule of the people by the people', or, at least, 'rule by the will of the people', is the entire aim of democracy. But the will of the people may be distorted and negated during elections, or even inside parliaments. Parliaments may also pass laws which restrict the freedom of the people or break their backs with taxes, making the poor poorer and the rich richer. They also may endorse treaties which undermine the sovereignty of the country or some of its rights. All this may happen in the name of democracy, leading inevitably to the rejection of democracy. So it becomes necessary to push people away from it and present alternative slogans, often attractive and poetic and, hence, blindly accepted. This is what happened in the Arab world in the late 1950s and throughout the 1960s. In those years, there was plenty of censure and abusive talk concerning democracy. Public libraries in many Arab countries are still full of such literature.

We do not doubt the good intentions of the authors of such reactions. The democratic experiences in the Arab countries in the 1940s and the beginning of the 1950s were truly disappointing. Though some violent and uncensored reactions may be justifiable at times, disappointment should lead to a review of the 'aspirations' themselves, which may have been greater than appropriate or mere 'castles in the air', or 'burying ones head in the sand'. Let us review this 'aspiration', our aspiration for democracy, and ask once more, 'Why democracy?'

Undoubtedly, the direct goal of democracy is to find the best solution for the problem of rule, by making or obliging the rulers to submit to the will of the ruled, through organizations and institutions freely elected by all mature members of the nation. If democracy were to realize only this aim, even as a minimum, we would have effected a coup in Arab situations past and present, and in every aspect. The state in the Arab homeland, in the past and at present, denies the 'partner' any role in government, while the very essence of democracy is 'partnership' (*al-shirk*) in the affairs of government. The principle of the unique oneness of God is the cornerstone in our faith, and this is what we must preserve. But we must at the same time believe that everything after God is multifarious and must be based on plurality. Foremost in this respect is the human governance which should be completely free of the principle of oneness. So long as we, Arabs and Muslims, do not accept partnership in government and politics any more than in the field of deity and divinity, we cannot derive any meaning from democracy, nor any clear conceptual and social dimensions from its content.

Let me cite for the record some of the aspects the demanded historical revolution of democracy might be expected to effect in our Arab nation, a revolution in thought and belief, a revolution in consciousness, a revolution in principles, in awareness, and a complete and final separation between oneness in the field of deity and partnership, and plurality in the field of government and politics. Some readers may not like the word 'partnership' (*al-shirk*), as it may suggest 'partnership in [the worship of] God', so they may prefer 'participation' (*al-mushārikah*) or a word of that kind. I think it is necessary to liberate ourselves from such psychological barriers, caused by the mere linguistic association of words. That would be the only way to eliminate our unconscious mental tendency to generalize the oneness principle of God as a principle of human governance, a generalization prohibited and proscribed by religion itself. The liquidity of language, causing such association of meanings, makes the generalization as true of the attitude towards the ruler as it is towards God.

Democracy, then, should aim at changing the mindset of the Arab individual, in order for that person to become accepting of democratic practice as an actual practice. Democracy is also necessary to change Arab society, in change oriented this time not from oneness to plurality and partnership (*al-shirk*), as in the case of its mindset, but from plurality to unity. Oneness is now dominant in the Arab political scene, while plurality, nay 'fragmentation', is dominant on the social level. By plurality, here, I do not refer only to the numerous provincial entities, but also to the numerous sects, minorities and ethnic groups within the same entity. Democracy, with its emphasis on the freedom of thought and expression, and the plurality of parties, is the framework suitable to make this plurality realize itself in a positive manner. The only alternative to sectarianism and tribalism is the plurality of parties, which is a basic aspect of democratic life. Parties, when their existence is focused and when their organizations are established on clear ideological choices, informed by class interests – without which a party does not deserve the name – which can easily penetrate the inherited organic social frameworks and mobilize the class contradictions within them and limit their effectiveness and hegemony. This would pave the way not only for social cohesion and coalescence, but also for the peaceful transition of power – all forms of it, the political, economic and educational – from the old aristocratic elites to the growing popular elites. This is the transition lurking behind the crisis from which the Arab society suffers at present.

The second aspect of the sought after historical revolution (*iniqilāb*) of democracy in the Arab nation is to replace loyalty to the person, alive or dead – whether a tribal chief or a sectarian leader – with loyalty to the ideas and the ideological choice of the party, and to let the dynamic organization of the party take the place of the stagnant tribal and sectarian organization. This will secure the peaceful transition of power and responsibility, in its broad sense, from the groups that have been ruling, but have now lost their privileges and competence, to the more comprehensive groups, the more competent in quantity and quality, the product of modern development. It is this revolution which makes national unity, through party plurality, transcend the old social frameworks, making the transition of power and its penetration in society proceed smoothly, and in keeping with the ongoing developments.

As democracy is a national necessity on the provincial level, it is equally so, on a pan-Arab level. An Arab unity, of any type, has imposed itself of a necessity in this age of economic, political, regional and international blocs. It has become a vital necessity for the Arabs and a basic condition for their survival. It is no longer possible today to achieve unity except through democracy. The provincial state (*al-dawlah al-qaṭarīyah*) in the Arab Nation has now become a most prominent and established fact. To bypass this provincial state can only be achieved from within the state itself, through its own systems, potentials and needs. And that can only be achieved through democratic pressure and from within each country. It is natural that such pressure cannot be implemented except in a real democratic situation. Therefore, free, popular institutions must arise to supervise the government and its branches, so that the popular forces can exercise their influence to open the way towards unity.

Changing the framework of the Arab mindset, facilitating social cohesion and the transference of power to the new elites in every Arab country, and opening the way towards unity, are three historical functions for democracy in the Arab Nation. Without party plurality and the plurality of voices within the same party, unity can never be achieved, and, without a minimum of real and useful unity, there can be no renaissance and no progress in the Arab homeland.

CHAPTER 5

# Democracy and the Right to Speak

My companion said:

> In all your writings you have projected democracy as the only possible and necessary solution for the problems of the Arab Nation. You have made of democracy a 'magic talisman' for solving all the problems suffered by the Arabs as individuals, peoples, and as an *ummah*. Democracy is the way to unity, and maybe the only way according to you. It is also the way to socialism; and if not the only way, it is the one you choose. The problem of sectarianism in your view is due, mostly if not wholly, to the absence of democracy. For you, every problem finds its solution in democracy. If we were to ask you how to realize this democracy, 'this key that opens all doors', you would probably say: 'By democracy itself, isn't it so?'

I replied:

> Your objections, dear colleague, are quite reasonable. But this key that opens all doors, is counterfeit. It is only possessed by thieves and the like, those who enter houses without permission, that is 'in a non-democratic manner'. We must distance ourselves from 'this key that opens all doors' in order to grasp the fact that every lock has its key to ensure entering houses through their doors and after asking permission, without breaking in; that is, if the inhabitants are the owners of the house, who are not practising aggression against one another or against their neighbours. Only in cases of violation or aggression, is breaking in a necessary measure to put an end to wrongdoing (*al-munkar*).

My companion interrupted:

> Now you are talking about breaking in and the necessity of stopping wrongdoing by hand, and not only by word of mouth. You may say this is a special case, but is not the entire Arab Nation today experiencing a 'special case' in every way and on every level?![1]

Then, my companion went on to say:

> You are putting us in an impasse, an infernal ditch! You want us to choose between the defects of democracy and those of dictatorship. You are adopting 'the lesser of two evils' as in the case of an emergency. Moreover, have we not tried democracy, that of parties and parliaments, East and West? Have we not witnessed how the will of the people was misconstrued, here and there? Has not party plurality been brought down to political adultery? Were not the polls rigged, and the voters harassed, not only through enticement, but by threats and even by physical and psychological persecution? Was not the game of democracy disgraced in several Arab countries? Were not 'the tables turned' and the game disrupted by those in power and authority in some places, while, in others, everyone was 'tamed' inside the 'elected' parliaments and outside them? Has not the democracy you are proclaiming led to a despicable retreat in the 'revolutionary' thought, in all its avenues, the national, the progressive, and the reformist? Has not democracy, as exercised inside the parties themselves, been on the retreat? Have not many parties, in 'running behind democracy', been transformed from revolutionary entities into parties of reform? Then, last, but by no means least, have not those parties become parties of the status quo, accepting it, at first, only to slip into supporting and defending it? Are you ignorant of all this or are you simply ignoring it?

My companion was talking passionately, yet sincerely. He was talking with bitterness, the bitterness of experience, the bitterness of bitter reality that imposes itself upon the human being everywhere he turns which does not leave room for choice or even permit one to catch a breath. Therefore, I did not want to argue with him. Why argue, when all he said was true? I also did not want to sound like an adversary. How could I when he witnesses what I witness and is pained by what pains me, and when I know what he knows – or even more?

I said:

> All that which you have said is true. Your description of our reality is the truth itself, and I agree with you whole heartedly. But this reality is the premise from whence I start, though starting from the same premises does not incontrovertibly lead to the same results, just as correct premises do not necessarily lead to correct results. This is what the logicians concluded and it is the logic which each of us can test for himself. In the human fields of sociology, economics, politics and culture, the results should not only follow the premises but they should themselves be aims and objectives as well. If so, then in order to arrive at the same results in the human field it is not sufficient to proceed from premises alone, but rather, there is no doubt, and

> it is imperative to agree on unified and well-defined aims and objectives. It is also imperative, if possible, to pave the way itself, or to, at least, make sure that the chances of success are greater than those of failure and loss.

My companion said:

> So, we are agreed on the premises and the objectives. We are before a bitter reality; this is a premise. We want to change this reality for the better or the best possible; this is an objective. However, we differ on the means. The means you are suggesting, which you call democracy, we've tried, and they have not yielded anything except what you [already] know.

I did not want to ask my companion about the means which he suggests, because I did not want to reach with him a similar conclusion, that all other means also did not lead except to what he knows. I preferred to proceed from reality as it is, and not from its potentialities, which are not present now.

I said to my companion:

> It seems to me that we do not differ about the means as much as we do about the premises and the starting points. I start with reality as it is, and look for a way to change it. You start from reality as you would like it to be. You start from its potentialities, and I start from its givens. If you want to categorize me as an ideological opponent you may call me a 'reformist' or a 'realist' and describe yourself as a 'revolutionary'. But let us put aside all these labels. Let us agree that what separates us is that you hope to change the potentialities into givens, while I want to change the givens into potentialities. Your approach is shorter; but it is not the right one, unless you have the means. If you do not, the result is a serious impasse: either immediate suicide, or a beautiful but depressing dream, which is a gradual suicide.

He asked, 'What is to be done in your view?'

I said:

> The struggle in the Arab Nation and many other countries is a struggle over power. The side which speaks, rather I say, which senses and feels and suffers, because it is overpowered, persecuted and beaten, should start from the beginning, i.e. to demand 'the right to speak'. Our tragedy in the Arab Nation of today is that we are not only deprived of speech, but of demanding the right of speech, the right without which man loses his identity as man. But you must know that without putting the world 'speaking' in its place, you do not get a 'human'. If without 'speaking' [meaning the rational intellect (*al-'aql*)/the word (*al-kalimah*)], there can be neither revolution nor reform.

My companion gave me a straight, silent look, yet speaking in its silence. So I hastened to say:

> I do not want to place you in the position of the vanquished, though we are all vanquished. From my position and yours, the position of the defeated, I call for democracy, beginning with the ruler acknowledging for the ruled the first of human rights, 'the right of demanding speech'. At least we want to speak about our defeat, its subjective and objective causes. Do we have 'the right to speak' about this subject?

As we were taking our leave, he replied silently – with his eyes, 'No, we do not have the right to speak about our defeat.'

As he disappeared into the distance, I heard a voice within me saying, 'The word is not given. Rights are not granted. They are taken, and we must take them. We must impose democracy by force, however long it may take. We must pay the price, no matter how large or small.'

## Note

1. This dialoge is couched in terms which are part of Qur'ānic and Prophetic injunctions to only enter a house through its doors, i.e. properly, and only after having received permission from its occupants to do so. The reference to 'wrongdoing' or 'abomination' (*al-munkar*) refers to Qur'ānic exhortations, as well as a *ḥadīth* from the Prophet that every believer who witnesses a wrong is obligated to, first, correct it by hand; if this is not possible, to correct it by word of mouth; and if this is not possible, to correct it in one's 'heart', with those choosing the last recourse being 'the weakest in faith'.

CHAPTER 6

# No Way Out Except Through a Historical Bloc

Since the 1967 defeat, in several parts of the Arab world, voices have been heard lamenting 'the end of ideologies' and 'the decline of all standards', etc. Some voices say that 'we were defeated because we moved away from our fundamental principles and faith'. It is clear that these voices came as a reaction against the 'nationalistic tide' and the 'revolutionary tide' of the 1950s and 1960s. These were two ideological trends related to theories and principles, belonging to contemporaneous international thought, mostly ignoring what belongs to our own 'traditional' thought, which takes the Islamic heritage as its only authoritative referent. That reaction decreed the failure of all ideologies in the Arab world: nationalistic, socialist, liberal or secular. The alternative, proudly suggested, was the return to the 'authentic roots' (*al-aṣālah*) to 'Islam'. (What we mean by 'Islam' here is not entering into Islam anew, because no one has gone out from Islam, at least not openly. What is meant is the application of the Islamic ideal, as it was defined in the Middle Ages.)

With amazing speed, spreading in all the Arab countries, especially since the mid-1970s, was what came to be known since that time as the 'Islamic Awakening'. As it is well-known, the Iranian Revolution was, at that time, the centre of gravity of this 'awakening'. The main slogan which was and still is heralded by the Islamic movements which represented this awakening was 'the application of Islamic sharīʿah'. It goes without saying that a slogan with such deep roots in our history, a reminder of its main flourishing stages, and an epitome of the ideals rooted in the conscience of the Muslim masses throughout the ages, cannot be challenged with an opposing slogan, or even with an alternative. For who can question the necessity of 'applying the Islamic sharīʿah' in Islamic countries where most of the government systems derive their legitimacy from belonging to Islam in one way or another?

Two decades have now passed[1] since the Islamic Awakening reached its peak, represented by the victory of the 'Iranian Revolution' over the regime of the Shah, followed by the spread of Islamic initiatives and movements throughout the Arab and Islamic world. These ten years have witnessed a sort of 'consensus' on the necessity of 'returning to the origins (*al-uṣūl*)', to the 'authentic roots' and 'the heritage (*al-turāth*)'. Rulers and ruled, *'ulamā'*, intellectuals and the masses all raised the slogan of 'Islam'. Some were sincere, others hypocritical, biding time or opportunist, and the rest, who are perhaps the majority, were carried away by the current, not knowing whence or where they were going. As the current of 'Islamic Awakening' swept the ideological fields and those of concept and conscience, several parts of the Arab world began to witness certain types of behaviour, on the individual and communal levels, embodying what the West terms 'the return of the religious [person]'. Some examples are the growing number of young people frequenting mosques, wearing of so-called 'Islamic attire' by young men and women, and of the beard by men – young and old. In countries where the Islamic Awakening movement has been able to share in rule, in one way or another, laws have been promulgated to 'apply *al-sharī'ah*'. It began to actually be applied at the level of 'amputating the hand of the thief' in particular, as in the Sudan.

Today, there is no denying the fact, at present, that the Islamic Awakening is on the retreat,[2] or at least is going into a shrinking and inactive stage, in various fields, and in most, if not all, of the Arab countries. Many people would probably not hesitate to say the 'Islamic Awakening' has begun to wane and has begun to enter a bottleneck. One may even venture to guess that the majority of the ideologists who dominated the Arab scene in the 1950s and 1960s would be inclined to say to the 'Islamists' today: 'Here you are, you have failed too. Here are your principles which have failed or are beginning to fail.' The sincere among both groups (and some may not see the need to separate the two groups) may say, 'We have all failed, we are all equal in distress.'

It is true that we are all alike in this distress, because this failure is not that of individuals or a trend. It is the failure of a whole historical experience which lacked the prerequisites of success, and because the victor in this failure is despotism and exploitation exercised on the weak nations, locally and internationally. There is no denying the role of the foreign colonial and imperialist powers in the decline of the nationalistic and the revolutionary currents in the near past. And there is no denying the role of the same powers in the present retreat of the Islamic Awakening. Imperialist and colonial powers are no longer hiding their intentions, as they realize that they are targeted in any case, whether it is the nationalistic, the revolutionary or the Islamic current who wins the race in the Arab-Islamic countries.

This is a fact which we must keep in mind at all times. Nonetheless, there is another fact that may be even more vital, and that is external powers, even the most ferocious colonizers and imperialists, cannot defeat the internal movements in any country, except when those movements are weakened by the seeds of failure carried within their own structure. I believe that the Arab nationalistic movement, and the liberal and socialist currents which dominated the Arab arena before the 1970s, just like the Islamic Awakening movements, dominant since the mid-1970s, have all carried within them, and in all their stages, the seeds of their own failure. These seeds are embodied in a serious oversight which has bedevilled all the Arab movements in the second half of the twentieth century. The first two movements, the nationalistic and the revolutionary, centred on one part of reality and ignored the other part completely. They expressed the thoughts and the aspirations of one sector of society, the so-called modern elite, as well as the few it appealed to: the working classes, the students and the fluctuating unorganized masses. On the other hand, they completely ignored the so-called traditional elite, and their actual and potential followers from the wide sectors of farmers, and villagers, the poor city-people, and the large sectors of the unemployed or semi-employed citizens. This is the 'primary material' of what the modern elite used to call the 'popular masses'. The Islamic Awakening movements, on the other hand, appealed largely to the traditional elite and to that very 'primary material' of the popular masses, while it was oblivious of or unconvincing to the modern elite, the working classes, and the other powers known in the contemporary political language as the 'vital forces'. These are the people connected with the tools of production and the requirements of modern civilization. This is not because the modern elite or the other powers place themselves outside Islam, but because they do not agree with the Islamic revivalists on the type of Islamic application they want to adopt. That application, as they project it, boils down to the special type of dress, and to 'amputating the hand of the thief', regardless of the situation of poverty in society, as well as failing to make use of the more developed deterrents.

This difference, or rather ideological split, reflects accurately the current Arab situation. We have the 'modern' economic, intellectual and social structures which find their ideological expression in the thoughts and aspirations of the modern elite.

Similarly, we have the other 'traditional' structures which find their ideological expression in the thoughts and concepts of the traditional elite. Hence the inevitable conclusion: no movement of change can secure its basic means of success unless it starts from the Arab reality itself, taking into consideration all its modern and traditional components, the entire people, their minorities and majorities, the labourers and the students, and, above all, the congregations at the mosques.

It is clear that any movement, even if it were to start from this reality as described above and take into consideration all its variations and differences, would be stilted and fragile if it relied on compromise, fabrication and political alliances of an opportunist nature. What is needed is the rise of a historical bloc, based on the one objective [public] welfare and motivated by a bloc whose voice can reach all classes of the population, and the *ummah* at large. It is the objective interest expressed by the principles of freedom, authenticity, democracy, *al-shūrā*, socialism, justice, the rights of the privileged people, and the rights of the underprivileged, of minorities and majorities alike. This is because the only forfeited right in the Arab reality is the right of those outside the circle of the favoured group who benefit from the absence of the right people in the centres of decision-making and rule.

Without the rise of such a historical bloc, the likes of which were known in the Arab-Islamic history, at the time of the Prophet and the Companions, and in many later periods, the last of which was the period of national struggle for independence in various Arab countries and many others, it will not be possible to inaugurate a new historical stage, secure in growth, continuity and stability.

## Notes

1. This article was published in 1988.
2. Ibid.

# Part Two
# Democracy and the Current Arab Reality

CHAPTER 7

# The Problem of the Transition to Democracy

It may not be far from the truth when I say that the transition to democracy is the main problem facing the countries of what was called the 'Third World' on the one hand, and those that made up the 'Communist bloc' on the other. Due to the complexities of this problem and of the attempts to solve it, in addition to its interconnection with internal, provincial and international situations, and social, economic, political, cultural and ethnic considerations, it seems to be truly the 'problem of the age'. This is because of its interconnected theoretical and practical dimensions, its internal, subjective factors and its external, objective ones.

The transition to democracy is a theoretical problem which can be generally summed up in the following query: Bearing in mind that democracy is the result of capitalist-industrial developments in Europe, how can there be a transition to democracy in societies experiencing situations generally related either to a [stage of] pre-capitalism or to what was considered to be an alternative to it (state economy and socialist experiments), or to situations which are a mixture of both?

Moreover, the transition to democracy poses a practical problem which may be stated as follows: This transition needs to be achieved by the rulers themselves, who, in turn, must give up their powers and privileges 'of their own free will'. This may have happened once or twice, but this is the exception to the rule. The alternative is to force those rulers to step aside, which requires the emergence of democratic powers in the society, capable of enforcing democracy and of safeguarding against the rise of another type of undemocratic rule.

In other words, transition to democracy may be achieved by one of two ways. The first one is slow and 'gradual'. It gives the democratic powers in society a chance to grow and establish themselves, while trying to democratize the state by transforming it into a state of truly representative institutions, which requires the separation of powers, respecting liberties, etc. The second is for the democratic powers either to pressure the ruler into stepping down or to remove him by force. The problem with the latter measure is that the democratic powers cannot usually bring down a system of government unless they transform into undemocratic powers. For instance, they may become an organized, secret, revolutionary movement of a militant nature, or turn into reckless, unorganized forces, finding expression as a widespread popular movement or in civil disobedience, etc.

Does that mean that a gradual change is safer and more secure? In principle it is so. But 'transition' is a matter of applying a principle, a gradual movement which takes time and progresses in stages. How can we guarantee its continuity and safeguard against its demise in order to ensure the safety of the democratic process itself? Furthermore, how can we keep the pace of this gradual movement to the end and avoid its deterioration into a 'permanently temporary' one? Who can safeguard against the regression of this gradual democratic process into the previous undemocratic state of affairs? An operation of gradualism in transitioning into democracy means a constant stripping of the privileges of power and wealth from a whole class, a semi-class, a sect, a family, or the one and only party. So, who can ensure that those privileged classes would 'understand' and not react in a way that would jeopardize or completely abort the process of gradualism?

These embarrassing apprehensions and queries are not superfluous or pessimistic hypotheses. They have their justification in events and experiences witnessed in so many attempts of transition to democracy in many African, Asian, Latin American and Eastern European countries. In the Sudan, non-democratic rule was brought down, several times, through the mobilization of the masses on the street by national opposition forces. But, directly or a short while later, the process always ended with the return of the undemocratic rule, at times by the army under national and revolutionary pretexts. At other times it came as a result of the failure of the democratic parties, themselves, to abide by democracy, which opened the way before the 'salvation' aspirants, by undemocratic means. What happened in Algeria is common knowledge: the ruling power interfered and blocked the transition to democracy half-way through. Then came the repeated declarations and insinuations that the forces which were expected to win the elections had no intention to respect the 'game' of democracy when in power.

Do I need to add other examples from Africa, such as Zaire, Congo-Brazzaville, Angola, Madagascar and others? Do I need more examples from Latin America, such as Chile, Argentine and Venezuela? Or more from Asia, such as Pakistan or Thailand? Suffice it to say that these apprehensions about gradualism towards democracy have similar examples in the Arab world. In Tunisia, the process of gradualism is moving like a tortoise, taking one step forward and two backwards (with no leap so far). In Egypt, the 'ruling party' has the 'majority' through which the ruling military establishment exercises authority. It is the party which is meant to hold the reins of power for eternity, manipulating the democratic process to its aims. In Morocco, the steps of gradualism have been moving in the same circle for the last 30 years. In the Arab Gulf states, 'consultation councils' were declared, but 'difficult birth' blocked the emergence of some, and those which have come through are severely handicapped in their growth and progress.

The question of democracy in the Arab homeland, then, cannot be seriously and constructively addressed except by looking at it in the light of the reality as it is, including its attempts, experiments and facts. To theorize on democracy while ignoring reality is a futile effort. Therefore, we have to search for theory by analysing the real state of affairs and considering all its facts and details. That alone can ensure the release of democracy from its present impasse. It is the only way that facilitates discourse on democracy in the Arab Nation, opening up positive theoretical horizons and offering the opportunity for a real exercise of democracy and for its escape from a bottleneck.

Finally, I shall define what I mean by 'democracy' as seen in this realistic perspective, namely the one informed by the democratic experience as it exists at present. Democracy is a political-social-economic system based on three principles:

(i) Human rights to liberty and equality, and all their ramifications, such as democratic liberties, the right to work and to equal opportunities.

(ii) A state of institutions, where the state is based on political and civil institutions which transcend individuals, irrespective of their status, their ethnic, religious or party affiliations.

(iii) Alternation of power within those institutions among the various political powers, on the basis of majority rule, with due regard to the rights of the minority.

Therefore, when I address the problem of the 'transition to democracy', I mean transition from a state where the above three principles are non-existent to a state based on those three principles.

CHAPTER 8

# Objective Situations Conducive to Democracy

One of the basic features of our age is that the world has become interconnected in parts and interests more than at any time in the past. National boundaries, whether abstract ones, such as culture and ethnic and sectarian affiliations, or material ones, such as political or geographical boundaries, are no longer effective against external influences, whether deliberate, like foreign intervention and influence of the superpowers, or semi-deliberate, like the interconnection of cultures and the migration of ideas and ideologies. Added to this are economic interests which have overwhelmed relations among nations and countries, thus transcending all types of boundaries among states.

In countries where democratic life did not develop through a long process of industrial, economic, social and cultural modernization, which is what happened in Europe during the last three centuries, the question of democracy has been influenced by external factors, either directly or through the effect of those factors on internal provincial issues. These external or external-internal factors are what I shall call here the objective reasons for the absence (or presence) of democracy in one country or another. Hence, I shall address the obstacles which, in the past decades, jeopardized the transition to democracy and the absence of which today constitutes the objective condition necessary to establish that democracy. So, what are those obstacles?

If we go back to the 1970s and a short while earlier, to compare the Arab and international situations then with the present situation, we shall see that the developments which took place have helped the democratic question in the Arab Nation and in several other countries to break the siege that surrounded them for several decades and limited the chances of transition, to a great extent.

On the international level, and in the 1980s in particular, the world witnessed an international event of great importance, which changed the course of history: the disintegration of the Soviet bloc and the escape of

Russia and the Eastern European countries from the leadership of a single party, and their steering towards democracy. This helped the issue of democracy in the Arab Nation and in many other so-called Third World countries to liberate themselves from two large obstacles which impeded the serious advance of democracy in becoming a top priority.

The first obstacle was the model of the Soviet Union itself. It was the model that had hoped to effect a rapid and comprehensive growth for the benefit of the widest strata of popular masses, through mobilizing the latter within one party, under the leadership of the 'working class'. This is no place to explore the various reasons that led to the failure of this model in achieving what was hoped it would realize on the social and economic levels. Yet, it is necessary to point out that the fall of this model into the grip of party and administrative bureaucracy, and the ensuing, almost complete absence of democracy, led to the stagnation and confinement of this model, making it impossible to reform or rebuild. It was, therefore, inevitable that it should collapse with even the slightest crack in its structure. The breakdown of this model on its own grounds was highly discouraging to parties and leaders in countries that achieved their independence after World War II, at the forefront of which were some Arab countries of major significance. The collapse of this model naturally led to the fall of these, which delayed the exercise of political democracy under the pretext of giving priority to social democracy and comprehensive development. It has become evident now that working for social democracy and comprehensive development at the expense of political democracy leads only to fatal bureaucracy, whose first casualty is social democracy itself.

The second obstacle, inevitably, had lesser negative influence on democracy in the Arab Nation and in other countries of a similar position. The withdrawal of the Soviet Union as a competitive axis against the West eliminated its need for 'friends' whom it had previously appointed or supported as rulers over their own countries for the purpose of retaining them as allies and satellites in its struggle against the Soviet Union and its satellites. Democracy in the Arab Nation and in many Third World countries suffered from following the Soviet model in government and administration. But it suffered even more from the constant Western intervention against the will of the people, and consequently against democracy in countries the West had dominated, or hoped to dominate, under the umbrella of the prevailing world order since World War II. This was the Cold War between the two axes: the United States of America and its allies, on one side, and the Soviet Union and its satellites, on the other. The absence of the Soviet Union as a rival adversary to the West, which somehow hurt our national cause, made the West, somehow, less enthusiastic to support non-democratic situations in the world, as they no longer served its interests. However, this does not mean that the West will relinquish its imperialism and become a supporter of true democracy outside its frontiers. It is quite reasonable to speculate that since there is now no rival to threaten the interests of the West among the 'developing' countries, it will not interfere so much in their affairs. This may potentially open the door wider before the democratic struggle to shift those countries from states of one party and rigged elections to states possessed of real democratic institutions. This is quite noticeable in several African countries, where popular movements demanding democracy are on the increase. Yet the attitude of the West towards them is markedly different from what it used to be.

Such was the new international situation that was supposed to facilitate the emergence of democracy in the Arab nation from the state of siege it had suffered previously. There were other developments in the Arab countries during the 1980s, which contributed to removing the obstacles before democracy. Chief among those was the development of the modern Arab states from provincial states endorsing division into 'national' states, asserting themselves as a reality which cannot be ignored or forced into any unification process without the approval of the citizens of those states. The establishment of democracy in the Arab homeland was put on hold twice. The first time was during the struggle of the Arab countries to achieve their independence. The second was immediately after achieving independence. In the first instance, priority was given to the national issue of independence, since there could be no democracy under foreign rule. Later priority was given to the consolidation of independence and the furtherance of development. Moreover, many leaders of the national movement in the Eastern Arab countries viewed the Arab provincial states as artificial entities set up by imperialism. For them, the only real entity for which to fight was a united Arab nation; therefore, priority ought be given to 'unity', as democracy in the presence of 'division' is an endorsement of an artificial situation imposed originally against the will and aspirations of the Arab nation. As a result, democracy in the Arab Nation has been on hold since the 1950s. Instead, the one-party, the sham pluralism and elections, or the 'overpowering tribalism' *(al-'aṣabīyah al-ghālibah),* to use Ibn Khaldūn's expression, have prevailed as the bases of rule in the Arab Nation since the rise of the 'modern' state to the present day.

But the current developments, on both the Arab and international levels, no longer allow for a further postponement of the application of democracy. The provincial/regional Arab state, which was formerly viewed as a sham entity, has now become an international reality and a part of the world order. Moreover, it has become a national, political and economic entity, connected to its citizens by national, regional feelings which supersede the pan-national feelings, even among the nationalists themselves. Hence, it is no longer acceptable to use the national issue of unity as a pretext for putting off the application of democracy.

Similarly, the model of Soviet development, based on the single party, has failed and is disappearing. Therefore, the priority of development and social justice is no longer valid. Furthermore, neither issue runs counter to democracy; and experience has shown that democracy is the right framework for development and the necessary background to social justice.

To sum up, the obstacles which used to hinder the establishment of democracy in the Arab homeland have no justification nowadays. The internal and external objective conditions for the transition to democracy in the Arab countries are available now, or are on the way to being so. What remains are the subjective factors, as summed up in the desire for democracy and the effort made to achieve it. These are no less significant than the objective conditions. In fact, on them depends the future of democracy in the Arab Nation.

## Chapter 9

# Contemporary Arab Ideology and its Doubts about Democracy

It is possible to sum up the subjective conditions necessary for the establishment of democracy in any country in a simple phrase: the desire for democracy. This desire depends on the awareness of its necessity, which depends, in turn, on the depth of that awareness in the thought, the culture and the authoritative civilizational referent, in general. The Arab of today has not yet realized the necessary dissociation from pre-modern political ideology. One cannot escape the observation that modern Arab political discourse has generally been anti-democracy, whether overtly or covertly. When democracy has not been directly targeted, its postponement, avoidance or its erroneous interpretation has been enough to exclude it from the interests which inform awareness. Undoubtedly, the first step to establish the awareness of democracy is to see the way or ways in which it has been postponed or avoided. Here are some of the ways in which Arab ideological trends undermined democracy and cast doubts on its value.

While the *salafī* revivalist current did not wholly oppose democracy, it preferred to call it '*al-shūrā*', knowing only too well that *al-shūrā* in Islamic political jurisprudence is not considered binding. Moreover, it is the prerogative of 'the people in charge', who are the chieftains and the senior members in society. Though the *salafī* revivalists did not openly abide by this jurisprudential concept of *al-shūrā*, they could not, on the other hand, put it in a contemporary positive context. So, Sheikh Muḥammad Abdu was content to say that *al-shūrā* means the absence of 'absolute despotism', namely 'the enforcement of one person's will upon all others, in accordance with *al-sharīʿah* and law or in dissent from them'. By 'limited despotism' he means 'the prerogative of the ruler to apply the enacted law and specified *sharīʿah*', which, in his opinion, does not negate *al-shūrā*. In any case, *al-shūrā* to him does not imply more than the 'exchange of opinions with chieftains and princes'. Its application, he says, 'is not limited to one way. The choice of the way is governed by what was originally permitted and possible.' But he unhesitatingly specifies the way of his own choice. In his essay 'A Renaissance in the East Needs a Just Despot', he looks forward to the rise, in the entire East, of 'A despot from among his own people, just to his people, where justice enables him to achieve in fifteen years what reason alone cannot achieve in fifteen centuries.' The attitude of the contemporary *salafis* and the Islamic groups branching from them is no different from that of Sheikh Muḥammad 'Abduh, if not more extreme. They actually view democracy with suspicion, as they assert that it cannot beget anything different from the present situation, where the rule is monopolized by a 'minority imitating the West'. In their view this marginalizes the vast majority of the Muslim masses.

The Marxist current in Arab thought has based its political discourse on the vilification of political democracy. It was viewed as a tool in the hands of the bourgeoisie to tyrannize the enslaved working classes and exploit them, as is evident in Marxist literature. Despite its support for democracy, the liberal Arab current did not refrain from proclaiming its doubts about the possibility of applying unlimited and untainted democracy in countries where social and economic conditions lag far behind the standards achieved in the West, when the bourgeoisie assumed the reins of power. Salama Musa, for instance, says, 'Democracy was a system of society before it became a system of government. Nay, it is a system of government only because it is the result of a certain system in society.' By that he means the rise of democracy in the West was the result of the rise of the middle class after the collapse of the feudal system. Therefore, he believes the Arab middle class should be left to grow and flourish, in order to make it possible to apply democracy. We must remember the same attitude is expressed, also, by many liberals in the Arab Nation at present.

Although Arab nationalistic thought did not exclude freedom from its list of slogans, the parliamentary experience in some Arab countries in the early 1950s and earlier, which were mostly corrupt, led to questionable reception of the idea with doubts about the validity of political democracy before realizing social democracy. In the draft charter presented by Gamal Abd al-Nasr to the National Convention of the Popular Forces on 21 May 1962, we read the following:

> Political freedom, or democracy, is not the adoption of constitutional orientations in form. Counterfeit democratic orientations are nothing but reactionary democracy. And reactionism is not willing to sever its relations with imperialism and end its cooperation with it. All this rips to shreds the conviction about false orientation and exposes the terrible deception in

> reactionary democracy. It also affirms, with absolute certainty, the futility of political democracy or political freedom without economic democracy, or social freedom.

In nationalist thought, social democracy is not the only condition that should precede political democracy, as absolute priority is given to popular/nationalist issues. A nationalist thinker from Syria asserts unequivocally:

> The freedom of expression and thought, which should be allowed in Arab society in its progress towards real democracy, is the freedom which does not exceed the basic objectives of democracy or undermine the major principles of nationalist life. This clearly means that freedom in our Arab society should be within the limits of the nationalist cause.

Should we add to the above a statement ascribed to some leaders of the Islamic Front for Salvation (FIS)? They unequivocally declared, during their election campaign that was about to bring them to power in Algeria, that they would discontinue the application of democracy as soon as they assumed power. Should we, accordingly, conclude that every dominant ideology which calls for democracy, while in the opposition, considers itself the sole representative of the people, and consequently it is its right, if not its duty, to seize power and monopolize rule?!

Even though this 'conclusion' does not rise to the level of a general rule, one cannot ignore the fact that, in contemporary Arab thought, there are actually plain and disconcerting doubts about the possibility of applying democracy in a society that has not yet developed to the level of a capitalistic, industrial society. More doubts centre on the problem of establishing real democracy within a dependent state with a dependent economy. There are also those who believe that the economic and social bases in the Middle East lack the depth to qualify them for managing political democracy and performing their historical role. I may add one more doubt, if not the last, about the possibility of applying democracy in a society where the rentier economy depends on revenue from the sales of oil or the income of immigrant workers, gifts and donations, and loans, rather than on taxes levied on the forces of production in the country to cover its needs. It is well-known that the demand for accountability of the state in its spending of revenues from taxation was the impetus for the operation of democracy in Europe. Doubts are mounting, and there is no doubt that work must be done to disperse them.

## Chapter 10

# Dispersing the Doubts about Democracy

There is no arguing the fact that the call for democracy in the Arab Nation is getting stronger and has been increasing since the 1980s. It has increased so much that one can safely say it is the only axiom which is openly proclaimed today without a need to defend its credibility and legitimacy, or even to explain its implications. Yet, one cannot help noticing that most people who advocate this ideal and are enthusiastic about it do not really have a deep awareness of the need for democracy or the sacrifices that have to be made to realize it. They rather act upon momentary and circumstantial desires that may not last after the disappearance of their immediate incentives. There are those who call for democracy only to get rid of the rule of the tribe, or that of the sect, the sole party, the military or tyrannical rule that hides behind sham parties and elections which are neither free nor unbiased. Others call for democracy when they are in opposition, but it does not mean they are ready to embrace it when they come to power. Yet there are others who call for democracy while thinking of only some of its aspects, like respecting the rights of minorities, or securing economic freedom. Moreover, some call for democracy without hiding their fear; it may bring to power an ideology that would appeal to the majority to which they themselves do not belong.

Democracy, then, still needs to be established in the contemporary Arab conscience. It still needs to be transformed, within the Arab conscience, from an issue surrounded by doubts to an unshakable conviction, like the conviction of the mind concerning fundamental necessities. How can we, then, realize this difficult task?

Among the facts that somehow have weakened and distorted the image of democracy in the Arab conscience are the distortion and falsification which have plagued the parliamentary experience in the Arab Nation. Added to this are the flaws of the parliamentary system itself, which are easily exacerbated in societies not yet developed to meet the required standard for the sound application, at least relatively, of the democratic system. But the corruption in certain parliamentary experiences, as well as the flaws of democracy itself, no matter how serious they both are, should not be taken as a pretext to denounce democracy, as the only alternative would be dictatorship and oppression. There is no third alternative to the flaws of democracy and those of dictatorship and oppression. The latter should be eradicated completely and replaced by democracy, and the former may be alleviated by adopting more democracy. As for the 'just dictator' or the 'charismatic leader', if one were to be found, there is no guarantee that his successor would follow in his steps. Thus, wisdom decrees not to bet on what may come and may never come. The only bet that has sure results, no matter how long it may take or what struggle it may require, is the bet of democracy.

However, democracy does not involve the parliamentary system only, so we should not blame it on all the defects and the distortions of this system. Democracy requires, first and foremost, the respect for human rights, i.e. democratic rights such as the right of expression, of founding societies and parties, of movement, of work, of equality, of justice, etc. These democratic rights cannot be compromised; they are above the parliamentary system and are independent of fair or biased elections, corrupt or untainted parliamentary life. It is truly deplorable to see our people reticent about the forfeiture of these rights, under one slogan or another, or because of fear or indifference. This means that human rights still need to be established in the Arab conscience, as well as to take root in individual and collective conduct, in the educational system and in every aspect of social life.

Experience has proven the fallacy of the claim that political democracy does not work except where social democracy is prevalent. To put off political democracy on the pretext of realizing social democracy first has only bolstered bureaucracy, dictatorship, intellectual and doctrinal stagnation and failure to provide the most basic of needs, such as foodstuffs for the masses. In contrast, political democracy has been successful in realizing social democracy wherever the latter was chosen, as in the case of the Scandinavian countries. Therefore, it must be stressed that political democracy is the regulating framework for democratic rights and the political system which serves and respects those rights. At the same time, experience has shown that social democracy as an economic choice cannot be realized in the absence of political democracy.

The claim that democracy has to wait for the 'maturity of the people', in order to be safe against anarchy, may be easily refuted. The maturity of the people cannot be realized except through the exercise of democracy. A child does not learn to walk except by actually practising walking.

To monopolize authority, even with good intentions, which is rarely the case, does not lead to the maturity of the people. On the contrary, it will always stifle the growth potentials of the individual and the community. In addition to that, social, economic and cultural problems, which weigh heavily on the Arab countries nowadays, cannot be covered up or made lighter and less painful by oppressive measures. The people's participation in a sound democratic atmosphere is alone capable of recruiting the energies and potentials sufficient to overcome those problems and difficulties in an atmosphere of responsibility and bearing the necessary burdens.

As for the connection of democracy to nationalist objectives, it was absolutely justified to defer democracy during the national struggle for independence, because it cannot ever be sound and genuine under foreign rule. The foreign rulers may even exploit democracy to entrench and prolong their presence. If this justification could be supported by national logic, it cannot be equally supported in the independent countries on the pretext of recruiting the entire public opinion for unity and giving no chance to its adversaries to take counter measures. In any case, experience has shown that democracy has become a national necessity as much as a provincial necessity.

Arab unity, of whatever form or size, is imposing itself nowadays more than at any other time in the past. It has become a national necessity in a world of economic and political coalitions, on every level. Unity is no longer an ideological slogan; it has become a vital necessity for all Arabs. The Arab countries cannot individually achieve the needed development and secure other necessities such as regional security and solving the problems of water and food, etc. This desired and necessary Arab unity cannot be achieved today except through democracy. It can only be built brick by brick, through mutual cooperation and concession among the Arab countries and within mutual democratic relations. Therefore, the concept of 'basic territory' should be replaced by what I have previously suggested as the 'model country' because of the sound democratic life it can offer.

Also, democracy is a necessity for the Arab nation as a whole and for each of the Arab countries at the same time. That is because the Arab homeland is one country in reality, whereas its unity is, in fact, based on plurality. What distinguishes the Arab Nation is the diversity within its unity, not only as a result of the multiplicity of the Arab countries, but as it persists within the same country, the same district or even the same tribe. In addition to that, there is the diversity that characterizes the transition period current in the Arab Nation, where the old and the new co-exist in different areas. Therefore, democracy is a necessity at the pan-Arab level as well as on the patriotic and provincial levels, because it is the only means that can realize national integration on the level of the village, city, country and the Arab homeland as a whole.

It is true that democracy may lead to struggles, but these are horizontal conflicts, between one class against another, one ideology against another, or one mentality against another mentality. Such conflicts end in the emergence of the new manifestations from within the old, which yields new revelations leading to progress. But the absence of democracy does not eliminate conflicts; it only shifts them to their old moulds of tribe or sect, making them vertical conflicts, where the rich and poor in one class fight the rich and poor in another, thus turning the conflict into one of rebellion and self-destruction.

So democracy, as far as the Arab Nation is concerned, is not only a political issue, but a national issue, an issue of integration between the different and the diverse in the Arab Nation. It is also a 'historical issue', because it alone provides the conditions necessary to permit social struggles to end in progress and manifestations of the new from within the old.

## CHAPTER 11

# The State that Swallows up Society

I have reviewed the ideological obstacles which have hindered the establishment of a democratic consciousness in modern Arab thought, in a manner that crystallizes the necessity of democracy as political will and intellectual conviction. Those obstacles are not merely theoretical or ideological, as there is also the reality of the 'modern Arab state' itself, with all its structures and institutions. It is imperative to analyse this reality in connection with democracy to deepen our awareness of the obstacles facing the transition to democracy in the Arab homeland.

How does the modern Arab state look from the democratic perspective? Needless to say the modern Arab states were founded under European occupation. Economic, administrative, political and cultural institutions were copied from liberal democratic models in the colonizing countries. It must be stressed, once more, that those liberal democratic institutions in the modern European state have grown as a result of internal development, parallel to the development of the state itself. This led to the rise of a civil society, independent of the political society (the state), a society based on economic institutions (corporations, banks), social ones (unions, societies) cultural institutions (schools, information centres), etc. Such institutions in the modern Arab states, and other previously colonized countries in general, were implanted, by force at times, by the colonizing states. Thus, it was the state, or the ruling authority, which set up for itself the institutions it needed, giving them the support, the guidance and the power they required. But the liberal democratic benefits of these institutions were sucked up by the state. So, democracy was applied only among the people in office (the colonial powers) and the European community living in the colonized countries.

When the Arab countries gained their independence, their experience was similar to what happened in most of the newly independent countries. The national movement which realized independence inherited the modern state structure which was implanted by the colonialists. Thus independence was more or less tantamount to a 'nationalization' of those structures by taking over power and replacing the foreign officials with local people. The relations between state and society remained the same as they had been under colonial rule, with apparatuses and matrices with the task of full control and repression of the people. In the countries with representative governments (Egypt, Syria, Iraq, then Morocco and Jordan), the system was subject to the same old colonial measures, whether during elections or inside the parliaments. This rendered the 'democratic experience' one of a people under surveillance by the state rather than being a means whereby the people can monitor state.

It was no surprise that the defects of this type of democracy, whereby the state controls the people by means of it, should be exposed with the occurrence of the first shock or crisis. The 1948 Arab-Israeli war witnessed the defeat of the Arab armies which were managed by governments produced by this kind of democracy. The defeat was an open indictment to this 'democracy', its governments, parliaments, institutions and all. The reaction of the defeated Arab armies came first in the movement of the 'Free Officers' in Egypt. They assumed power with the intention of realizing what the previous governments, the heirs of the colonial state, could not. They wanted to set up a national state, strong enough to confront imperialism and Zionism and to realize complete sovereignty and economic independence. To speed up the achievement of these goals, the Free Officers found it necessary to begin by 'purging' political life from parliamentary and party manoeuvrings and contentions. Whether or not this vision was justifiable and genuine, the result was the same: the rise of a 'military state' which controlled the people by using the same old repressive apparatuses made even more powerful and prevalent by the military regime.

As the Free Officers' government became involved in open confrontation with colonialism and Zionism, Egypt found itself (and consequently Syria, Jordan and Iraq to a certain extent) in a 'state of war'. They began to feel the repercussions of the state of war among the people as a whole, on all levels: economic, social, political, intellectual and cultural. Little by little, Egypt came to join the Soviet Union in a front against colonialism and imperialism. Thus, the Soviet Union, the state of the sole leader and the sole party, came to present to Egypt, and to many other previously colonized countries, a new 'model' contrary to the one presented by the colonial liberal state: a model based on excessive centralization, economic planning, and cultural and ideological control. It was a model that swallowed civil society, where there was no place for institutions independent of the state. Instead, all institutions were an extension of the mother institution – the state itself. The only difference between the Soviet model and its 'copies' outside the Warsaw Pact is that the original model was based on a party (Communist party) which had a state and an army. This is while its copies, whether in Egypt and elsewhere, it is the army that has a state and a party.

In addition to the military state which blocked democracy in the name of the revolution, there was what might be described as the 'traditional state'. It exploited the status quo (creed, tribe, booty) to seize absolute power. This form of state strove to limit society in a 'traditional framework' and did not allow the founding of modern institutions such as societies and unions or any others.

Besides the 'revolutionary state' and the 'traditional state', there were the semi-democratic states. In the latter, democracy was not completely absent. Some democratic aspects were present, but that did not deter autocracy in such countries from asserting itself, from time to time, especially when the active forces in the country succeeded in using that margin of democracy to address the basic political, economic and social issues.

In both traditional and semi-democratic states, one can easily see the role of international imperialism in hindering the pursuit of democratic rule. It is a role not substantially different from the subversive one played against the 'revolutionary state' and its programme of liberation and development. In both cases, the first and the last victims were the institutions of civil society.

They were the first victims because the revolutionary state, just like the traditional and the semi-democratic states, could not tolerate the rise of genuine and independent institutions that could seriously compete with those of the military, the sole party, the tribe, the sect or the artificial parties. They were also the last victims, because of the subversive role played by imperialism, whether against the national policy of liberation in the revolutionary state or against sound democratic development in the other two types of states that had a strong negative impact on the process of elite formation and their activities. Imperialism created a sense of failure, frustration and despair among the elite generations. It is well known that civil society, which is the field of democratic application, is constructed by modern elites who have managed to realize their projects and aspirations, and to gain enough power and experience to institutionalize their activities and recruit other active forces to their side. Consequently, they were fit to establish democracy and lead the progress of modernization. This remark will lead me to review the elite classes and their succession in the Arab homeland.

CHAPTER 12

# Civil Society and the Elites in the Arab Nation

Regardless of the disagreement about the definition of 'civil society', it is first and foremost 'a society of cities'. Its institutions are those founded by urban people to organize their social, economic, political and cultural life. They are, therefore, voluntary, or semi-voluntary institutions, formed by the people who may subscribe to them, withdraw from them or dissolve them at will. This is quite contrary to the institutions of the Bedouin/rural society, which are 'natural' institutions. The individual belongs to those institutions and is part of them by birth, so he or she is unable to withdraw from them, from their tribe or their sect, etc. Therefore, research into the presence or absence of the institutions of civil society in any country requires that we should start with the situation in the cities of that country: Are they controlling the people through their economy, institutions, conventions and traditions? Or is it the Bedouin/rural society with its institutions, traditions, code of conduct, values and thought that has control?

As far as the Arab Nation is concerned, it is quite obvious that the peoples of the desert and the countryside have been in control, through their institutions, codes of conduct, traditions and mentality. This is an addition to the demographic domination, not only in the mountains and the plains, in the deserts and the countryside, but also in the cities themselves. The majority of inhabitants there are immigrants who came in successive waves 'from the desert into the city'.

I will overlook the history of the relation between the city and the desert in the Arab homeland, the pivotal point of the analyses by the famous Ibn Khaldūn. I am rather concerned, here, with the modern Arab Nation which took shape at the beginning of the colonial era, the era when the modern Arab city started to grow either around the old towns or outside their area. I will also focus mainly on the rise of the elite classes and their development. The institutions of the civil society are nothing but the social framework which regulates the activities of the modern elite classes on political, economic and cultural levels.

The colonizers implanted the institutions of the modern European state in the colonized countries, thereby contributing to the rise of the modern elite classes. The first generation of those classes stemmed from the civil aristocratic classes, in particular, as they were more in touch with the colonizers and their institutions. As a result of the relatively fast growth of these elite classes and the development of their national, social and economic awareness, due to their connection with the liberation movements in the world, they emerged as the powers that were to lead the national struggle towards independence. Although 'independence' always meant, before anything else, a restoration of national sovereignty, we have to consider the difference between the project of this new elite class and the popular reaction of the traditional elite, basically Bedouin. The latter confronted the colonial invasion from the start in order to preserve the status quo of the traditional non-civil society, that of the tribe, the sect and their state. The modern elite forces, though the product of colonial modernization, arose to call for independence, along with a modernizing programme. They sought to lend a national character to the modern institutions and structures introduced by the colonizers and to develop those structures to involve all the activities of society. In a word, they wanted to establish a modern state with the institutions of a civil society.

Without going into unnecessary details, we must assert a basic fact involved in the process of social development witnessed in the Arab countries and beginning with the struggle for independence. It is the quick succession of the elite classes which is an example of 'the emergence of an opposite from within a thing itself'. Such succession can be outlined as follows: There is first that elite class which led the national movement to independence. It emerged from the traditional civil aristocracy, as we have seen, as a result of the 'modernity shock' caused by contact with the West (the West as colonizer and the West as a model, at the same time). This elite class, which endeavoured to recruit and enlighten the 'people' through modern education, etc., was soon to find itself confronted with an opponent, emerging from within. It was an opposing power coming mostly from the people who emigrated from the desert into the cities, which began to grow in the early stages of the colonial period. This was virtually a new elite class standing behind the leading elite. They urged the escalation of the national struggle from a mere peaceful political action (civil party action) into confrontation and conflict (demonstrations, strikes, armed resistance). If things develop in that direction, the new elite class will take over the leadership of the 'national violence', it will gain status and legitimacy over the old elite in the leadership of the national movement and the liberation endeavour in a new takeover.

With independence, the two elite classes came into open confrontation, this time, not due to disagreement about the right way of confronting the colonizers, but about status and social rank and benefits, and gains should be allotted to them or be provided by the independent state. The elite coming from the civil aristocracy held the reins of power in the independent state. They were naturally the only class qualified for the job by virtue of their political experience, social status and educational level. They were also on 'peaceful' terms, or what became peaceful, with the state which 'granted' the independence at the negotiation table. With the dawn of independence, the aristocratic elite started two contradictory schemes. One was to support their economic, institutional, political and cultural positions, which deepened the gap and augmented the conflict with the nascent elite class. The other was to address some of the urgent popular demands such as work opportunities and education. This was to provide the 'opposing' elite with new means to look for better and higher positions.

If we add to this the pressure of 'Neo-Colonialism', which was incessantly creating hurdles before the independent state to jeopardize its national programme, we can see that this explains why the disagreement about confronting colonialism surfaced once more to confer the conflict with an ideological cover, derived from 'nationalist thought'. This ha-s now come to be nourished more than ever before by the ideology of the international liberation movement of revolutionary and socialist orientation. Thus, the next practical step finds its justification: the 'Free Officers' in the army, or the 'radical elements' in the party, seize power in the state or in the party, or in both. They speak in the name of the new elite (of a Bedouin-rural origin) which becomes the 'sole' representative of the people, giving themselves the 'civil' means to extend their domination over the entire society.

The process of development follows another, similar cycle, reminding us of the cycle proposed by Ibn Khaldūn. The ruling elite, with its military and civil members, embark on vying against the old elite for their economic, social, political and cultural positions, usurping some or all. They create new positions for their members and supporters and erect new industrial, cultural and rural institutions, in an atmosphere of media hype and revolutionary ideologies. The result is the fuelling of social awareness of class differences and the monopoly of positions, etc.

In their monopoly of the state and the public sector, this new elite class fails to cater for the new masses of job-seekers, especially graduates of universities and higher institutes. The new 'opposition' begins to form in new elite classes, as if historically aware of the failure of the ruling elite of the 'revolutionary state' in realizing their principles and commitments. So, the ruling elite is plagued with economic and political crises aggravated by increasing foreign debts. Therefore, the ruling elite confronts the popular demands with more 'oppression' that can no longer be justified by revolutionary national principles as before. Voices are raised, calling for democracy, mostly from among the classes of the old elites removed from power, or from their branches or offshoots who have not yet attained their share of power. Stronger voices, at present, are heard from different groups; the strongest among them are those proclaiming the slogan 'Islam is the solution'. These are the voices of the new opposition, namely the newer elites produced once more by the process of development described above: transition from desert and rural areas to the city and from the peripheries to the centre, by virtue of a wider education and an awareness of the need to move upwards in status and positions.

Three successive generations of elite classes appeared on the stage of modern Arab history. Their politicians and leaders are well known to the citizens of every Arab country. What is common to all of them is their fear of democracy.

## Chapter 13

# Elites Fear Democracy

Three successive generations of elite classes in modern Arab history have feared to take the game of democracy to its conclusions. There may be some partial differences among the Arab countries regarding the method or the time of addressing the issue of democracy. The image is not much improved if we disregard some slight differences among the various types of elites and 'states' in the Arab world. Basically, they are all the same if we look at the outcome of 'opposites' formation. This outcome is the current Arab reality, where those elite classes struggle violently in one place and tacitly in another. They struggle for power and positions which 'lead to wealth', as Ibn-Khaldūn would say, for the sake of power and interest.

There are also the remaining members of the traditional city aristocracy and their followers. There is the 'controlling class', the product of the public sector, or that which grew around that sector and somehow exploited it. There are also the opposing, protesting groups (from the extreme right to the extreme left), who somehow express the demands of the crushed majority of the people. No talk about democracy or civil society in the Arab world will be realistically significant without taking this social map into consideration, or the ability of its component classes to handle democracy and give a chance to civil society institutions to operate. What is common to these three elite classes is their fear of democracy or its outcome. This is because the relations of those classes with society do not penetrate the institutions of the civil society, which are the channels capable of respecting the principles of the democratic process.

City aristocracy fears democracy as that class is no longer in control of the channels influencing the numerical majority of the people to gain their votes. The controlling class also fears democracy because it realizes that the definite result of every real democratic application would cost that controlling class their positions and power. The other groups of opposition and protest see 'democracy' in their assumption of power, as they consider themselves the 'numerical' representatives, and sometimes the legitimate and historical representatives, of the nation. They do not accept democracy which leads to the assumption of power by the 'modern elite' of a city origin through the 'game' of election as it is played in the West, where publicity and the media play a decisive role.

Undoubtedly, this fear of democracy among all these elite classes, which confers a problematic character upon the issue of democracy itself, finds its reflection in the type of dominant economy. This economy is not controlled by an institution independent from the state. Such an institution is the basis of modern society, and consequently the basis of the social, political and cultural institutions of civil society. In the Arab Nation, economy is dominated by two factors or sectors not conducive to the formation of institutions. One is natural, non-mechanized agriculture which underlines the Bedouin-rural aspect in society, basically contrary to civil society in its institutions, traditions and orientation. The second sector is state revenue, not from the production process inside the country itself, but from oil revenues, emigrant labour, grants and loans. This type of income, which forms the basic element in the economies of most Arab countries at present, is absolutely at the disposal of the state. The state uses this income to protect itself and support its authority and its channels. It enables the state to be, partially or totally, independent from the taxpayers (whose demand of their right to monitor the ruler's disposal of tax money formed the source of modern democracy in Europe). Moreover, the state uses that revenue to finance public projects and social services, and to pay the salaries of its employees and subsidize foodstuffs, etc. This gives the state the upper hand in every field and makes the livelihood of individuals and institutions dependent on it, while the state has its own resources and is in no need of any outside its own.

Then there is the capital flight of national funds to foreign banks for fear of being under the control of men in authority; only enough is left to finance small enterprises which yield quick profit. On the other hand, international capitalism controls the world economy, exploiting and undermining 'the process of independent development in the countries of the South'. These facts make it clear that the general economic situation in the Arab world cannot, on its own, produce enough institutions to lend a modern civil aspect to society and to make political democracy a self-imposing choice, not only through the desire and the struggle of the people but also by 'force of things', the force of the growing institutional reality.

The economic situation in the Arab world is not of this type. It is a situation where one comprehensive institution, the state, holds the reins of power, with its internal systems and external connections. Therefore, it produces a similar 'spontaneous' political vision. By this I mean a type of vision inspired by the socio-economic situation, with its limitations and facts, as established by the dominant culture. People dream of change and expect what is better from 'another comprehensive institution' as an alternative, though it is of a similar nature. They may give alternative, different names and descriptions, based on ideological references (religious, nationalistic, revolutionary), yet the content remains the same: the just autocrat, the heroic leader, the unique leader, etc. The solution is seen in the alternative individual/institution; it is seen in the captain as if the boat that cannot sail has its defect in the captain and his steering only, and not in the structure and equipment of the boat as well.

My analysis, so far, may suggest that my aim here is to prove that it is 'impossible' to realize democracy under the present economic, social and cultural conditions in the Arab world, because of the ineffectiveness of civil society institutions or their absence all together. However, the objective treatment of the issue of democracy in the Arab world requires researching the hurdles that hinder its realization. This is the same as diagnosing a disease, which is not meant to prove that cure is impossible. A close diagnosis that discovers the causes of the disease, no matter how painful and horrible it may be, is the only way to prescribe the appropriate and effective cure for it. Democracy today is that cure; it is a basic demand and one of the essentials of our age.

## CHAPTER 14

# Democracy, a Necessity

How should we look at democracy in the Arab world? Through the historical circumstances that produced it in Europe, or through the current historical Arab situation, which makes democracy a historical necessity? In other words, should we look at it through what the historian may consider the reasons for its rise in Europe, or through the goals entrusted to democracy in the Arab world by the legislator for the future, the intellectual and the political activist?

Without any hesitation, I choose the second approach, because the first one, at best, can only produce a certain interpretation of history, with some degree of success. The second approach leads to the making of history, which is what we need most.

Democracy today is not merely a subject for history, it is also a basic necessity for the modern human being who is no longer a mere figure, but a citizen whose identity is defined by a great number of rights. These are democratic rights, such as the right to choose rulers, to monitor their conduct and to depose them; the right to freedom of speech, to hold meetings and form parties, unions and societies; the right to education and work; the right to equal opportunities in all fields, political, economic, etc. Therefore, democracy should be viewed not as a process that may be applied in one society or another, but as an essential process to be established and applied. It is the only atmosphere wherein the rights of citizenship can be enjoyed by the people, on the one hand, while it enables the rulers to enjoy the legitimacy that justifies their rule, on the other.

The democratic legitimacy, today, is the only acceptable legitimacy; there is no alternative to it. The revolutionary legitimacy, which called for the deferment of political democracy, on the pretext of giving priority to other objectives, in preparation for 'real democracy', has failed in realizing those objectives. Whether that failure was caused by internal factors or by foreign intervention, the only conclusion today is the assertion of the need for democracy as a right that cannot be suspended or compromised by any party. Any objectives posed by the state today cannot be put above the 'rights of the human being and citizen'. On the contrary, all objectives must stem from these rights and be in their service. The so-called historical legitimacy claimed by some rulers is a thing of the past; namely, it is no longer capable of justifying itself in the present age. It might be justified only if it were to conjoin itself to democratic legitimacy and adapt to its rulings. This is its only hope of survival.

On the other hand, viewing democracy as a principle, or a system whereby man enjoys his citizenship rights, gives it precedence over channels and institutions wherein these rights are exercised. This is like a patient's right to be cured, which takes precedence over the means by which that cure is effected, such as medicines and hospitals. It is clear that addressing this issue as a principle eliminates the problem of linking it to civil society, which is like the relation between the chicken and the egg. It is true that applying democracy comes through the so-called civil society institutions, but we should remember also that the rise of such institutions is part of democracy itself. The more the various democratic rights are exercised, the more these institutions grow; and the more these institutions dominate the society, the stronger the democratic system, and so on.

It is clear that the emphasis on democracy as a principle and a framework of citizenship rights does not undermine my previous analysis. Democracy is exercised in a society, and society is not merely a number of individuals; it is a multitude of relations, interests, groups, contentions and rivalries. Hence, democracy is a sound and positive method to regulate relations inside the society in a rational manner, directing the struggle towards the advancement of society as a whole, within the citizen's enjoyment of his rights. While democracy in Europe has played a part in regulating capitalist relations and addressing its internal conflicts peacefully, there is nothing to justify the notion that these are part of those same capitalist relations. On the contrary, capitalist relations are based on monopoly and exploitation, while democracy aims at reducing them to the lowest degree possible, through supervision, resistance and upholding the balance of power.

Arab societies today experience various types of intricate conflicts, as we have seen, among the elite generations. If we put aside the political, social and cultural analyses and look at those conflicts from the general historical and civilizational perspective, we will see that it is a matter of a great civilizational change, a transition from the desert-rural civilization, where agriculture and grazing predominate, to the city civilization of industry, trade and public services. This is a transition from the society of natural institution (the tribe) to the rational one. The critical aspect of this transition is that it is rapid and happening on a wide scale. This is because the incentives for this 'transition' do not stem only from within the society and as a result of internal development, such as what happened in Europe. It is a shift taking place under the pressure of an international civilization which has overwhelmed the world with its achievements; thus it imposed itself as the civilization for the entire age and a culmination of the previous stages of human history.

All this led to the succession of new elite generations in the Arab world and the developing world in general. It is such a fast succession that the outgoing generation has hardly a chance to establish its dominance through institutions engendered by accruing achievements and experience, or to fulfil its aspirations. What happens is that the prevalence of modern civilization through education and media and the availability of goods and facilities, along with the popularization of political and social awareness, encourage people, especially the new generations, to aspire to better positions. The son of a farmer is no longer destined to become a farmer, nor the son of a blacksmith a blacksmith, as was the case in the past, when personal and communal aspirations were limited to certain areas inherited from fathers and forefathers. Education, the media, and political and social awareness, have made all areas open to all. These aspirations were supported and made achievable by the need of the independent state for more qualified employees with the growing needs of modern life. It was natural, then, to see rivalry among the successive new generations, against the backdrop of a rise in birth rates. The elite class, in the final analysis, is nothing but a group of people from the same or overlapping generations, with the same aspirations generalized to become a future programme for the entire society. They work also to mobilize the entire population to realize that programme.

Such transition makes the move from one social, political or ideological position to another an easy and spontaneous process. Class and institution barriers, in such cases, become movable and easy to cross. To shift from the extreme right to the extreme left or the other way around, from poverty to wealth, from 'a harsh Bedouin life to a soft civilized one', as Ibn Khaldūn would say, is to shift allegiance to a person or a party, to shift from one ideology to another, to change attire (which has become an ideological symbol for some elites). These have all become quite uncontrollable, which opens the way to all possibilities.

This shows that democracy is a historical necessity. Democracy alone can institutionalize and mould this major process of transition. Free democratic expression, the recognition of difference and diversity, in addition to the rotation of power, are the basic conditions which ensure, or at least help to direct, the movement and the conflict within the process of transition properly and safely. This would open the way for the establishment of civil society institutions such as parties, societies, unions and elected councils. These institutions can lead the conflict, the movement and the transition inside society towards historical progress. Democracy is a historical necessity, because the only alternative, under the weight of such a major transitional process, is frustration and chaos, which will lead to civil wars, which are never an acceptable alternative. No one party achieves a historical victory over the other party, which might take social steps forward. On the contrary, civil wars always end with the same result, which is the defeat of all the parties; and nothing but democracy can offer an alternative to such a defeat.

# Part Three

# Cultural Implantation of Human Rights in the Contemporary Arab Conscience

Chapter 15

# Human Rights: Particularity and Universality

In recent years, there has been much ado about 'human rights'. The expression has become a slogan raised all over the world, and by all parties but with different aims and implications. This has made it quite legitimate to inspect the motives and considerations of those who herald that slogan.

There is, for instance, what we see and hear about the use of this slogan by the Western media against all parties viewed by the West as hostile to its interests and influence, or those who reject its domination. I still remember how the West used human rights as a weapon against the Soviet Union before its fall, against what used to be called the 'Communist Bloc' and against all the states that had policies and orientations incompatible with the interests of the West. The Western media have remained silent over other states which repeatedly, intentionally and blatantly violate human rights – to a degree that has made such violation a fixed policy of those states.

Major examples are seen in the human rights violations in occupied Palestine by both military and civil authorities in Israel. Other examples have been seen in South Africa, in Third World dictatorships allied to the West; in Bosnia and Herzegovina; and in the European states themselves, where foreign minorities, especially those from the countries of the 'South', are constantly subjected to various forms of harassment, oppression and racial discrimination.

On the other hand, there are those who criticize, in no uncertain terms, the Western form of human rights as promulgated in the Universal Declaration of Human Rights, issued by the United Nations (in 1948, under the control of the West). Similarly, there were the agreements to apply that declaration, concluded by the European states (such as the European Agreement on Human Rights, 1950, and the American Agreement on Human Rights, 1969), all of which derive from the 'constants' of Western culture, which differ from the constants and particularities of other cultures. Therefore, the universality of 'human rights' as expressed in those declarations is contested and the need to revise the Universal Declaration of Human Rights is stressed in order to come out with a new version, respectful of the constants and particularities of all cultures. Some of these reactions are seen in the initiatives taken to formulate Islamic versions of human rights or from an Islamic perspective. These are: (1) The Declaration of the Rights and Duties of Man in Islam; (2) The Universal Islamic Declaration; (3) The Universal Declaration of Human Rights in Islam; (4) A Draft of Human Rights in Islam; and (5) A Draft Declaration of Human Rights in Islam. Similar initiatives have also been taken in Africa and other countries.

Thus, I note two main features in the discourse of human rights at present. One is the use of this slogan as an ideological weapon against the adversary, by the Western media, both American and European. The second is the contention about the universality of the Human Rights Declaration, from the perspective of the cultural particularity. This provokes the question about the 'cultural legitimacy' of these rights.

I will leave aside the first feature as its aggressively antagonistic ideology is quite obvious, and I will discuss, instead, universality and particularity in the field of human rights. My approach will be to compare the facts in the European referential authority with those in Islam.

My purpose from such a comparison is to make use of it in the process of the cultural implantation of human rights as they are specified in the international conventions and endorsed by contemporary thought. To lend this process of implantation an institutional dimension, we have to extend the comparison further than the 'rights' themselves, namely to their theoretical and philosophical bases. Therefore, discussion here will deal with the philosophy of human rights, which will show the historicity of these rights. Yet this does not necessarily mean that the historicity of an issue makes it merely an outcome of certain circumstances. The contrary is also true, namely, that the historicity of an issue may highlight its role in demarcating and establishing a new historical era.

Thus, the Universal Declaration of Human Rights that was heralded in Western culture (like the American Declaration of Independence in 1776; the French Declaration of the National Assembly, in 1789; and the UN Declaration, in 1948) finds its authoritative historical point of reference in the givens of the Western nations and appears to be the outcome of situations experienced by those nations. Yet, this is not sufficient justification to contest the *universality* of human rights in its modern implication. A supporter of these rights may argue that this Declaration was a revolution both in and against that culture. It was a call to renounce the behavioural, intellectual, social, economic and political criteria established by that culture. Consequently, this Declaration was a universal declaration, calling for a new legitimacy to counter the one that was dominant in that culture. This is a historical fact not open to doubt. The same argument may be the right answer to those who object to the particular nature of the human rights in Islam; namely, that behind that particularity lies a universality which gives it a real historical dimension, the one that makes history, not the one made by it.

The process of the cultural implantation of human rights in our contemporary Arab thought must, in my opinion, highlight the universality of human rights in both European and Islamic cultures, to show that both are based on the same philosophical principles. The differences do not stem from the 'cultural constants', but they are due to the diversity of the 'occasions of revelation'. More specifically, the differences are due to the social, economic, political and intellectual circumstances which made it necessary for one legislator or another to take a certain stand on a certain issue. It is necessary to understand the rationale behind that stand, or the purpose (*al-ḥikmah*) as the Muslim jurisprudents would say. These are the objectives intended by the legislator in issuing his ruling in one case or another.

To realize the rationality of a ruling is also necessary to avoid that serious methodological error committed by some when they judge the issues of the past by the criteria and concerns of the present. Human rights specified by Islam at the time of the Prophet and his Companions cannot be judged by the criteria of contemporary human rights, as each has its own rationale. What is meant here by cultural implantation is not a compromise between the two rationales, nor the inclusion of one within the other. It is to stimulate the awareness of the universality of human rights within our culture by highlighting the universality of their theoretical bases, which are not radically different from the bases of human rights in Western culture. This would underline the universal, comprehensive and absolute nature of human rights within the cultural particularity itself. It would also affirm, once more, that particularity and universality are not two opposite attributes but two integral ones. Every 'particular' has something of the 'universal', as the universal is so only because it includes what is universal in all that is particular.

# Chapter 16

# Universality of Human Rights in the European Point of Reference

The 'Declaration of Human Rights' in modern Western thought is qualified as 'universal', which means 'comprehensive' in this context. Thus, the rights here are universal, in the sense that they are the rights of all human beings, with no discrimination against male or female, white or black, poor or rich. They are the rights of man as a human being, irrespective of any other consideration. The European philosophers of the eighteenth century based human rights on two major ones, from which stem all other rights. Those two are the right to freedom and the right to equality. The question now is: how did those philosophers establish the universality of those two rights, and what was their authoritative referent?

To describe human rights, as heralded by the European philosophers, as universal, in the sense I have explained above, there must have been an authoritative referent to resort to, which necessarily fell 'outside' the European culture dominant at the time, which was a culture of oppression and inequality. So, their referential authority must have been independent, transcending time and place; a self-justifying authority, transcending history.

What then was this referential authority? We learn from the history of human thought that religion has ordinarily provided a referential authority that transcends all other authorities. To refer a matter to God means establishing that matter on the basis of an absolute comprehensive authority, not affected by cultures and civilizations. It is an authority which transcends time and history and consequently transcends man himself, whoever and wherever he may be. Did the European philosophers of the eighteenth century resort to religion in their effort to establish the universality of the human rights as mapped out in the US Declaration of Independence in 1776 and later on in the Declaration of the French National Assembly, on 26 August 1789?

In the articles concerning human rights in the US Declaration of Independence, straight religious concepts are used, such as 'the Creator', 'the Highest Ruler of the Universe' and 'Divine Providence'. Besides this, the 'Declaration of the Rights of Man and Citizen', issued by the French National Assembly, refers in the preamble to the 'Providence of the Highest Being', meaning God. Yet the philosophers of the eighteenth century were basically opposed to all the ruling powers that tyrannized the peoples of Europe at the time, especially the powers of tradition and the Church.

Thus, religion was not the universal, comprehensive referential authority on which those philosophers based the universality of the human rights they were heralding. They resorted, instead, to an independent rational referential authority which transcends the authority of the Church and which comprised three main premises: the correspondence between the rational and the natural systems; the hypothetical 'natural condition'; and the concept of the 'social contract'. Here, then, is a quick review of each of these basic premises:

> (i) The advances made in science (especially mathematics and physics) in the sixteenth and seventeenth centuries culminated in a mechanical outlook on nature, in the eighteenth century, as crystallized by Newton. This new outlook unseated the entire predominant epistemological system and disrupted all previous scientific and philosophical conceptions. That led to the rise of the Age of Enlightenment and Reason. As is well known, Newton formulated the general theory of gravity as a mathematical (i.e. rational) law. According to this law the natural and the rational systems are two aspects of the same fact. Thus, the concept of 'nature' came to mean not the inanimate things exhibited before the human being, but 'the rational order of things as a comprehensive order comprising all that is in nature, inclusive of man himself'. As a result, people began to correlate the natural with the rational, on the assumption that whatever existed in nature is subject to a precise system just like the parts of a machine being subject to the machine as a whole, which makes the natural easy to grasp by reason. Similarly, everything that sounds rational or justifiable by reason is natural, namely, compatible, or must be compatible with nature.
>
> Hence, the function of the mind is to discover the natural, that is the rational aspect in every field, and discard all that is not natural; namely, the inaccuracies which accumulated in people's conceptions of things, as a result of imitation rather than using the mind. If the scientific law that brings together scattered phenomena in a comprehensive, constant relation, is an expression of the truth about nature, there is in human life, also, what may be called its nature and comprehensive law. It is the ideals described as universal, which can be found everywhere, East and West, among civilized and primitive

nations alike. Hence comes that phenomenon in European culture of the time, the phenomenon of judging European society by 'Persian' or 'Chinese' epistles, or by those written about the 'primitive man'. All this was to highlight the universal values that define the ideal to be sought after.

As the advance in mathematics and physics led to a correspondence between the rational and the natural, so did the expanding information about the life of human societies (Eastern and primitive) lead to the correspondence between the natural and the primitive 'primordial' – innate – in human life. This gave rise to visions of a 'golden age' enjoyed by early humanity, when men followed a 'natural religion which they accepted because it was basically rational'. This is the innate religion in the Islamic sense: 'But the conniving clergy and monarchs in the later ages corrupted and debased it to the level of superstitions to serve their own interests.' This is the hypothetical 'state of nature' I will address next.

(ii) The philosophers of modern political thought in Europe in the seventeenth and eighteenth centuries did assume the existence of a 'natural state' of man. Some thought it existed prior to social systems and political authorities. Others thought it only represented what man could be like if he were not subjected to education or the authority of law or government. While all such philosophers referred to the natural state hypothesis in one way or another, it was the British philosopher John Locke (1632–1704) who developed this hypothesis, to make of it a potential referential authority that could serve to establish the universality of human rights. He said:

> In order to understand political authority correctly, and verify its origin, we must explore the natural state into which all individuals were born. It is a state of complete freedom in managing their actions, persons and possessions in the manner they consider suitable to them, within the limits of the natural law, without asking anyone's permission or depending on the will of another. It is also the state of equality, where authority and legislation are parallel, no side takes more than the other. There is no truth more self-evident than that all creatures belonging to the same race enjoying the same benefits offered by nature, and using the same faculties should also be equal to one another.

The natural state, then, is the state of freedom and equality enjoyed by people before the rise of an authority to limit their right to enjoy that freedom and equality, except for the 'natural law' itself, the law which aims at 'protecting the human race and ensuring its safety, the law which every human being is responsible to apply'.

> The natural state hypothesis was not a mere imaginative or illusory idea. It was, rather, based on the new concept of 'nature' formulated by modern science, as we have seen. Therefore, the word 'natural' does not refer to inanimate objects separate from man. It denotes 'the complete and real order of things including man', who is part of the work of nature, as he exists in nature and is subject to its laws.
>
> In this, all men are free and equal with one another because the right of man to freedom and equality is his natural right – hence the correspondence between the two expressions 'the rights of man' and 'natural rights', i.e. the rights of man are his *natural* rights. It is clear that the reference to 'nature' here means basing those rights on an authority prior to any other, as nature came before any culture or civilization, any society or state. Consequently, it is a total and absolute authority and the rights based on it are equally total and absolute.
>
> (iii) However, the natural state does not mean chaos, it is a state subject to 'natural law'. Since it is quite likely that contentions will break out among people when everyone is exercising his natural right, it becomes equally natural that they will try to interpret and apply the natural law in a way that ensures everyone's rights. This can only happen when 'they unite among themselves to protect each one, to enable him to exercise his rights, and allow him, while in union with the others, not to submit except to his own self, and, consequently, continue to enjoy the freedom that he used to enjoy initially'. This led to the hypothesis of the 'social contract', which explains the transition from the 'natural state' to the 'civil state' as specified by Jean-Jacques Rousseau (1712–78).
>
> While John Locke more than others elaborated on the natural state, Jean-Jacques Rousseau was the first among the eighteenth-century philosophers to elaborate on the hypothesis of the social contract. This hypothesis purports that man, by his nature, cannot live alone, but he needs to live with others of his kind. And since the wills of people differ and conflict, their life together cannot be in harmony unless it is based on a 'contract' among them, where everyone surrenders all his rights to the group which is represented by the state as a moral entity responsible for organizing people's enjoyment of their rights. In so doing, those natural rights become civil rights, with freedom and equality as their essence.

So, the submission of people's rights, in accordance with this social contract, to the collective will as represented by the state, is only a formal one. Its aim is to endorse the right to freedom and equality on a social basis, as nothing else can justify the rise of the state. The laws promulgated by the state gain legitimacy only because they express the general will of the people that will work for the common interest and seeks the common good. Thus, the natural rights of man find their realization in turning into civil rights, based on an absolute, comprehensive referential authority, namely, the 'public will', which transcends all other wills, while being, at the same time, the will whose only aim is the common interest and the common good.

This makes it clear that the establishment of human rights achieved by modern European philosophers bypasses all cultural particularities. It relates those human rights to the point of origin, prior to all cultures and civilizations: first to the natural state, then to the social contract which is the basis of human society, and ultimately to culture and civilization. Does that lead us to say that the universality of human rights, including those specified in the Universal Declaration, have a philosophical basis that makes it insignificant to seek 'cultural legitimacy' for these rights? This is the question I will address next.

CHAPTER 17

# Universality of Human Rights in the Islamic Authoritative Point of Reference: Reason and Innate Nature

We highlighted previously how the philosophers of Europe worked, during the eighteenth century, to establish 'human rights' in modern European thought by employing three suppositions or 'theoretical bases' which were: 'the correlation of the natural system and the rational system [of the reason]'; the 'natural state'; and 'the social contract'. At the end of our analyses of these premises, we posed the question of whether or not this was a type of philosophical establishing the 'universality' of 'human rights' which made demanding 'cultural legitimacy' or posing the matter of cultural specificity a moot point. We are concerned here with discussion of this matter.

It is possible to say at the outset that this type of establishing the 'transcendence' of the major issues of the human being, the cases of truth, obligation, good, the ideal, being, destiny, etc., were not something invented by the European philosophers in the seventeenth and eighteenth centuries. Rather, the 'transcendence' of the human issues which were of this type was a general phenomenon in which all cultures and civilizations participated. If we restrict our attention to Arab and Islamic culture, we find that this type of establishing of the 'transcendence' of the 'major' human concerns is present in various forms: Islam functioned from the beginning to establish its call (*al-da'wah*), and among that was what we term today 'human rights' on theoretical bases which almost correlate identically to those which we have mentioned previously. It is no doubt clearer here if when we use the expression 'almost corresponds' that we mean, first and foremost, to indicate the necessity of taking all the differences in time and civilization completely into consideration so that we will not slip into the danger of projecting the present onto the past. Aside from this precaution, a correspondence becomes evident between the means whereby Islam elevates human rights to a position of transcendence – as it might be imagined in that age – and the path tread by the philosophers of Europe in the modern era. It is, I believe, an operation justified by its function in implanting consciousness of human rights in our contemporary thought. This is how that correspondence may be addressed in this connection:

(i) The European philosophers used the principle, or the premise, of 'correspondence' between the 'natural and rational systems' to make the mind the ultimate authority and the first and last arbiter. I believe this kind of correspondence can be seen in the Islamic call and in the Qur'ān, in particular. The Qur'ān has urged its audience over and over again to meditate upon the system of nature and derive there from the correct conclusions (i.e. the existence of a Creator who alone has to be followed, disregarding all other authorities). Those admonitions are often concluded by expressions suggesting that the natural system is, itself, the rational system, or at least they indicate and stress that meaning:

> Behold! In the creation of the heavens and the earth; in the alternation of night and day; in the sailing of the ships through the ocean for the profit of mankind; in the rain which Allāh sends down from the skies and the life. He gives therewith to an earth that is dead; in the beasts of all kinds that He scatters through the earth; in the change of the winds, and the clouds trailed between the sky and the earth, [here] indeed are signs for people that are wise (2, al-Baqarah, 164).

The system of nature here (i.e. the heavens and earth, day and night) are signs the significance and indications of which are grasped by the mind. It is obvious that the mind could not realize the significance of the natural system if its own system were not correspondent to the system of nature, or if its judgments did not correspond with the laws of nature. The European philosophers themselves declared that God made the natural system and the rational system in such correspondence and harmony.

On the other hand, we find the Qur'ān using the mind (*al-'aql*), over and over again, as an arbiter and authority, reproaching those who submit to imitating tradition (*al-taqlīd*) and calling on them to follow the judgment of the mind alone:

> They said, 'We worship our idols, and we remain in constant attendance to them.' He said, 'Do they listen to you when you call [on them]. Or do they benefit you or harm you?' They said, 'No, but we found our fathers doing thus [what we do]' (26, al-Shūrā, 71–4).

(ii) This call to follow reason and leave aside traditions and conventions, guided by the signs of the universe (the natural system), is coupled in the Qur'ānic discourse with a call to return to *al-fiṭrah* (innate nature). Islam is the 'religion *al-fiṭrah*' (the religion of innate nature). The Arabic *fiṭrah* is almost identical, in Qur'ānic discourse, with the concept of the 'natural state' [in European thought]:

So, set up your face steadfastly and truly to the faith; the *fiṭrah* of Allāh upon which he created (*faṭara*) the human being. There is no change in the creation of Allāh. That is the upright religion, but most people know not (30, Al-Rūm, 30).

The 'upright faith' (*al-dīn al-qayyim*) or the 'pious religion' (*al-dīn al-hanīf*) or the 'religion of *al-fiṭrah*' is the religion of Abraham preceding the religions – the Jewish and Christian – which were being practised in the Arabian peninsula prior to the call of Muḥammad on the basis of [the Qur'ānic text]: 'Abraham was neither a Jew or a Christian, but he was true [in faith] (*hanīfan*), a Muslim [one who submits to Allāh] , and he was not of those who worshipped [other things] in partnership' (3, Āl 'Imrān, 67). The faith of Abraham is Islam itself, which is the only religion accepted by Allāh: 'The religion with Allāh is Islam [i.e. submission to His Will]' (3, Āl 'Imrān, 14). Islam is the religion of *al-fiṭrah*, it is the right religion, as it covers:

> What has been revealed to us and what was revealed to Abraham, Ishmael, Isaac, Jacob, and the Tribes, and in [the books] given to Moses, Jesus, and the prophets from their Lord. We make no distinction between one and another among them, and to Allāh we bow our will [in Islam]. If anyone desires a religion other than Islam [submission to Allāh], never will it be accepted of him, (3, Āl 'Imrān, 84–5).

What is meant by 'Islam' is the faith of Abraham, which is the origin of every religion, and it is prior to any religious controversy, as it is the religion of *al-fiṭrah*: 'Nor did the People of the Book dissent there from except through envy of each other, after knowledge had come to them' (3, Āl 'Imrān, 19).[1]

There is, therefore, a justification in comparing the 'state of *al-fiṭrah*' in the Qur'ānic sense with the 'natural state' on which European philosophers of the eighteenth century based the concept of human rights and its modern connotations. This comparison can be augmented by quoting other Qur'ānic verses: 'Mankind was but one nation but they differed [later]' (10, Yūnis, 19); also, 'Mankind was one single nation, and Allāh sent messengers with glad tidings and warnings' (2, al-Baqarah, 213). We can also refer to the famous *ḥadīth*: 'Every newborn is born according to *al-fiṭrah* (innate nature). His parents turn him Jewish, Christian, or Magian.' It is useful to refer to what the exegetes had to say in this respect. They understood *al-fiṭrah* to mean initiation and origination. It is the way God created people. The meaning of 'Islam is the religion of *fiṭrah*', according to Zamakhshari, is God created people:

> inclined to believe in the unique oneness of God and in thre religion of Islam, not deviating from it or objecting to it, because it is concordant with reason and with sound judgment. If men were to be left alone they would not choose another religion. Those who dissent are misled by demons and Satan.

Fakhruddīn al-Rāzī comments on the relevant *ḥadīth* by saying:

> The *ḥadīth* indicates that if the newborn were to be left to its original innate nature (*'alā fiṭrahi al-aṣīlah*), it would not follow any of the false religions. If it were to embrace a false religion that would be caused by an external factors, such as the parents' efforts or exposure to corrupting influences.

Would it be a deviation from the truth to say that the basic Islamic authoritative referent, not to say the only one, that establishes the universality of Islam is the 'state of *al-fiṭrah*'? And, consequently, what is established by Islam is the 'law of *al-fiṭrah*' according to which God created (*faṭara*) people.

This is not to prove correspondence between certain elements in European and Arab-Islamic cultures; it is only to serve as a comparison, where the logic of absolute right and wrong does not apply. The matter under consideration here is not composed of 'scientific facts', but of 'revolutionary facts' if one could coin such a phrase. These are the facts used by revolutions and all movements of reform, which derive their veracity or rather their credibility from their function as the motivating factor behind the revolution or the slogans of the call [for revolution/reform]. The European philosophers of the eighteenth century, by expounding upon the 'natural state' and the supposition of the 'social contract', were establishing a revolution, the one known as the bourgeois revolution, or the middle-class revolution. The Islamic call, by using the concept of *al-fiṭrah*, was in turn establishing the revolution of the 'oppressed' (*al-mustaḍ'afīn*) against the 'arrogant oppressors' (*al-mustakbirīn*), the revolution of monotheism (*al-tawḥīd*) against polytheism (*al-shirk*), and the revolution of the connection to the one God and the liberation from all [other] authorities and bonds. This comparison will look for elements in the Islamic discourse which can be compared with the concept of the 'social contract'.

## Note

1. A common misconception is that 'Islam' is understood to be exclusive to or a religion 'originated' by Muḥammad when he began his teaching sometime around the year 613CE – three years after the first revelation. According to both the texts of the Qur'ān, as well as to the understanding of Muslims throughout history, 'Islam' means

'submission' to the law and commandments of God – whatever they may be at any particular period in time. Thus, to have been a 'Muslim' in the time of Abraham or Moses or Jesus mean to be 'one who submits' to the law given, respectively and sequentially, to each of those prophets. Muḥammad is distinguished, according to the Qur'ān, by being simply the 'seal (*khātim*) of the prophets' – that is, the last in the long chain of human interlocutors for God going all the way back to the primordial human being, Adam. It is for this reason that Jews and Christians are considered 'People of the Book' (*ahl-al-kitāb*), as there is never any question about the legitimacy of their 'book' which constitutes, in Muslim understanding, the same 'book' and the same religion of 'submission' – 'Islam' – at early stages. Thus, by this usage, the author should not be misunderstood as asserting a type of 'exclusivity' for 'Islam', but rather a 'universal' inclusiveness.

CHAPTER 18

# The Universality of Human Rights in the Islamic Authoritative Point of Reference: Covenant and *al-Shūrā*

The supposition of the 'social contract' upon which the philosophers of Europe based the universality of human rights – the right to freedom and the right to equality and what derives from these, as we have seen – narrows down to two principles: the surrender of people's natural rights to the 'public will', which transcends every other will and is motivated only by the public good and the common interest; and the regaining of those rights in the form of civil rights, organized and ensured by the state which acts on behalf of the public will, the will of society as a whole.

We have, therefore, a three-dimensional structure of relations:

(i) Individual human beings, the possessors of natural rights.

(ii) The public will to which people surrender their natural rights.

(iii) The organized group wherein the human being exercises those rights, which have been returned to him in the form of systematized civil rights (to be exercised without violating other the rights of others).

Can there be a comparison between the suppositional framework of the 'social contract' and what is propounded by the Islamic discourse with regard to transcendence in its call (*daʿwah*)?

The hypothesis of 'the contract' reminds me of the 'covenant' verses in the Qur'ān. These are the verses which establish that God took a vow from the children of Adam not to worship anyone except Him; therefore, He honoured them by making them His vicegerents (*khulafā'*) on earth, and entrusted them with that responsibility, sending them messengers to bring them glad tidings, to warn them and to guide them to the right path. Among these verses we have: 'When your Lord drew forth from the children of Adam from their loins their descendants and made them testify concerning themselves, [saying] "Am I not your Lord?": They said, "Yes! We do testify"'(7, al-Aʿrāf, 172). Other verses mention the covenant per se:

> And [remember that] We took from the Prophets their covenant as [We did] from you, from Noah, Abraham, Moses, and Jesus, the son of Mary, We took from them a solemn covenant (*al-mīthāq*), that [Allāh] may question the truthful concerning the truth [they were charged with] and He has prepared for the unbelievers a grievous penalty (33, al-Aḥzāb, 7–8).

So, on the one hand, there is the covenant between God and the children of Adam, by which they testified to His Lordship and bore witness upon themselves not to associate anyone or anything with Him. On the other hand, there is the covenant between God and the Prophets by which they pledged to convey the message to the people, the message of 'guidance and right religion', which honours them over all other creatures: 'We have honoured the sons of Adam, provided them with transport on land and sea, given them for sustenance things good and pure, and conferred on them special favours, above a great part of Our creation' (17, al-Isrā', 70). Therefore, what is needed of them is: 'Let there arise out of you a community (*ummah*) inviting to all that is good, enjoining what is right and forbidding what is wrong; they are the ones to attain felicity' (3, Āl 'Imrān, 104).

From these and similar verses, we can easily derive elements for comparison with elements from the hypothesis of the 'social contract'. The submission of rights by the human beings to the 'public will' in the 'social contract' is close to the admission of the children of Adam and their testimony to ascribe divinity to God alone with no other associate. By such admission, they have surrendered their 'right' to worship other gods like idols, stars or angels, and committed themselves to worship God alone, and to recognize Him alone as a power that liberates man from the control of other powers. This is comparable with the 'public will' in the hypothesis of the social contract. On the other hand, this submission is not without reward. God sends prophets to the people to show them the path of righteousness and prosperity. This is to say that their surrender of their 'natural right' to worship whomever they choose – 'Let he who wills believe, and let he who wills disbelieve' (18, al-Kahf, 29) – will be rewarded by being shown the path of righteousness by the prophets.

This primordial covenant, which was concluded upon the creation of Adam and his progeny and which establishes religion – namely the relation between God and human beings, turns into a 'real' social contract with the initial rise of Islamic society. The Qur'ān calls this *al-shūrā*, which is a contract establishing the society: '[They conduct] their affairs by mutual consultation' (42, al-Shūrā, 38). It is, as well, a contract that organizes the relation between the people and the state: 'And consult them in the matter' (3, Āl ʿImrān, 159). All this is intended in that primordial covenant, which makes *al-shūrā* the embodiment of that covenant in the reality of social life. Hence, this is the significance given by the Qur'ān to *al-shūrā*, when it was put forth in a single context with what constitutes the essence of Islam.

The Qur'ān equates *al-shūrā* with belief, the avoidance of the major sins, the performance of prayer – that is, with what constitutes the essence of Islam as a religion and a social system:

> Whatever you are given [here] is [but] an enjoyment of this life; but that which is with Allāh is better and more lasting; [it is] for those who believe and put their trust in their Lord. Those who avoid the greater sins and shameful deeds, and when they are angry, they forgive; those who answer their Lord, and establish regular prayer; who [conduct] their affairs by mutual consultation (*al-shūrā*); who spend out of what we bestow on them for sustenance; and those who, when an oppressive wrong is inflicted on them [are not cowed but] help and defend themselves (42, *al-shūrā*, 36–8).

Some commentators say that these verses were revealed about the Ansar, 'who, before Islam and the Messenger's arrival in Medina, used to meet and consult among themselves about affairs of moment, so the Messenger commended them for that, as they would not follow a single opinion until it won consensus' (al-Zamakhshārī). Others think that these verses are Meccan, and the address is general. In any case, *al-shūrā* is a sublime Islamic principle, as it is equated with the qualities of 'those who believe', those who are the pillars of the Islamic society.

On the other hand, the Qur'ān mentions *al-shūrā* in the context of the qualities which regulate the relations between the head of the Islamic group and the Muslim community. This came as a command:

> It is part of the mercy of Allāh that you deal gently with them. Were you severe or harsh-hearted, they would have broken away from about you; so, pass over [their faults] and ask for [Allāh's] forgiveness for them, and consult them in the matter (3, Āl ʿImrān, 159).

Moreover, there are many *ḥādīth* ascribed to the Prophet commending consultation and encouraging its exercise. Although the ascription (*isnād*) of many of those *ḥādīth* does not attain a level of certitude such as that which al-Bukhārī, for example, would specify, the above verses vouch for their veracity at the level of content, which is more important than veracity of ascription. Moreover, those *ḥādīth* are vindicated by the Prophet's practice of *al-shūrā*, which was followed by the Companions after him in selecting a caliph (the meeting in the bower of Banī Sāʿidah, ʿUmar's appointment of a consultative committee to choose a caliph after him and the mutual consultation of the Companions on important matters). We may add to this that the *ḥādīth on al-shūrā* remained as an expression of the Islamic conscience throughout the ages. Consensus (*al-ijmāʿ*), which is a principle of Islamic legislation, is not endorsed except after mutual consultation.

The natural state, the state of *al-fiṭrah*, social contract, *al-shūrā* and the comparison may be extended to other rights, such as the right to 'resist injustice' which is specified by article 2 of the '*Rights of Man and the Citizen*', issued by the French National Assembly in 1789. A better expression of that right is found in the Islamic principle of 'Enjoining what is right and forbidding what is wrong'. Then, there is the famous *ḥadīth*: 'Whoever sees an evil, let him redress it by his sword; if he cannot, then by his tongue; if he still cannot, then by his heart, and these are the weakest in faith.'

I need not carry the comparison any further, as my point is not to prove the precedence of Islam in one field or another. My intention is simply to establish that the claim of the European philosophers about the universal aspect of the human rights, and the human being's right to freedom and equality and what is derivative of these, is not particular to European civilization alone. The cultural, civilizatoinal dimensions of human rights are *human* dimensions shared by all cultures and they transcend the current civilizational, cultural reality and all civilizations. The demand to respect human rights is always directed against a certain cultural civilizational reality (an intellectual, political, social, economic reality and a call to change that reality). All cultures and civilizations join in establishing this call, based on an authoritative referent which presents itself as the beginning and the origin, like the natural state or the religion of *al-fiṭrah*.

There may be some objection to my claim of universality in the Islamic authoritative referent for human rights. Some may say that there is a 'particularity' in that authority, as those rights are closely connected with Islam as a religion and also because of the restrictions imposed by Islamic jurisprudence on some of these rights. This problem will be addressed in later sections in this work.

## Chapter 19

# Philosophy of Human Rights and Religion

I have shown the way by which we can comprehend the universality, i.e. the all-encompassing and comprehensive aspect of human rights in Islam, by relying upon the same or similar theoretical focii to those used by modern European philosophers to establish human rights. These rights are based on freedom and equality.

There is no doubt that my method and conclusions could lead to some objections and queries, most notable of which may be the following two: First, the credibility of my comparison may be questioned. It may be said that the theoretical framework of human rights in modern European thought is 'secular', while that in Islam is 'religious'. Second, universality of freedom and equality may be undermined in Islam by referring to certain jurisprudential rulings, such as sentencing the apostate to death, which is at the expense of the freedom of belief or religion, or those rulings which cover inheritance, testimony, marriage and divorce, which accord the man more rights or recognition than the woman.

These two observations may sound 'embarrassingly' valid. But rationale is relative, not permanent or unchangeable. It is always possible to build different rationales, which form the bases of different philosophies, religions, political persuasions, or scientific theories about the same subject. Every theory is different from other theories in the type of rationale it constructs to interpret matters. The scientific revolution of the late nineteenth century was built on the acceptance of multiple rationales. Various geometrical theories were developed, each with a rationale equal to that of Euclidean geometry, which had no rival until the mid-nineteenth century. In the early twentieth century, new theories in physics were developed with new rationales about time and space, and the relation between both. Thus, the theory of relativity developed its own rationale to counter the one that was dominant about time and space. On the other hand, the 'partical theory' of light became the opposite of the 'wave theory' of the same phenomenon. Then a new theory was developed to join both theories in one, with one rationale.

Therefore, the validity of an objection to an opinion does not necessarily disprove it as contradictory to the truth. It only means that there is more than one possibility to establish the rationale of the issue under discussion. This does not undermine the 'truth', as man cannot reach the 'ultimate truth' all at once. Man builds up the truth by various steps of trial and error. What is correct in the sciences is established by experimentation, while in the field of rights and legislation it is what most realizes the public good and what is best for the individual and the community.

Based on this assumption, I shall address the two objections, starting with the first. To say that human rights in modern European thought derive from secularism, while those in Islam stem from religion, is an assertion which needs to be tested. First, that which must be examined is the term 'secularism' itself. The European philosophers who initiated the Enlightenment and worked towards the establishment of human rights in modern thought did not oppose religion as such, but they opposed the way the Church practised religion. Diderot, a leading figure of the Enlightenment, said:

> If a man testifies to the existence of God, to the existence of the moral good and evil, the eternity of the soul, the reward and punishment in the other world, why is it necessary for him to preserve the traditional ideas (that is, the Church). If we suppose this person has learned, as well, all the sacraments of the Eucharist, Trinity, hypostasis, destiny, the incarnation, etc., do these beliefs help him to be a better citizen?

It is true that those philosophers built their theories on the hypothesis of the correspondence between the rational and the natural. But the 'natural' in their Enlightenment discourse was not a substitute for the 'divine'; in fact, they united the two together. The so-called natural religion or rational religion, describing the ideas of the Enlightenment philosophers of the eighteenth century concerning human rights in Europe, did not then mean replacing the divine by the natural, or religion by reason. On the contrary, natural religion for them meant the same as divine religion, but man adopted it without the mediation of the Church, and understood its issues only by virtue of reason. Those philosophers saw that natural religion is based on the same three principles as the divine religion:

> There exists an omnipotent God, expecting man to lead a righteous life by his obedience to the Divine will. There is another life in the Hereafter, where the good is rewarded, and the evil punished. If man could use his talent in deriving results from the given facts, he could see the benefits of righteous life and run his life on rational bases to realize the reward in the Hereafter.

On the other hand, John Locke, the founder of the human rights theory based on the idea of the 'natural state', tried to prove the 'rationality of Christianity', which meant to dispense with the Church and its rites. He searched through the New Testament and 'could not find more than two conditions for salvation: the belief that Jesus is the saviour and the belief in the ideal life'. Although the ideas of these Enlightenment intellectuals were described as 'rational religion', they did not all believe in dispensing with the 'revelation', they rather distinguished between reason and revelation. For instance, John Locke himself distinguished matters as: (1) those that agree with reason; (2) those that contradict reason; and (3) those that transcend reason. The first and second types are the concern of reason; the third of revelation. He says, 'To believe in the existence of one God goes with reason; to believe in the existence of more than one God goes against reason; to believe in the resurrection of the dead transcends reason.' As for Rousseau, the founder of the 'social contract' theory, we find that, though he lived in the age of reason, historians of modern European thought put him 'outside' that age, assuming that he was not as rational as the Enlightenment philosophers, but emotional and romantic. Though he criticized the Church practice of religion, he was not against religion per se. He emphasizes the necessity of religion, provided 'it be limited to the basic doctrines for life', like the belief in the existence of God, the divine Providence, reward and punishment in the Hereafter, without the need for Church rituals. Therefore, we find him, in *Emile*, his book on education, specifying that, when a child becomes 15 years old, he should learn he has a spirit and that God exists; and he should embrace, at a later age, the doctrine of religion specified by revelation, taught to him by a priest, without being subjected to the Church and its rituals.

This shows that the 'secularism' of human rights in modern European thought did not mean to dispense with religion as such, but simply to be liberated from the authority of the Church and its rituals. They have built the rationality of human rights by reliance on reason alone, without being against religion, but against the understanding imposed by the Church and collateral rituals. They have retained religion and dispensed with the tradition and the authority of the Church, replacing them by reason and its authority. Does this outlook conflict, in any way, with the Islamic attitude which establishes human rights on reason (*al-'aql*) and *al-fiṭrah* (nature), covenant and *al-shūrā* (consultation), as I have shown above? If not, to object to my argument concerning the basis of human rights in Islam, because of the claim the theoretical basis of those rights, in the Western context, is purely 'secular', is not a valid objection. This is because it imposes on the concept of 'secularism' meanings that did not hold among the European philosophers who established that theoretical basis.

The other objection, concerning the jurisprudential rulings such as rulings against apostasy and against women regarding inheritance, marriage and divorce, and which seem at first look not to respect the principles of freedom and equality, will be discussed in the following chapter.

## Chapter 20

# Freedom is One Thing, Apostasy Another

Some raise certain issues to object to the 'universality' of human rights in Islam, and to undermine it. Others raise the same issues to affirm the 'particularity' of those rights in Islam, and to justify their rejection of those rights as specified by modern international thought, on the pretext that they are a product of the culture of the West, and part of the history of its development. Some of these issues belong to the right of freedom (the rulings on apostasy and slavery), while others relate to equality (the rulings on women's rights to inheritance, testimony and marriage) and are familiar Islamic jurisprudential issues. Before addressing those two objections, it is necessary to give an idea about the background of my stand on this issue.

The Islamic sharīʿah comprises general fundamentals (*kulliyāt*) as well as particular rulings (*juzʾiyāt*), principles and applications. The origin of a ruling issued in a particular case is an application of a general, fundamental principle. Should a discrepancy exist, it must be for a reason. The reasons that justify the particular ruling and show its rationality are either the 'occasions of the revelation' (*asbāb al-nuzūl*), which are normally the special circumstances that necessitated the ruling, or they may be the general intents (*al-maqāṣid*) which stem from the public good. There are three keys which are all necessary in order to understand the rationality of *sharīʿah* rulings in Islam: general fundamentals of *al-sharīʿah*, particular rulings, the intents of *al-sharīʿah*, and the occasions of revelation. In the light of these facts, let us look at the two objections: the one against the ruling concerning the apostate; the other against the rulings concerning the 'status' of women.

Islam specifies the right to freedom as a general principle, in absolutely clear terms, but we shall be making a methodological mistake if we expect the Islamic or any other old texts to discuss freedom in the language we use today. Freedom and other issues differ, in some aspects at least, from one age to another, in accordance with level of development, concerns and aspirations. Despite all this, I can affirm that Islam specifies the principle of freedom in all fields. The reference in all this is the Qur'ān and the *sunnah*: "We offered the trust (*al-amānah*) to the heavens and the earth and the mountains but they refused to undertake it, being afraid thereof; but man undertook it" (33, al-Aḥzāb, 72). This is an indication that man freely chose to undertake 'the trust' which amounts to God's vicegerency on earth, reason, and responsibility. It was not imposed on him. As the 'time' when God offered this trust to Adam was the time before Adam's descent to earth, i.e. the prehistoric time of 'eternity', it means that freedom has been an essential part of man since that primordial time. The application of this principle proves this fact on the level of man's personal freedom and his freedom of belief. On the first level, where the question of 'slavery' comes in, suffice it to say that there are no rulings in Islam which corroborate slavery. There are certain rulings concerning prisoners of war; others which consider the manumission of a slave a form of worship (atonement) and a social exigency (ransoming captives). Slavery is a historic phenomenon addressed by revealed religions such as Judaism and Christianity, as well as by Greek philosophy; and it was not proscribed except in the modern ages. But the general tendency in Islamic legislation is definitely towards abolishing this phenomenon, based on the principle that man is born free. Is there anything more touching than the exclamation of 'Umar bin al-Khaṭṭāb: 'Since when did you enslave people when their mothers gave birth to them free?'! And is there anything more significant in this connection than the fact that some prominent Companions were originally slaves, but after embracing Islam they rose to the same level of eminent members of Quraysh?

So much for freedom in contrast to slavery in Islam. The freedom of faith and its relation to the ruling on the apostate need a detailed consideration. We have to start with the attitude of the call of Muḥammad for freedom of belief as specified by the following verses, where God addresses His Messenger: 'Say: "The truth is from your Lord. Let him who wills, believe, and let him who wills, disbelieve"' (18, al-Kahf, 29). And, 'Therefore, admonish [them], for you are one to admonish. You do not have control over them' (88, al-Ghāshiyah, 21–2). Moreover, 'If then they turn away, We have not sent you as a guard over them. Your duty is but to convey [the Message]' (42, al-Shūrā, 48). And, 'If it had been the Lord's Will, they would all have believed, all who are on earth. Would you coerce people until they became believers?' (10, Yūnis, 99). Also, 'We have created man from a drop of mingled sperm, in order to try him: so We gave him [the gifts] of hearing and sight. We have guided him to the way: whether he be grateful or ungrateful' (76, al-Insān, 2–3). It is quite clear that these verses specify man's freedom of faith. He is free to embrace

Islam, but if he turns away, not even the Messenger has the right to compel him to join Islam.

Here, an objection may arise about the apostate whose punishment is execution, as is well known in Islamic jurisprudence. But, in addressing this issue, we have to realize that this is a marginal issue, wherein the ruling differs from the demands of the general principle which is specified by the quoted verses. To understand the reason behind this discrepancy, we have to refer to the 'occasions of revelation', and to look into the way the Qur'ān dealt with the apostates at the time of the call in Mecca, then to look into what happened at the time of the state in Medina.

In the Meccan verses, we read the following, to quote only a few examples: 'And if any of you turn back from his faith and dies while he is an unbeliever, it is those whose deeds will come to nothing' (2, al-Baqarah, 217); and 'As for those who sell their pledge to Allāh and their faith for a petty sum, they shall have no portion in the Hereafter' (3, Āl 'Imrān, 77). Also:

> How shall Allāh guide those who reject faith after they accepted it and bore witness that the Messenger was true and that clear signs had come unto them? But Allāh does not guide a people unjust. Of such the reward is that on them [rests] the curse of Allāh, of His angels and of all mankind (3, Āl 'Imrān, 86–7).

Moreover:

> If anyone contends with the Messenger, even after guidance has been plainly conveyed to him, and follows a path other than that becoming to men of faith, We shall leave him in the path he has chosen, and convey him to Hell, and what an evil refuge! (4, al-Nisā', 115).

Also:

> Anyone who after accepting faith in Allāh, utters unbelief-except under compulsion, his heart remaining firm in faith – but such as open their breast to unbelief – on them is wrath from Allāh, and theirs will be a dreadful penalty (16, al-Naḥl, 106).

In all these verses, we find the ruling on the apostate, as prescribed by the text, is a curse by God, His wrath, and hell but not execution. Moreover, there is always a chance for repentance.

This is what the Qur'ān specifies, but jurisprudence specifies that the apostate is to be killed. The *fuqahā'* rely for support in this on a *ḥadīth* which says, 'Whoever changes his religion, kill him.' How do we explain this discrepancy?

There is no reason to doubt this *ḥadīth*, as fighting the apostates at the time of Abū Bakr is a historic fact. Moreover, the execution of the apostate is a point of convergence among the jurisprudents, and it is also a subject of consensus (*al-ijmāʿ*) as well. That is because the 'apostate' (*al-murtād*), after the rise of the Islamic state, was not merely a person who changed his faith. He was also a person who renounced Islam as a faith, a society and a state. If we take into consideration that the Islamic state in Medina, at the time of the Prophet and the four Rāshidūn Caliphs, was in constant war against the Arab pagans at first, then against the Romans and Persians, we will realize that in modern terms the apostate at that time was equal to a traitor who betrays his country and colludes with the enemy at the time of war. The 'Apostasy Wars' at the time of Abū Bakr were against people who did not only 'betray' the Islamic state, which they joined at the time of the Prophet, but organized themselves to attack that state after violating its laws (by withholding payment of *al-zakah*). Therefore, the apostate in this sense is one who renounced the Islamic state as a 'fighter', a conspirator or a spy for the enemy.

The ruling of Islamic jurisprudence on the apostate in this sense is not a ruling against the freedom of belief. It is one against treason to the nation, the state and religion, against collusion with the enemy or turning into a thief or enemy in arms. This explains why the jurisprudents equate the apostate with the fighter who rebels against the state and society, and threatens public safety. The apostate, in the Islamic jurisprudential discourse, is a type of adversarial fighter. The rulings in his case vary, depending on whether the apostate actually fights against the state or not. The one who does deserves execution, by consensus of the *fuqahāʾ*. However, even before the apostate takes up arms against the state his case is controversial. Some *fuqahāʾ* see that he should be given a chance to repent, others believe that he should be executed straight away. There is also a distinction between the apostate who fights while he is in the precincts of Islam, or the apostate who leaves to join the enemy. All this shows that Muslim jurisprudents were thinking of the apostate not as a person exercising freedom of faith, but as a betrayer and a rebel against Islamic society.

In summary, we must realize that the legal position of the apostate in Islam does not come under the rubric of freedom of faith, but under what is nowadays called 'high treason', by taking up arms against society and the state. Those who talk about human rights today, with emphasis on the freedom of belief, do not mean by it 'freedom to betray one's own country, society and religion', or 'freedom to usurp other people's property', or 'freedom to collude with the enemy'. Therefore, freedom is one thing, apostasy another. What the modern jurisprudents are expected to do is to decide whether or not a Muslim who chooses to follow another faith, on personal bases, which do not affect the Islamic society or the state, should be considered an apostate in the traditional jurisprudential sense or in the sense explained by the verses quoted above, where the apostates are threatened with great punishment in the hereafter, without reference to execution.

CHAPTER 21

# Women's Rights in Islam: Between the Fundamental Principles of *al-Sharīʿah* and its Particular Rulings

I have observed that human rights in Islam are based on three principles: the fundamental rulings of Islamic *sharīʿah*, the particular rulings, and the rationality bestowed on these rulings by the intents of *al-sharīʿah* and the occasions of revelation.

Concerning a woman's rights, Islam specifies her equality with man as a general and absolute principle:

> O mankind! We created you from a single [pair] of a male and a female, and made you into nations and tribes that you may know each other. The most honoured of you in the sight of Allāh is the most righteous (49, al-Hujurat, 13).

> And their Lord answered them, Never will I suffer to be lost the work of any of you, be he male or female (3, Āl ʿImrān, 195).

Also: 'If any do deeds of righteousness, be they male or female, and have faith, they will enter Heaven, and not the least injustice will be done to them' (4, al-Nisā', 124). Moreover, 'The believers, men and women, are guardians, one of another' (9, al-Tawbah, 71).

In addition to these verses, there are numerous *ḥādīth* which elevate the status of woman. The Prophet also asserted, 'Paradise is under the feet of mothers'; and He said, 'Women are on a par with men'. It is well known that Islam charged women and men with the same religious duties, putting them on the same level of responsibility. Islam also prohibited female infanticide which had been a custom of pre-Islamic Arabs.

It is therefore clear that the general tendency in Islamic legislation is towards equality of men and women in rights and duties. The particular rulings that may appear contrary to this tendency must be referred for their rationale to the intents of *al-sharīʿah* and the occasions of revelation, which will be addressed next.

## The Question of Testimony

The Qur'ān stipulates that two men, or one man and two women, are needed to give testimony:

> And get two witnesses, out of your men, and if there are not two men, then a man and two women, such as you choose for witness, so that if one of them errs, the other can remind her (2, al-Baqarah, 282).

The verse makes it clear that the only consideration taken by the Legislator in demanding two women instead of one man is the chance that one woman may err or forget. Error and forgetfulness are not in the nature of women, but they are only due to the social and educational situation at the time.

The question now is: How would Islam rule on this issue, on the assumption that the situation of women has improved and has risen to a level on a par with that of men? Should we apply the principle which says: 'When impediments cease to exist, matters return to their original status'; namely, that of equality between men and women. Or, should we remain constrained to the letter of the text? This, I will address next.

## Women's Rights to Inheritance and Marriage

The Qur'ān specifies that a daughter has a half-share of the inheritance, while the son has a full share: 'Allāh [thus] directs you as regards your children's [inheritance]: to the male a portion equal to that of two females' (4, al-Nisā', 11). As in the case of testimony, the Qur'ān does not mention reasons for this distinction. Therefore, we have to refer to the intents of *al-sharī'ah* and the occasions of revelation.

If we consider the environment wherein the Qur'ān was revealed, we shall find a justification for this ruling. Pre-Islamic society was a tribal, pastoral one. Property was common and shared, especially in pastureland. The relation among pastoral tribes was one of contention about pastures. On the other hand, marriage was not simply a relationship between man and woman, but between the families of both, and, consequently, among their tribes. Arabian tribes preferred mostly to marry a girl to a man from another tribe. This would create problems concerning inheritance in case of the father's death. If she had the right to inherit from her father, her share in his livestock or, at least, in his right to a common pasture, would go to her husband's tribe, at the expense of her father's, which would lead to contention and wars. To avoid such conflicts, some tribes in pre-Islamic Arabia barred the woman from any inheritance, while others granted her only a third or less.

If we add to this the limited amount of wealth in circulation in tribal society, we shall see that a woman's inheritance might disrupt the economic balance among tribes, especially with polygamy, which was often practiced in pre-Islamic Arabia. When men and women have equal shares of inheritance in a polygamous tribal society, the man may inherit from several tribes, through his several wives. This will lead to the accumulation of assets in his hands, causing an imbalance which leads to contention and wars. To deprive the woman of any inheritance was a measure taken by some tribes in those social situations. Certainly Islam had taken that situation into consideration and apprehended the common good, which is the avoidance of contention and dissent. Hence, the happy medium to suit the new stage inaugurated by the rise of the Islamic state in Medina. The woman was allotted half a share of the inheritance, the man a full share, while the expenses and needs of the woman (wife or mother) were made the responsibility of the man.

Bearing in mind these facts about Arabian society at the time of revelation, we may find a rational justification for the female share of inheritance. In the same manner, we can find a rational justification for the amputation of a thief's hand, which was a common practice before Islam, due to the absence of prisons or authority to arrest the thief. A physical sign was the only way to make the thief recognizable, hence avoidable. With the advent of Islam, this measure continued in observance of the same situation, as the state was not quite established yet. Other measures were kept, also, for the same reasons.

The common good and social conditions stand behind these rulings. This was the case when 'Umar bin al-Khaṭṭāb refused to divide Iraqi lands among fighters, as the Qur'ān specifies. He determined the public good to be in leaving the land to its proper owners and imposing land-tax thereon. It is known that some *fuqahā'* derived from this precedent, and from the spirit of the entire Islamic legislation, a principle that specifies if the public good does not agree with the text, priority is given to the public good over the text, as it is the basis of the text. Islamic jurisprudence has adopted this principle, in some cases, concerning a woman's share of inheritance.

One example comes from Morocco, where, in the nineteenth century, some *fuqahā'* issued a *fatwa* that stated that if a woman was made rich enough by her husband she had no right to inherit from her father. This was a measure to ward off harm and contention. In the mountainous areas of Morocco, tribes live in common pasture land. When a woman inherits, this can lead to conflict and dissent among tribes, similar to the case in pre-Islamic Arabia. Other *fuqahā'* took a contrary measure by advising that the wife take half of what her husband left, as in certain areas the wife is considered a partner with the husband in his work and production. It is useful to mention also that Shī'ite jurisprudence is very flexible concerning a woman's rights to inheritance.

## Divorce and Polygamy

I can see no justification in making an issue of the questions of divorce and polygamy when discussing women's rights in Islam. Islam does not enjoin or recommend either divorce or polygamy. In fact, these two phenomena were common in pre-Islamic Arabia, and Islam limited them by imposing conditions short of proscription. Islam specifies the condition of justice and fairness in polygamy: 'But if you fear that you shall not be able to deal justly [with them] then only one' (4, al-Nisā', 3). Then, 'You will never be able to be fair and just between women, even if it were your ardent desire' (4, al-Nisā', 129). This is definitely a tendency towards prohibition. As for divorce, there is a well-known *ḥadīth*: 'Divorce is the most hateful permitted act in the eyes of God'. Hence, it cannot be claimed that Islam undermines women's rights through divorce and polygamy, as the first is almost prohibited and the other is heavily restricted to almost impossible conditions.

Moreover, the *fuqahā'* distinguish between matters of worship, which are not open to rational justification, such as breaking the fast in Ramadan at sunset, and such matters as the transactions which are open to *ijtihād* because they are related to the intents of *al-sharī'ah* and the occasions of revelation, and what *fuqahā'* consider causes of those transactions. There is also the problem of whether or not it is permissible to relate the rulings to the intents instead of the causes. I see no reason to stick absolutely and constantly to the rule specified by the *fuqahā'*, namely that 'rulings follow their underlying causes not their legal significance'. This rule is only an outcome of *ijtihād,* which is not a binding legal opinion. The causes of rulings are not given by the text, they are rationally deduced by the *faqīh*, who admits that induction is built not on conviction and absolute certitude, but on assumption and preponderance. What is more correct in my opinion is to pull back from the particular rulings of *al-sharī'ah* when they no longer agree with the common good, and go back to the fundamental principles of *al-sharī'ah*, as these are equal in weight to the 'operative/categorical verses' (*al-maḥkamāt*) in the creed. Since it is necessary to refer the analogous/ambiguous (*al-mutashābih*) to the operative/categorical, why cannot we consider the contradiction that may arise between a ruling issued on a particularity and the public good at present as an example of the analogous/ambiguous which must be referred to the operative/categorical; namely, the fundamental principles of *al-sharī'ah*.[1]

Finally, the universality of human rights is established in Islamic thought in the same manner as in any other human thought. To prove and verify that quality we have to refer to the fundamental principles. What is particular is ruled by practical application, which differs from one age to another according to the change that may affect the public good. Islamic *sharī'ah* is for the good of humanity as a whole, but God is not in need of the world(s).

## Notes

Issued by the Muslim World League, 1979

Issued by the European Muslim Council London, 1980

Issued by the European Muslim Council London, 1981

Presented to the Summit of the Muslim Conference Organization Ta'if, Saudi Arabia, January 1989

Presented to the Fifth Conference of Human Rights, Tehran, December 1989

1. Here, the author is referring to a concern of both Qur'ānic commentators (*mufassirūn*) as well as *fuqahā'*, which centres on a mention of two kinds of verses in the Qur'ān *maḥkamāt* and *mutashābihāt* (3, Āl 'Imrān, 7) – the former being referred to as the 'mother of the book' – *umm al-kitāb*. While there was debate about the signification of these, especially in the circles of *al-kalām*, general consensus was that the *maḥkamāt* were the 'operative' verses containing the *ḥikmah* and the commands and prohibitions of Allāh. On the other hand, the *mutashābihāt* were verses which were analogous or 'ambiguous' – commonly understood as those which defied possible or literal explanation such as characterizations of Allāh and references to the 'hands' and 'eyes' (using Arabic plural forms indicating three or more), especially given the admonitions in the Qur'ān that 'There is nothing like Him' (46, al-Shūrā, 11). Consensus was that it was the operative verses – the *maḥkamāt* – which were to be followed and applied leaving the nebulous *mutashābihāt*, which were likely to cause disagreement, aside. The author is arguing for an analogous approach to *al-sharī'ah* where the particular rulings (*al-juz'iyāt*), which are often derivative and the product of the inductive process of *ijtihād* applied by the *faqīh*, ought to be considered *mutashābihāt* in contradistinction to the universal or fundamental universal principles (*al-kulliyāt*) which ought to be considered as operative *maḥkamāt*. This also rests on the presumption that the fundamental principles of *al-sharī'ah* are 'intended' to correlate with the public good (*al-maṣlaḥah al-'āmah*), and, therefore, the 'particulars' can be assessed or measured according to this.

# Part Four

# Enhancing Awareness of Human Rights in Islam

CHAPTER 22

# The Concept of the Human Being in Modern Thought

Having addressed the problem of 'the cultural roots of human rights in the Arab-Islamic thought', we now have to try and single out a number of rights which Islam accords to man, by referring to the Qur'ān and *sunnah*, in particular.

There is a methodological problem which must be settled first, while the concept of man and the fields of human rights in Islam are addressed. This is the attempt to establish a kind of relation between a concept which belongs to our present times and current concerns and a type of thought based on ideas and views that belong to a cultural field which is an inseparable part of the Middle Ages. Those ages are supposed to have come to an end more than three centuries ago and were followed by the modern ages, which are radically different from the previous ones. How can we look for origins to such a modern concept, so unrelated to the past and its concepts in a thought informed by texts and anecdotes 14 centuries old?

It is clear that posing this problem methodologically differs completely from posing it ideologically, with self-assertion and a claim of historical precedence. Yet, this methodological problem changes into a theoretical one, which cannot be completely severed from ideology in its broad and flexible sense. This is because religious texts, whatever the religion, are like traditions, in general, always open to interpretation. Therefore, people usually find in them what they want to find; hence the resulting multiplicity of religious sects and denominations, each claiming to be the only right-minded and 'saved' group.

However, the Islamic *mujtahids* on matters of worship and operational practice (or the *fuqahā'*) have been more modest and open-minded, as they admit that their *ijtihād* was based on mere assumption and preponderance. Some of them went as far as saying, 'Every mujtahid is right'.

But *ijtihād* in the view of the *fuqahā'* is not merely the expression of an opinion or a conviction. It is an opinion which has to be most objective, and completely free from any subjectivity. This requires that the opinion expressed in *ijtihād* be based on genuine texts, on an accurate knowledge of the language, the style and the historicity of those texts, the 'occasions of revelation' and the intents of *al-sharī'ah* relative to those texts.

The last two conditions form the objective basis of jurisprudential *ijtihād*. A question may arise here about the possibility of using those two conditions in addressing tradition or related topics. We think the answer should be in the affirmative, especially in methodological questions connected with objective scientific thinking. Considering the occasions of revelation is almost similar to what is nowadays called the 'historicity' of the issue, namely looking at the issue in the light of its time and place, and avoiding a projection of the present on the past or transferring the past to the present arbitrarily. The 'intents' to the *fuqahā'* are the 'incentives' of today, i.e. the aims and the objectives behind the issue. In modern philosophical terms, occasions of revelation and intents, in their interconnection and integration, would be called 'what is thought of'. Both the 'thought of' and the 'thinkable' in a certain age had occasions of revelation and intents, but what had neither is termed as 'what is not thought of' and could also be 'unthinkable'. Close to this is what the old logicians termed as 'the possible' and 'the impossible', simultaneously.

Now, we can approach our subject with more objectivity if we adopt these four concepts: what is thought of; the thinkable; what is not thought of; and the unthinkable. So, instead of projecting our current views on man and his rights, we can focus on what was thought of and the thinkable in our tradition and texts, especially in the Qur'ān, *sunnah* and in the *ijtihād* of the *fuqahā'*.

On the other hand, we are governed in our view of the human being, of his development and rights, by the 'occasions of revelation' and the 'intents' which are compatible with our own times and aspirations. This means that our reading of what was thought of, or thinkable, in our tradition would be directed by a desire to find a historical reference that could help us engraft the modern implications of the concept of man and his rights in our awareness and authoritative references. In other words, our work is like compiling a dictionary of the thought of in the past, about man and his rights, which could act as a mirror that reflects today's thought on the same subject, without exaggeration or distortion.

Hence, it is necessary to stress that the concept of 'man' in our religious and traditional texts did not carry the same implications that are thought of in our modern world, which have their authority basically in the European Renaissance, especially in the so-called humanism of the sixteenth and seventeenth centuries. The concept of man in the European referential authority was established and conceived of as the basis of restoring dignity to man, by liberating him from the burden of the 'original sin' of Adam, who disobeyed the orders of his Lord and tasted the forbidden fruit of Paradise and was punished by expulsion to Earth, where he and all his progeny will suffer forever in the wake of that sin – according to the Christian view. On the other hand, man was to be restored to his original inseparable unity of soul and body by liberating his soul (or spiritual life) from the authority of the Church; and his body (or physical life) from the authority of the 'ruler'. Hence, the first human right in the European authoritative point of reference was man's right to his body, its ownership, its pleasure and enjoyment. Hence, man was no longer viewed as a 'tainted' being, but as the supreme ideal to which all other ideals were subservient; a being that has to direct all his activities to develop his body, soul, freedom and dignity; in a word, his humanity.

The concept of man in the modern European authoritative referent, therefore, presents a model of human perfection, on the intellectual, moral and aesthetic levels, completely contrary to the model which was dominant in the Christian Middle Ages. That model was part of a general view based on a distinction between the so-called Kingdom of God and the Kingdom of Satan where man is bonded to the first with his soul, and with his body to the second; namely, the soul belonged to the holy, the body to the profane. The salvation of man was represented as being in atonement for original sin, engendered by the body and its lusts. Atonement connects man's life with the Kingdom of God, represented on earth by the Church.

The concept of man in the European Renaissance, therefore, came to eliminate that duality and put an end to that division by restoring recognition of the body as an inseparable part of the entity of man himself. Man came to be considered as transcending his humanity itself, not with anything outside it, above all defects and shortcomings, aspiring to perfection with his soul and body, striving to control the world and to subject it to his own good and benefit.

CHAPTER 23

# The Concept of the Human Being in the Qur'ān

Having discussed the concept of 'man' in both the Medieval Christian and European Renaissance perspectives, I will move now to the concept of the human being as defined by the Qur'ān. I will try to explain how close it is to the concept of man in the European Renaissance perspective, while assessing the distance that separates it from the Medieval Christian concept of man.

I have to stress, first, that what I find in the following verses was always present there, namely, that it was 'thinkable'. In fact, the old commentators have actually thought of those issues, in their own way and in the light of their occupations. Yet it must be said that those issues were not 'thought of' or 'thinkable' in the same manner I look at them at present. On the other hand, do not forget that my reading of our traditional texts is governed by a desire to establish a concept of man and his rights, on every level, on roots that go deep into our tradition and culture. Moreover, the texts to be quoted below are not the only ones dealing with man. There are other texts that deal with the other side of man: his shortcomings, defects, injustices, tyranny, etc. However, these and similar texts fall outside the 'thought of' in medieval and modern European thought, as far as this subject is concerned. Islam is not alone in that. All religions and philosophies address this other aspect of man, which is a theme for another study.

Here is a review of the most significant Islamic texts which establish a concept of man fully compatible with the modern European concept, adopted by modern international thought.

The first among such texts which asserts my view is: 'We have honoured the sons of Adam, provided them with transport on land and sea, given them for sustenance things good and pure, and conferred on them special favours, above a great part of Our Creation' (17, al-Isrā', 70). In his *al-Kashāf*, often considered the best commentary on the Qur'ān, al-Zamakhshārī says:

> About honouring the sons of Adam, it was said that man was honoured by reason, speech, discernment, writing, goodly form, upright stature, management of the affairs of this life and the hereafter, and, also, by controlling whatever is in the Earth and subjecting it to his good. It was also said that all creatures pick up their food by mouth except man.

Despite the extent of 'what is thought of' as described by al-Zamakhshārī, it does not cover all what is 'thinkable' and could really have been 'thought of' at the time. This becomes clearer if we approach the verse through a concept which was present in Arab-Islamic thought at the time of al-Zamakhshārī, especially with Ibn Khaldūn, i.e. the concept of 'human development', which takes us directly across to the contemporary complementary concept of 'civilization' to that of 'development' in its comprehensive meaning, including human rights. Honouring human beings with 'reason and discernment' came coupled with and explained by the Qur'ānic verse: 'We provided them with transport on land and sea, and gave them for sustenance things good and pure, and conferred on them special favours, above a great part of Our creation.' It is obvious that travelling by land and sea and enjoying the good things in life are among the bases of human civilization. The concept of man, as it can be conceived through the verse, has two dimensions: one rational (reason and discernment), the other civilizational (writing, managing the affairs of life, taking food by hand, travelling by land and sea, and enjoying the good things in life).

Moreover, honouring of man (*takrīm al-insān*) covers his preference to other created things. These, in the religious texts, are the inanimate, the plants, the animals, human beings, the *jinn* and the angels. An argument erupted between the Mu'tazilites and Ash'arites about which was highest in status before God: human beings or angels? The Mu'tazilites follow the direct meaning of 'great part' in the verse 'conferred on them favours above a great part of our Creation'. They say there are other creatures, like the angels, who are not included in that 'great part' of creation over which man was favoured. The Ash'arites looked at other verses which imply God's preference of man over the angels, especially the verse that relates how the angels fell prostrate before Adam and about their ignorance of the 'names' taught to Adam by God. Therefore, they say, the verse means that God created Adam and a 'multitude' of other creatures besides him and preferred him over all that multitude of other creatures. In fact, if we look closely into the Qur'ānic verses which tell of God's honouring of man, we will find what supports the Ash'arite view. It may suffice to say that if the angels are also like man in possessing reason – accordingly they are called the 'independent minds' by the Islamic philosophers, i.e. the pure minds which are self-sustained, without the need of inhabiting a body – then man alone, among all other creatures mentioned in the Qur'ān, has a civilizational dimension. Man is the maker of civilization. This dimension in the human being is vital in this context, as it is the dimension which establishes the concept of human rights and related concepts.

Now we may go back to read the verse in the light of 'what is thought of', as defined by the text. This verse was revealed on the occasion of an argument with the pagan people of Mecca who rejected the call of Islam to desist from the worship of idols. The Qur'ān reminds them of several phenomena and events which prove that Allāh alone is God and that no one is His associate. Among the incidents related by the Qur'ān in this context of honouring man is the refusal of Satan (Iblīs) to fall prostrate before Adam:

> Behold! We said to the angels, 'fall prostrate before Adam'. They did so, except Iblīs. He said, 'Shall I fall prostrate to one whom You created from clay?' He [then added] 'Do You see this, the one whom You have honoured above me! If You will but grant me respite until the Day of Judgment, I will surely bring his descendants under my sway, all but a few' (17, al-Isrā', 61–2).

The Qur'ān relates the story of Iblīs in more detail in another context, giving the concept of 'honouring' man another dimension, which liberated the Islamic thought from the feeling of guilt [over original sin] which dominated European thought in the Middle Ages:

> Behold! Your Lord said to the angels, 'I will create a vicegerent on Earth'. They said 'Will You place therein one who will spread corruption therein and shed blood, whilst we celebrate your praises and glorify Your holy [name]?' He said, 'I know what you do not know.' And He taught Adam the names of all things, then He placed them before the angels and said, 'Tell Me the names of these if you are truthful.' They said, 'Glory be to You, of knowledge we have none, save what You have taught us' (2, al-Baqarah, 30–2).

Then:

> And behold, We said to the angels: 'Fall prostrate to Adam.' And they did, except Iblīs; he refused and was haughty and was of those who reject faith. We said, 'O Adam! Dwell you and your wife in the Garden and eat of the bountiful things therein [wherever and whenever] you will; but approach not this tree, or you will be transgressing.' Then Satan made them slip from it [the Garden] and took them out of the state [of felicity] in which they had been. We said, 'Get you down, all [you people] with enmity among your-

> selves. On Earth will be your dwelling place and your means of livelihood for a time.' Then Adam received words from his Lord Who pardoned him, for He is the ever pardoning, the ever merciful (2, al-Baqarah, 34–7).

These verses show that the concept of man in the Qur'ān covers, other than the rational and civilizational dimensions, like the vicegerency of man on Earth, teaching him all the names and pardoning him. The vicegerency on Earth means developing it, as many verses show: 'It is He who has produced you from the Earth and settled you therein [to develop it]' (11, Hūd, 61). Also, 'They tilled the soil and populated it' (30, Al-Rūm, 9). Moreover, 'Then We made you heirs in the land after them to see how you would proceed' (10, Yūnis, 14). To develop the land and establish civilization needs knowledge of the land and that is the implication of 'And He taught Adam the names of all things', which leads to discernment and knowing the difference between things and their particulars, etc.

Then comes the question of 'error' (*al-khṭi'ah*) in the disobedience of Adam and his wife to the orders of God and their allurement by Satan to taste the fruit of the forbidden tree. But Adam and his wife repented and asked God's forgiveness. So God pardoned them, which is explained by the Qur'ān thus:

> And their Lord called unto them, 'Did I not forbid you that tree, and tell you that Satan was an avowed enemy to you?' They said, 'Our Lord! We have wronged our own souls. If You do not forgive us and bestow Your mercy on us, we shall certainly be lost' (7, al-A'rāf, 22–3).

This invocation is what is referred to in the previous verse, 'Then Adam received words of inspiration from his Lord', which means that God taught Adam how to pray to Him for His forgiveness: 'then He pardoned him, for He is the ever-pardoning, the ever-merciful'. So Adam's sin was removed by his repentance and he and his progeny were liberated from that sin. What is left is the work of Adam on Earth, where he and his progeny were ordered to descend. They will be held accountable for their action there, whether good or bad.

What comes under 'thinkable' is that the Qur'ān has no reference to the duality of the soul (*al-nafs*) and body (*al-jasad*) which occupied the religion and philosophical thought in Europe. Man in the Qur'ānic perspective is a soul (*rūḥ*) and a body (*jism*), and there is absolutely no reference in the Qur'ān which belittles the body. On the contrary, the Qur'ān mentions the body in a context of merit and superiority:

> Their Prophet said to them, 'Allāh has sent you Ṭalūt as a king over you.' They said, 'How can he exercise authority over us when we are more fit than

> he to exercise authority, and he is not even gifted with wealth in abundance?' He said, 'Allāh has chosen him above you, and has gifted him abundantly with knowledge and bodily prowess' (2, al-Baqarah, 247).

And, 'We have indeed created man in the best of moulds' (95, Al-Tīn, 4). Also, 'He has given you shape, and made your shapes comely, and has provided for you sustenance of things pure and good' (40, Ghāfir, 64). The human body and its goodly form, the like of which no other creature has, are really aspects of God's honouring of man, as al-Zamakhsharī would say. Therefore, the body has rights as well as the soul and man has to recognize them. There is a *ḥadīth* which says, 'Your soul has a right over you, and your body has a right over you' (reported by al-Bukhārī). Therefore, honouring man, who is soul and body, means that man must enjoy a number of rights. The Islamic vision of rights of the human being will be discussed next.

## Chapter 24

# The Right to Life and Its Enjoyment

It is necessary to point out, once more, that we have to distinguish between the 'thought of' and the 'not thought of' in the old Arabic-Islamic texts. In talking about human rights, we have to note that the word '*ḥaqq*' in modern Arabic discourse is a translation of the French word '*droit*' and the English word 'right'. On the other hand, it must be realized that the term '*ḥaqq*' in Arabic is one with multiple connotations wherein it might be used to denote what is 'vrai' or 'true' in juxtaposition to what is 'faux' or 'false', as it is said 'certainty proceeds from doubt'. And the definite term 'al-Ḥaqq' is used to mean God. Among the most important considerations is that interconnection in meaning between '*al-ḥaqq*' (right) and '*al-wājib*' (duty), Arabic *ḥaqq* meaning right, is interconnected in its meaning with *wājib*/duty. The meaning is decided by the preposition after the word. Therefore, we find the concepts of right and duty overlapping in the Arabic language and the Arabic-Islamic cultural field. What is a right for a person is a duty due to him. The significance of this remark will be appreciated later. Hence, it is wrong to look into the tradition by thinking of 'human rights' through 'what is thought of', both of which belong to modern European thought, which makes a distinction between rights and duties. If we follow the European approach, we will find nothing in the field of rights in the Arabic-Islamic 'thought of', or it may be interlocked with 'duties'.

This means that, in order to look for the rights in the Arabic-Islamic 'thought of', we have also to look at the duties. The 'rights of God', for instance, are the duties due to Him in the way of worship and obedience, etc. Similarly, the 'rights of man' are the duties due to him in the forms of 'honouring', explained in the previous chapter. Therefore, it can be said that the rights of man in Islam are all the material and moral duties due to him, in accordance with God's honouring and favouring him over all His creation. If we look for human rights recognized by Islam in the light of 'what is thought of' in the present age, we shall easily distinguish, particularly in the Qur'ān, two types of rights. These are general rights, which are for all human beings, and special rights, which are for certain categories of people, like the rights of the weak and oppressed, the rights of women, the rights of non-Muslims in a Muslim society, etc. Here is a brief review of these rights.

## The Rights of Man in General

### *The Right to Life*

From the Islamic perspective, life is a gift from God to man, so it is his right: 'It is He who gave you life, will cause you to die, and will again give you life' (22, al-Hajj, 66). God honoured man by breathing into him some of His spirit and gave him the faculty of hearing, sight and feeling:

> He Who has made everything which He has created most comely. He began the creation of man with [nothing more than] clay, and made his progeny from a quintessence of despised fluid; then he fashioned him in due proportion, and breathed into him of His spirit (*rūḥ*). And He gave you [the faculties of] hearing and sight and feeling [understanding] (32, al-Sajda, 7–9).

Therefore, man's life is his own right, which he has to protect physically and psychologically. No one has the right to harm man in body or soul. It is for that reason that God prohibited suicide, irrespective of circumstances: 'Do not kill yourselves, for Allāh has been most merciful to you. If any do that in rancour and injustice, soon We shall cast them into fire' (4, al-Nisā', 29–30). God also prohibited the killing of any human soul except for a just cause: 'Do not take a life, which Allāh made sacred, except by right (*illā bi-l-ḥaqq*). And if anyone is slain wrongfully, we have given his heir authority to demand retribution, but let him not exceed in the matter of taking life' (17, al-Isrā', 33). The killing of prisoners of war and the mutilation of dead bodies was also prohibited. In pre-Islamic Arabia some people killed their children if they could not provide for them: 'Do not kill your children for fear of hunger. We shall provide sustenance for them as well as for you. Truly, killing them is a great sin' (17, al-Isrā', 31). God also prohibited female infanticide, which some pre-Islamic Arabs did for fear of shame: 'When the female [infant], buried alive, is questioned, for what crime was she killed?' (81, al-Tawkīr, 8–9). In addition, He prohibited putting an end to the life of the foetus (abortion). Islamic sharī'ah considers abortion as premeditated murder, deserving the death penalty. God also prohibited execution of the death sentence on a pregnant woman until she delivers her baby, because the foetus's right to life should be considered first. As a general rule:

> If anyone slays a person, unless it be for murder or for spreading corruption in the land, it is as though he has slain all whole people. And if anyone saves a life, it is as though he has saved the lives of all people (5, al-Mā'idah, 32).

The punishment which specifies the execution of the criminal was greatly alleviated by Islam to a degree of suspending the punishment when there is doubt around the case. The Ḥadīth says, 'Avoid the *ḥudūd* penalties in doubtful cases.'

*The Right to Enjoy Life*

God granted life to the human being to live and to enjoy. He subjugated to the human being whatever is in it for his enjoyment and the fulfilment of his needs, except what may harm him, or cause harm to other creatures, animate or inanimate. The Qur'ān terms what people are allowed to enjoy as 'the good things', an expression which recurs often in various verses. This covers all the permitted things, which are not prohibited by God. They are the opposite of 'the impure', which are prohibited. Here are some of the many verses which deal with this subject: 'They ask you what [food] is lawful to them. Say, lawful to you are [all] things good and pure' (5, al-Mā'idah, 4); 'O you who believe! Do not make unlawful the good things which Allāh has made lawful for you' (5, al-Mā'idah, 87); 'Say, who has forbidden the beauty of Allāh which, He has produced for His worshippers, and the things clean and pure [which he has provided] for sustenance?' (7, Al A'rāf, 32); 'O you who believe! Give of the good things which you have [honourably] earned, and of the fruits of the earth which We have produced for you' (2, al-Baqarah, 267); 'And [He] made for you out of [your mates and companions] sons and daughters and grandchildren, and provided for you sustenance of the best' (16, al-Naḥl, 72).

Enjoying spouses, children and grandchildren, which is family life, is, like enjoying the 'things good and pure', a right of man, exactly like enjoying his good form and all that adds to its glamour: 'And He has given you shape and made your shapes beautiful, and has provided for you sustenance of things pure and good' (40, Ghāfir, 64). Also, 'We gave them for sustenance things good and pure' (45, al-Jāthiyah, 16). Perhaps the following verse sums up all the above:

> O children of Adam! Wear your beautiful apparel at every time and place of prayer: eat and drink, but waste not by excess. For Allāh does not like the wasters. Say: Who has forbidden the beautiful [gifts] of Allāh, which He has produced for His servants, and the things good and pure [which He has provided] for sustenance? Say: 'they are in the life of this world, for those who

> believe, [and] purely for them on the Day of Judgment'. Thus do we explain the signs in detail for those who understand. Say: 'The things that my Lord has indeed proscribed are: shameful deeds, whether open or covert, sins and trespasses against truth or reason, assigning of partners to Allāh, for which he has given no authority, and saying things about Allāh of which you have no knowledge' (17, al-A'rāf, 31–3).

It must be noted in this context that the movements of asceticism and mysticism in Islam were a reaction to excess and extreme luxury, as well as to the oppression of rulers. Most of these movements penetrated Islam from previous ancient cultures. Like all other religions, Islam considers life in this world a passage to the hereafter. Yet, Islam also considers this life an end in itself and urges man to take his share of enjoyment while he lives, provided that he 'does not harm to himself or others':

> But seek, with the [wealth] which Allāh has bestowed on you, the home of the hereafter, and do not forget your share in this world, but do you good as Allāh has been good to you, and do not seek [occasions for] corruption in the land: for Allāh does not love those who spread corruption (28, al-Qaṣaṣ, 77).

One *ḥadīth* says, 'Work for your after life as if you were to die tomorrow; and work in your worldly life as though you were to live forever.' Another *ḥadīth* says, 'If Allāh granted you wealth, let the signs of His favour be seen on you.'

CHAPTER 25

# The Right to Freedom of Belief, Knowledge and Difference

## The Right to Freedom of Belief

The Qur'ān recognizes the freedom of belief as one of the rights of man. This is because God created man and gave him a mind and power of discernment, showing him the way and leaving the freedom of choice to him: 'We created man from a drop of mingled sperm, in order to try him. So we gave him the [gifts of] hearing and sight. We showed him the way, whether he be grateful or ungrateful [rests on his will]' (78, al-Insān, 2–3). Having encouraged belief and following in the path of Islam, the Qur'ān concludes the *sūrah* by saying, 'This is an admonition: Whosoever will, let him take a [straight] path to his Lord. But you will not, except if Allāh wills. For Allāh is All-Knowing, All-Wise' (78, al-Insān, 29–30). This meaning is stressed in another *sūrah*: 'Let there be no compulsion in religion. Truth stands out clear from error' (2, al-Baqarah, 256). In commenting on this verse, it is said that Ibn 'Abbās reported that

> This verse was revealed about a man from the Anṣār called Abū al-Ḥusayn, who had two Christian sons, while he was a Muslim. He said to the Prophet: 'Shall I force them, they chose no religion but Christianity?' So this verse was revealed.

al-Zamakhshārī comments:

> No compulsion in religion means that God has not made the question of belief a matter of incontrovertible force (*al-ijbār*) or of compulsion, but of choice. Similar to that is the verse, 'If it had been your Lord's will, they would all have believed all who are on earth. Will you then compel mankind against their will, to believe!' (10, Yūnis, 99). This means that Allāh could have compelled them, but he did not, and left the matter to choice.

## The Right to Knowledge

As the Qur'ān specifies the right of man to the freedom of belief, it does not follow that all religions and creeds are equal before God. Like all religions and creeds, Islam sees that the right creed is the one specified by the religion of Islam, which is the creed of monotheism. The Qur'ān threatens the unbelievers with punishment, yet God does not punish those who were not aware of the message or the call. Hence, knowledge is a right of man who is not blamed or punished for something he does not know:

> Who receives guidance, receives it for his own benefit; who goes astray does so to his loss. No bearer of burdens can bear the burdens of another; nor would We punish until We have sent a messenger [to give warning] (17, al-Isrā', 15).

Then, 'Every community (*ummah*) has a messenger; when their messenger comes their matter will be judged between them with justice, and they will not be wronged' (10, Yūnis, 47).

Very often, the Qur'ān couples the creation of man with ascribing knowledge to him, as if knowledge were his first right. At the beginning of creation, 'He taught Adam the names of all things' (2, al-Baqarah, 31), and 'He has created man. He has taught him [intelligent] speech' (55, al-Raḥmān, 3–4). Also:

> Recite! In the name of your Lord Who has created. Created man out of a [mere] clot of congealed blood. Recite! And your Lord is most Bountiful. He, Who taught [the use] of the pen. Taught man that which he did not know' (96, al-'Alaq, 1–5).

It is well known that this is the very first *sūrah* revealed in the Qur'ān.

There are many *ḥādīth* which encourage the search for learning, considering it a duty: 'Seeking knowledge is a duty imposed on every Muslim man and woman.' Also, 'Seek knowledge from the cradle to the grave.' It is also reported of the Prophet to have said, 'Among the signs of Doomsday are the elimination of knowledge, the establishment of ignorance, the popularity of wine-drinking, and the resurgence of adultery.' This *ḥadīth* equates ignorance with wine-drinking and adultery, which are prohibited. Another *ḥadīth* says:

> God does not eliminate knowledge by wrenching it away from those who have it. He eliminates it by taking unto Him the men of knowledge. When none is left, people will have their chieftains from among the ignorant, who, when asked, give erroneous counsel. So, they go astray and lead others astray.

Concerning the right to seeking knowledge, Islam makes no distinction between men and women, free men or slaves; it is the right of all. 'Ā'ishah said, 'How good are the Ansar women! Their shyness did not stop them from being erudite in religion!' The Prophet is reported to have said:

> Three types of men have two rewards each: a man from the People of the Book who believed in his prophet and in Muḥammad; a slave who performed the rights of God and his master; and a man who had a slave-woman whom he brought up well and taught well, then he manumitted her and married her.

## The Right to Differ

The Qur'ān recognizes difference as a fact of existence and an element of human nature. The difference among human beings in colour, language, race, and their division into nations and tribes, was all by the will of God, exactly as He willed the difference in the elements of the universe to make it a sign of His existence:

> And among His signs is that He created for you mates from among yourselves. And among His signs is the creation of the heavens and the earth, and the variation in your languages and your colours. Truly in that are signs for those who know (30, Al-Rūm, 21–2).

This is on the natural level. At the level of creed and belief, the Qur'ān recognizes the multiplicity of religions and the differences among them in several verses. 'If your Lord had so willed, He could have made people one community (*ummah*), but they have not ceased to dispute, except those on whom your Lord has bestowed His mercy; and for this He created them' (11, Hūd, 118–19). Also:

> To each among you We prescribed a law and an open way. If Allāh had so willed, he would have made you a single community (*ummah*), but [His plan is] to test you in what He has given you, so strive for virtues, the goal of you all is Allāh: It is He that will show you the truth of the matters in which you dispute (5, al-Mā'idah, 48).

In the text of the Qur'ān, Islam specifies that belief in all prophets and messengers is part of Islam itself. The monotheistic religions at the time of the Prophet were three: Judaism, Christianity and Sabianism. The Qur'ān stresses the recognition of those religions on two occasions, using almost the same expressions:

> Those who believe [in the Qur'ān], and those who follow the Jewish [scriptures] and the Christians and the Sabians – any who believe in Allāh and the

> last day, and work righteousness, shall have their reward with their Lord. On them shall be no fear, nor shall they grieve (2, al-Baqarah, 62).

By 'Islam', in the verse, 'If anyone desires a religion other than Islam [submission to Allāh] never will it be accepted of him' (3, Āl 'Imrān, 85), is meant Islam as the absolute monotheistic religion, which is the religion of Abraham, indicated by the context of the verse. This is agreed upon by consensus of commentators.

The question of apostasy may come up here, as it is not covered by the right to differ or the right to freedom. At the time of the Prophet and the Companions, it meant a betrayal of Islam as a society and a state. Therefore, Abū Bakr fought the apostates. The apostate is like a 'fighting adversary' who revolts against Muslim society. Therefore, the *fuqahā'* equated them in rulings and punishment.

But the 'apostate' in the narrow sense of the word is a person who embraced Islam, then turned away, without antagonizing Islam or causing harm to Muslims. There are several verses where such a person is mentioned, but there is no reference specifying his execution. The verses do not go further than stressing God's wrath and curse on him and that his abode is hellfire: 'And if any of you turn back from their faith and die in unbelief, their work will be for naught in this life and in the hereafter' (2, al-Baqarah, 217). Also, 'Anyone, who, after accepting faith in Allāh, utters unbelief, except under compulsion, his heart remaining firm in faith, but such as open their breast to unbelief, on them is wrath of Allāh, and theirs will be a dreadful penalty' (16, al-Naḥl, 106). Yet repentance is always an option for the apostate, as has been explained in a previous chapter.

So much for disagreement with Islam. However, disagreement within the locus of Islam is a right, because it is *ijtihād*. As is well known, *ijtihād* is one source of Islamic legislation; but the disagreement among imāms and the *'ulamā'* in respect to different ages and countries and changes in circumstances is a historical reality. It is according to this meaning the *ḥadīth* which states, 'The disagreement [in opinion] among my people is a mercy.'

However, it is necessary to stress that the right to differ and disagree which is guaranteed by Islam does not mean an encouragement to disunite and quarrel. On the contrary, Islam protects the unity of the *ummah*, and it condemns religious disagreement which leads to contention and strife:

> And hold fast, all together, by the rope which Allāh [stretches out for you] and be not divided among yourselves. Let there arise among you a community (*ummah*) inviting to all that is good, enjoying what is right and forbidding what is wrong: They are the ones that attain felicity. Be not like those

> who are divided amongst themselves and fall into disputation after receiving clear signs. For them is a dreadful penalty (3, Āl 'Imrān, 103–4).

To secure the unity of the nation, without impinging on the right to disagree and engage in *ijtihād*, Islam calls for the avoidance of fanaticism and extremism and advises moderation: 'Invite [all] to the way of your Lord with wisdom and good preaching, and argue with them in ways that are most gracious' (16, al-Naḥl, 125). Also, 'Say to my worshippers that they should [only] say those things that are best' (17, al-Isrā', 53). The Qur'ān stresses that Islam makes things easy not difficult: 'Allāh intends every facility for you. He does not want to put you to difficulties' (2, al-Baqarah, 185). Also, 'Therefore, do you give admonition, for you are one to admonish. You are not one to control their affairs' (88, al-Ghāshiyah, 21–2). All these aspects of tolerance, the adoption of the easiest and best of ways, the avoidance of exaggeration, extremism and fanaticism give 'the right to differ' its positive and constructive content which guards against sedition and contention, and develops the healthy multiplicity which is the essence of fruitfulness and creativity.

Chapter 26

# *Al-shūrā* between the Qur'ān and the Circumstantial Interpretations

Connected with the right to differ and disagree is the right to *al-shūrā*, which is specified by the Qur'ān, the *ḥādīth* and the conduct of the Companions. There is a clear text in the Qur'ān which considers *al-shūrā* one of the basic qualities of the believer, on the same level as avoiding major sins and performing religious duties:

> Whatever you are given [here] is [but] a convenience of this life. But that which is with Allāh is better and more lasting: [It is] for those who believe and put their trust in their Lord; those who avoid greater sins and shameful deeds, and when they are angry, even then forgive; those who harken to their Lord and establish regular prayer; who [conduct] their affairs by mutual consultation; who spend out of what We bestow on them for sustenance, and those who when an oppressive wrong is inflicted on them [are not cowed but] help and defend themselves (42, al-Shūrā, 36–9).

As noted above, the commentators say that these verses were revealed with reference to the Anṣār who 'before Islam, and the advent of the Messenger to them, used to meet and consult. The Messenger commended them. They would not take a decision unless they achieved consensus on it' (al-Zamakhshārī).

Although the expression '[they conduct] their affairs by mutual consultation' comes as a statement, it is an implied command as well, which is a recurrent pattern in the Qur'ān. The command to adopt consultation is quite clear on other occasions, where the Prophet himself is addressed:

> It is part of the mercy of Allāh that you deal gently with them. Were you severe or harsh-hearted, they would have broken away from about you. So, pass over [their faults] and ask for [Allāh's] forgiveness for them, and consult them in the matter. Then, when you have taken a decision, put your trust in Allāh (3, Āl 'Imrān, 159).

Commenting on this, al-Zamakhsharī says, 'Consult them in the matter means: the affairs of war and the like where there is no revelation, in order to benefit from their opinion and to elevate their positions.' While al-Zamakhsharī and other commentators stress the idea that *al-shūrā* is a duty on the Prophet, they are also clear in showing that it is also a right of the believers. In this connection, it is reported of al-Ḥasan bin 'Alī bin Abī Ṭālib to have commented on this verse: 'God knew that he [the Prophet] had no need for their opinion, but He meant to start a precedent for his followers.' It was also reported of the Prophet to have said, 'No people have ever consulted each other without being guided to the better in their affairs.'

Abū Hurayrah said, 'I have never seen any people who consult each other more than do the Companions of the Messenger.' It is said that matters became more difficult for the Arab chieftains if they averted consultation, so God enjoined it on His Messenger to consult his Companions in order to avoid distressing them if he held on to his own opinion and did not regard theirs.

It is clear from all this that *al-shūrā* in Islam is a duty on the ruler and a right of the ruled. It is rather a right of the ruled first, as the caliph at the time of the Rāshidūn was not installed until after *al-shūrā* was conducted. The Companions consulted and discussed [matters] with each other for a long time before they elected Abū Bakr. The strong character of 'Umar imposed itself on the matter of a succession to Abū Bakr so that he appeared to be the sole candidate. So when Abū Bakr consulted the Companions about 'Umar, no one objected, and he chose him to succeed him in the caliphate. When 'Umar bin al-Khaṭṭāb was stabbed, he realized that there were several possible canditates to succeed him. So, he chose six from among the Companions who were the primary candidates owing to their stations in society and asked them to choose a caliph from among them (excepting his own son 'Umar), provided the choice be accepted by the people. The six Companions had long negotiations and asked the opinions of various groups before 'Uthmān was appointed caliph, as a result of consultation. *Al-shūrā* does not end with the choice of the ruler; it rather begins at that moment as a duty on the caliph and a right of those he represents: the people of authority, the *'ulamā'*, the dignitaries and the tribal sheikhs and everyone who has a representative quality.

Though the *ḥādīth* about *al-shūrā* reported of the Prophet are numerous and clearly-worded, scholars of *ḥadīth* categorize most of them as 'weak' or 'spurious'. But doubting the authenticity of the chains of transmitters in these *ḥādīth* does not undermine their content, because they specify what is specified in the Qur'ān itself and seen in the conduct of the

Prophet and His Companions. But the authors of *al-adāb al-sulṭānīyah* [*Mirror for Magistrates*] and *al-siyāsah al-mulukīyah* [*The Royal Polity*] are, in turn, supportive of *al-shūrā*. Perhaps the longest of such texts is what we read in Ibn al-Azraq's *Badā'i' al-Sulk fī Ṭabā'i' al-Mulk* [*The Best Behaviour in the Nature of Sovereignty*]. The author quotes several opinions on *al-shūrā*, which he tries to categorize and re-organize. He quotes al-Ṭarṭūshī, who said that *al-shūrā* is 'considered by wise men as the basis of kingship and of the principles of sovereignty. It is needed by the ruler and the ruled alike.' He quotes Ibn al-'Arabī, the Andalusian Ash'arī *faqīh*, who said:

> Consensus (*al-mushāwirah*) a source (*aṣl*) of religion, a *sunnah* (normative law) of Allāh in the worlds, a duty on the people from the Messenger, down to the lowest human being in status. It is a consensus of opinion on a matter where everyone contributes his own opinion.

Then Ibn al-Azraq discusses the legitimacy of consultation, referring it to the two Qur'ānic verses quoted above. He gives a quotation from al-Nawawī, referring to the verse 'And consult them in the matter', that runs as follows: 'This verse is enough; it leaves us in need for no more. If God enjoins consultation on the Prophet in such unequivocal terms, knowing that he is the most perfect among men, then what can be said of other human beings?' Ibn al-Azraq goes on to cite the benefits of consultation. He says it saves one the regretful consequences of following one's own opinion alone; it leads to the right decision in most cases; it keeps away from whims; and builds action on solid grounds. Then he talks extensively about the consulting person, the consultant, and the subject of consultation and what is expected of the consulting person after consultation. But in all this, Ibn al-Azraq did not go beyond the traditional view dominant found in the literature on advice to rulers, where consultation is merely a suggestion; he did not treat it either as a right or a duty.

In fact, there were lengthy discussions among *fuqahā'* and commentators about whether *al-shūrā* is binding on the ruler or whether it is simply for information, and whether the ruler is free to follow the opinion given or not. Those who say that *al-shūrā* is not binding refer to the verse, 'And consult them in the matter, and when you decide, put your trust in God.' They say this verse implies two stages: one is *al-shūrā,* which is asking the opinion of the consulted party; the second is the stage of decision and action taken by the ruler, whether in accordance with the opinion given or not. They believe that 'put your trust in God' abrogates *al-shūrā*, so they say the meaning of the verse is 'if you decide on a certain action, then put your trust in God not in the opinion arrived at by *al-shūrā*'.

There is no need to point out that such interpretation of the verse is highly arbitrary. It breaks up the sequence of the verse and ignores its vital unity which commends the Prophet for being lenient towards his people, not cruel or overbearing, but affable and easy going. The verse enjoins on him to forgive them, pray God to forgive them, and consult them. To couple decision making with putting trust in God does not undermine *al-shūrā*. The consulting person is expected to follow the advice of the consulted party and, in every case, he has to put his faith in God when he decides and carries out his decision. Putting faith in God, in this connection, means that success in the future is not definite, even if it were based on *al-shūrā*. Therefore, it is necessary to put faith in God and ask for his help and guidance.

It is quite obvious that the above interpretation implies biased intention, namely, to justify the despotism of the ruler. In any case, such interpretation would not have occurred to the interpreter had the idea of human rights, in its modern sense, been among 'what is thought of' in his time. The old *fuqahā'* and commentators, who claimed that *al-shūrā* is merely advisory and not binding, must have been thinking of it, not as a right of the *ummah*, but merely as a desirable quality in the ruler. Some were reluctant to say that *al-shūrā* is compulsory in order to avoid the sense of ordering the Prophet in the verse 'And consult them in the matter'.

There is no doubt that this approach to *al-shūrā* is governed by what had been and not by what must be. But if we look at *al-shūrā* from the perspective of 'the thought of' in our times, namely as a right of the *ummah*, then all past objections to *al-shūrā* as binding would disappear. Those objections, made in good faith as they may be, were dictated by a desire to avoid saying that *al-shūrā* is compulsory on the Prophet, as 'compulsion' does not befit the station of prophethood. Added to this is the desire to bypass the dispute that cannot be resolved about the conduct of the four caliphs and the Companions in general concerning certain matters and incidents where *al-shūrā* was not in order. But if we leave the past aside and think of the present and the future, then there is nothing that can undermine *al-shūrā* as a right of the *ummah*, judging by the text of the Qur'ān and the *sunnah*. The nation has the right to exercise *al-shūrā* in a manner concordant with the times.

CHAPTER 27

# The Right to Equality and the Question of 'Preference'

The Qur'ān emphasizes equality among people; in a well-known, categorically clear-cut, decisive verse, is the speech of the Almighty:

> O mankind! We created you from a single [pair] of a male and a female, and made you into nations and tribes, that you may know each other. Truly the most honoured of you in the sight of Allāh is [he Who is] the most righteous of you (49, al-Hujurat, 13).

Commentators believe that equality in this verse eliminates differentiation and preference because of ancestry, emphasizing words in the verse such as 'male', 'female', 'nations' and 'tribes'. Commenting on the verse, al-Zamakhshārī says 'of male and female' means 'of Adam and Eve'. It was also said: 'We created each of you of a father and a mother, so each one of you is equal to the other, and there is no reason for you to boast preference because of pedigree'. Concerning 'peoples and tribes that you may know each other', al-Zamakhshārī says, 'The purpose of your being organized in peoples and tribes is to let you know each other's pedigrees and guard against claiming different forefathers, boasting about your parents and forefathers, claiming preference because of pedigree.' Then he adds a comment on 'except in piety', saying, 'Then [He] mentioned the quality by which a person is preferred to another and gains honour and favour in the sight of God: The most honoured amongst you is [he who is] most pious', not the highest in pedigree. And 'piety' means 'good deeds'.

It is obvious that such interpretation of the verse, stressing pedigree is limited to 'what was thought of', which was the main factor if not the only one about which the pre-Islamic Arabs used to boast. So, this limitation to the tribal 'thought of' is not legitimate, as there are other *ḥādīth*, quoted by the same commentators concerning this verse, which enlarge the circle of boasting and preference, to include other elements such as colour, wealth and position, or anything that elevates the individual. In his speech, on the day of the conquest of Mecca, the Prophet declaimed 'Praise be to

God who removed from you the burdens and haughtiness of *al-jāhilīyah (the "time of ignorance")*. O you people! Men are of two types: pious believers, honoured by God, and wretched reprobates, disdained by Him.' Then, the Prophet went on to quote the verse above. Among the decisive *ḥādīth* in this respect is, 'No Arab is favoured over a non-Arab, or a white over a black except in piety.' He also said, 'People are equal, like the teeth of a comb.'

The context of 'the most honoured amongst you in the sight of God is the one most pious' confirms this absolute rejection of all types of differentiation and preference other than piety. The verse comes in a context which specifies the morals that must characterize the believers:

> The believers are but a single brotherhood. So make peace and reconciliation between your two [contending] brothers, and fear Allāh, that you may receive mercy. O you who believe! Let not some men among you laugh at others; it may be that the [latter] are better than the [former]; nor let some women laugh at others: it may be that the [latter] are better than the [former]. Nor defame, nor be sarcastic to each other, nor call each other by [offensive] nick names. Ill-seeming is a name connoting wickedness [to be used of one] after he has believed and those who do not desist are [indeed] doing wrong. O you who believe! Avoid suspicion as much [as possible] for suspicion in some cases is a sin; and spy not on each other, nor speak ill of each other behind their backs. Would any of you like to eat the flesh of his dead brother? Nay, you would abhor it. But fear Allāh, for Allāh is Forgiving, Merciful. O mankind! We created you from a single [pair] of a male and a female (49, al-Hujurat, 10–13).

But this has come within the context that speaks of 'good' manners and in a comprehensive way, and so urges the avoidance of pride and limits virtue to piety, i.e. to good conduct, generally.

As the Qur'ān stresses equality among individuals, it also specifies it among nations and peoples. The Qur'ān does not prefer the Muslims as an *ummah* except for the good they do, which is recognized by people in general as common good: 'Let there arise out of you a nation inviting to all that is good enjoining what is right and forbidding what is wrong. They are the ones to attain felicity' (3, Āl 'Imrān, 104). It is reported that the Prophet was asked while he was on the pulpit, 'Who is the best among men?' He answered, 'The one who most enjoins good deeds and prohibits bad deeds, and the most pious and God-fearing.'

There are, indeed, certain verses which prefer certain people over others:

> Not equal are those believers who sit [at home], except if they have an ailment, and those who strive and fight in the cause of Allāh with their wealth and their persons. Allāh has granted a grade higher to those who strive and fight with their wealth and persons than to those who sit [at home, inactive]. To all [in faith] has Allāh promised good, but those who strive and fight has He preferred above those who sit [at home, inactive] by a great reward (4, al-Nisā', 95).

It is clear here that the preference is due to matters which fall under the meaning of 'The most honoured amongst you in the sight of God are the most pious.' Thus, *jihād* in the way of Allāh in wealth and person is the pinnacle of piety. The verse, therefore, does not establish a difference or inequality, but defines the reward deserved by those who strive in the cause of Allāh, which is why they are favoured by God. There are two more verses which mention God's preference of some people over others, and they appear in the same context:

> O you who believe! Do not eat up your property among yourselves in vain. But let there be amongst you traffic and trade by mutual good will. And, do not kill yourselves, for truly Allāh has been to you Most Merciful...do not covet that which Allāh has bestowed more freely on some of you than on others: to men is allotted what they earn, and to women what they earn: But ask Allāh of His bounty. Men are protectors and providers for women, because Allāh has given the one more [in strength] than the other, and because they support them from their means (4, al-Nisā', 29–34).

The context of these verses is clear in prohibiting people from illegal gain, like theft, treachery, usurpation, gambling and usury. On the other hand they permit trade which is conducted by mutual consent between seller and buyer, without any pressure from either side. After a reminder of the necessity to avoid major sins such as suicide, slander, adultery and usurping the orphan's property, the verse warns against envy of other people for the gain or success they have achieved, since all people, men and women, have their share of gain.

'Men are protectors and providers for women' is concerned with profit and trade. Men have always been more active in trade and consequently making more money. Women's work was at home. Hence men were protectors of and providers for women. Not all men are equal in wealth, or in providing for women. It is God Who apportioned the sustenance(s) [of people], preferring the working and active over the lazy in their sustenance – i.e. what they earn (*al-kasb*).

Another significant verse is:

> Allāh has bestowed His gifts of sustenance more freely on some of you than on others: those more favoured are not going to throw back their gifts to those whom they possess, who are equal in that respect. Will they then deny the favours of Allāh? (16, al-Naḥl, 71).

This verse does not establish difference. On the contrary, it calls for equality between masters and slaves. al-Zamakhshārī comments on this verse:

> He made you different in sustenance. He gave you more than He gave to your slaves, though they are human beings like yourselves, and are your brothers. You should give the surplus of what you have to them so you become equal to them in clothing and food. But you do not really do that, which is an act of ingratitude and denial of Allāh's favour on your part.

Therefore, there is nothing in the Qur'ān or *ḥādīth* that undermines the principle of equality which is based on 'the most honoured amongst you in the sight of God is the most pious'. The Qur'ānic reference to difference is related to a person's actions, whether those actions that favour them in the afterlife, or those which lead to their privilege in this world in wealth or other favours. The Qur'ānic principle here is, 'the human being can have nothing but for what he strives' (53, al-Najm, 39), and, 'If any deserves a reward in this life, We shall give it to him; and if any does desire a reward in the hereafter, We shall give it to him. And We shall reward those who are grateful' (3, Āl 'Imrān, 145).

## Chapter 28

# Slavery and the Rights of Women

Among the most significant issues raised concerning the right to equality is the question of slavery and the question of [status of] women. It may be appropriate here to point out that in ancient civilizations, from the Middle Ages and up to the end of the nineteenth century, slavery was considered a normal and necessary practice. The Greek philosophers considered the slave less human than the 'citizen'. They considered it his duty to carry out heavy chores, and they compared him to the hand and the foot in contrast to the mind and the head. Greek intellectuals, other than philosophers, had the same attitude. The Romans followed along in the same mode and were known for their oppression of slaves, considering them like animals or even lower. The situation was not different in the European Christian Middle Ages, and it continued throughout the Modern European era. In other words, slavery was considered a normal social phenomenon, so its abolition was among 'what is not thought of' and also among 'the unthinkable' matters. Women were in no better situation. In the ancient civilizations, from the Middle Ages and up to recent times, women were put on a lower level than that of men. A woman could not enjoy all the rights of men; even after the declaration of 'The Rights of Man and Citizen' by the French National Assembly in 1789, women remained deprived of the right to vote in some parts of Europe until the early decades of the twentieth century.

The matter is different in Islam. The manumission of slaves was in the category of 'what is thought of'. The Qur'ān does not endorse slavery. On the contrary, it considers manumission a work of worship. Most of the prohibited actions and errors committed against religion may be atoned for by certain deeds, among these forms of atonement is the manumission of a slave, or literally the 'liberation of a neck', either by liberating the slave from the owner, or by buying him from the owner and then setting him free. There was also 'ransoming the captives', which Islam considers a religious and social duty. We have already seen how the Qur'ān calls for equality between master and slave, in food and clothing. Abū Dharr reports the Prophet to have said of slaves, 'They are indeed your brothers, so clothe them like you clothe yourselves, and feed them of your own food.' The general tendency in Islamic legislation is to eliminate this phenomenon of slavery, on the principle that man was born free and that 'the most honoured amongst you in the sight of Allāh is the most pious'. 'Umar bin al-Khaṭṭāb emphasized this meaning in his famous dictum, 'When did you enslave people even though they were born free?' Again, we have to remember that a number of eminent Companions were slaves before Islam, but this did not bar them from reaching high status in Islamic society. However, the decisive and absolute proscription of slavery was not feasible under those historical, economic, social and cultural conditions. Yet, it is possible to say that proscription of slavery remained in Islam among the matters that 'can be thought of'. In our present age, abolition of slavery is completely in keeping with the teachings of Islam.

Similar to that is the equality between men and women which falls under 'what is thought of' in the Qur'ān. The general tendency in the Islamic religious texts, the Qur'ān and *ḥādīth*, is towards equality of both men and women, with a special consideration for a woman as a mother. A *ḥadīth* says, 'Paradise is at the feet of mothers'. Women are charged with the same duties as men, except where the nature of women is not suited to that duty (such as *jihād* which is not a duty on women). There are numerous references in the Qur'ān to 'of males and females' and 'Muslim men and Muslim women', and 'believing men and believing women' in the context of equality between both.

True, there are certain secondary rulings which recognize a degree of difference between men and women, especially in cases of testimony and inheritance. As for the conditions of the Qur'ān which specify two women in testimony along with a single man, instead of a single woman, this was justified due to the woman's greater tendency to be exposed to forgetfulness and error as the Almighty said: 'Take as witnesses two men, and if you do not find two men, then one man and two women of those whom you are pleased to take as witnesses, so that if one of the two [women] goes astray, the other can remind her' (2, al-Baqarah, 282). Error and forgetfulness do not naturally pertain to the nature of woman to the exclusion of men, but these go back simply to the social circumstances at that time.

As for the share of the woman in inheritance, it was half the share of the man: 'To the male is the like of two shares of the female' (4, al-Nisā', 11). That was the practice in some of the tribes of the Jāhilīyah, whereas some other tribes forbade the woman to inherit at all. The issue of inheritance finds its rationality in the conditions of tribal society that depended on the scarce resources of land and herd in what made the inheritance of a girl into a source of discord and conflict between the tribes. If most often a girl would be married into a tribe other than hers, and if she were to inherit, then that would mean her husband's tribe would inherit the wealth of her family's tribe and that would cause conflict to no end. There was no doubt that the Qur'ān would deal with the givens of these circumstances and look to the public good – that is the avoidance of conflict – so it put forth something of an intermediate solution: it did not forbid the girl from inheritance absolutely but rather it gave her half the share of a boy and made the male responsible for her welfare whether she was a wife or a [widowed] mother. It made that a kind of compensation. In sum, the equality between the man and woman is the starting principle, and the Qur'ān and the *ḥadīth* textually specified this principle. Additionally, equality between them is in all spheres from the category of 'tribe' to what is 'thought of' in order that public good should be the intent of *al-sharīʿah* in all states.

Polygamy was a dominant phenomenon in pre-Islamic Arabia and was recognized by the Qur'ān, but with a strong leaning towards prohibition, as the Qur'ān demands justice and fairness among the wives in every respect, which is a formidable task. But the question of polygamy, as related in the Qur'ān, is open to more than one interpretation, as the Qur'ān connects polygamy with the property of orphans. The order to the guardians of orphans is to be fair and just in handling that property. A man in pre-Islamic Arabia could marry a number of widows, which could exceed 10, because he coveted the property of their orphans. The Qur'ān prohibited that practice and limited the number of wives to the maximum of four, provided the husband be fair to them all, in every material and moral aspect:

> To orphans restore their property; nor substitute [your] worthless things for [their] good ones; and do not devour their substance [by mixing it up] with your own, for this is indeed a great injustice. But if you fear that you shall not be able to deal justly with the orphans, then marry women of your choice, two or three or four, but if you fear that you shall not be able to deal justly [with them] then only one (4, al-Nisā', 2–3).

Commentators have different opinions about the relation between orphans and polygamy. The fact of the matter is that abolition of polygamy at the time of the Prophet or the Companions was among 'the unthinkables' of that age. Polygamy was an acceptable social phenomenon, in fact a desirable one, especially in a tribal society where relations were strengthened by intermarriages, which lessen the chances of friction and contention. But at the present time, polygamy undermines the rights of women, and its abolition falls under 'the thinkable' in the light of the Islamic principle of equality between men and women in rights and duties. On the other hand, the Qur'ān stipulates justice among the wives; and since justice in this case is difficult, if not impossible, and in all cases it is questionable, abolition of polygamy would not be discordant with the teachings of Islam. The Qur'ān does not *enjoin* polygamy, it rather encourages monogamy for fear of injustice in treatment.

CHAPTER 29

# The Right to Justice: The Strength of the Qur'ānic Text and the Vacillation of the 'Advisory Discourse'

Justice occupies a significant part in the Qur'ān and *ḥadīth* and in the work of commentators, *fuqahā'*, muhājirūn, in addition to the writers of 'advise to rulers' literature – *al-adāb al-sulṭānīyah* [*Mirror for the Magistrates*]. In the Qur'ān, the order to act justly is recurrent on all levels. The Messenger is ordered to act justly, not among Muslims only, but also among non-Muslims if they seek his judgment: 'Say, I believe in the book which Allāh has sent down; and I am commanded to judge justly between you. Allāh is our Lord and your Lord. For us [is the responsibility for] our deeds, and for you for your deeds' (42, al-Shūrā, 15). And, 'If they [the Jews] do come to you, either judge between them or decline [to interfere]. If you decline, they cannot hurt you in the least. If you judge, judge in equity between them. For Allāh loves those who judge in equity' (5, al-Mā'idah, 42). God addresses the prophet David: 'O David! We made you a vicegerent on earth, so judge between men in truth (and justice); nor follow the lusts [of your heart]' (38, Sad, 26). The command to do justice occurs in general terms in many verses: 'Allāh commands you to render back your trusts to those to whom they are due; and when you judge between men that you judge with justice' (4, al-Nisā', 58). Also, 'Allāh commands justice and the doing of good' (16, al-Naḥl, 90).

The Qur'ān insists on avoiding discrimination between people, poor and rich, relatives and non-relatives, and stipulates justice to all:

> O you who believe! Stand out firmly for justice as witnesses for Allāh, even as against yourselves, or your parents, or your kin, or whether it be [against] rich or poor; for Allāh can best protect both. Do not follow the lusts [of your hearts], lest you swerve, and if you distort [justice] or decline to do justice, truly Allāh is well-acquainted with all that you do (4, al-Nisā', 135).

Moreover, 'O you who believe! Stand firmly for Allāh, as witnesses to fair dealing, and let not the hatred of others to you make you swerve to wrong and depart from justice. Be just; that is closest to piety' (5, al-Mā'idah, 8).

The *ḥādīth* reported about justice are various and numerous. Although some of them are considered 'weak', they, nevertheless, express the Islamic conscience and confirm what is stated in the Qur'ān. Therefore, those *ḥādīth* are correct in implication, even if some may be of questionable authenticity. However, of the authentic *ḥadīth*, reported by al-Bukhārī and Muslim, states, 'Seven are graced by the shade of Allāh, when there is no shade but His.' The first of the seven is a 'just ruler'. Al-Tirmidhī reports the Messenger to have said:

> The most favoured man by Allāh on the Day of Judgment, and the nearest to His seat is a just imām [ruler], and the most detested man by Allāh on that day and the most remote from His seat is an unjust imām.

The books of the 'advice to rulers' genre – *al-adāb al-sulṭānīyah* – repeat the expression that 'justice is the basis of rule', explaining and confirming its meaning by sayings ascribed to Greek philosophers, Persian and Indian wise men, and Muslim dignitaries.

Yet one cannot help note that all statements on 'justice', ascribed to the Prophet, the Companions or the wise men of the world, are less in strength from what is stated in the Qur'ān. The writers on *al-adāb al-sulṭānīyah* [*Mirror for the Magistrates*] avoid quoting the Qur'ān on 'justice', though they quote sayings by wise men that encourage and enjoin justice. This is due, in our view, to the fact that those authors were not thinking of justice except in the context of preaching, while the Qur'ān poses the issue of justice as a command, which renders the establishment of justice a duty. To believe justice is an enjoined duty entails certain consequences, the foremost among which in Islamic *sharī'ah* is the position of the unjust ruler: Is revolt against him a duty, or should he be left to the Judgment of God? Since the Muslim rulers, after the Rāshidūn Caliphs, did not abide by justice (with the exception of 'Umar bin 'Abd al-'Azīz), and since revolting against them led always to anarchy and civil wars, which never resulted in a just ruler, and since to have a rule, though unjust, is, according to the *fuqahā'*, better than having no rule and the rule was necessary to execute many religious rulings, the *fuqahā'* maintained a kind of silence about the issue of justice. They interpreted the Qur'ānic texts which enjoin justice, implicitly or explicitly, as merely of advisory nature and addressed the issue of justice in that context. Therefore, as those *fuqahā'* could not place justice within the duties of the ruler, it was, consequently, not possible for them, politically, as well as jurisprudentially, to place that justice within the rights of the 'ruled', as they understood the concept of the ruled. Human rights, in the modern sense, were not among 'the thought of', as explained above.

Nowadays, conditions have changed. Human rights have become an international demand. Respecting and enjoying those rights became a necessity of life. Therefore, the silence of the *fuqahā'* is no longer justifiable. And it has become necessary to approach the issue of justice as one of human rights and place it among 'what is thinkable' within the context of the basic religious texts (the Qur'ān and *ḥadīth*). These texts, quoted above, are of an authenticity and clarity not open to debate. They present the issue of justice as a 'command' and demand placing justice as a duty on the rulers and consequently among the rights of the ruled. When we do this, as the Qur'ān demands, the issue presenting itself directly would be: How can the rulers be forced to abide by this duty of justice, and how can the ruled enjoy this right?

Here comes the issue of *al-shūrā*, presenting itself not only as binding, but also as a right of the ruled which must be practised in a way that turns it into 'constant *shūrā*' in the service of 'justice', a means to constantly monitor the rulers: their political, judicial and socioeconomic conduct. This is what nowadays is called 'democracy'. Justice, then, which accompanies equality, is a basic democratic right, which Islam orders to be respected and secured by providing conducive conditions.

From the Qur'ānic perspective, justice is not limited to the narrow meaning assigned by the *fuqahā'* which is to rule justly between two adversaries. It covers different relations among people: men and women, parents and children, rulers and ruled. This meaning is clear in 'Allāh commands you to render back your trusts to those to whom they are due; and when you judge between men that you judge with justice (*bi-l-'adl*)'; in another verse, 'in equity (*bi-l-qisṭ*)' (5, al-Mā'idah, 42). Justice and equity have the same meaning. We also read, 'Allāh commands justice, the doing of good and liberality to kith and kin, and he forbids all shameful deeds, and atrocity, and injustice' (16, al-Naḥl, 90). It is clear that connecting justice with all the good deeds mentioned in the verse bestows a comprehensive meaning on justice.

These are the human rights in general: the basic rights as specified in the Qur'ān and *ḥadīth*, for all human beings with no exception. They are the right to life, to the enjoyment of good things in life, to freedom of belief, to knowledge, to be different, to consultation, to equality and to justice. Without the enjoyment of these rights the human being falls short of the basis of his or her existence and the means of growth and development.

In addition to these general rights there are other special rights for a special group of people, namely, the 'weak oppressed'. These rights are no less important, as they form the bases of the full enjoyment of the general basic rights.

CHAPTER 30

# The Rights of the Weak Oppressed: The Right of the Poor to the Wealth of the Rich

The term '*al-mustaḍ'afūn*' as it occurs in the Qur'ān denotes weak people. It is used as an antonym to the term '*al-mustakbirūn*' – the arrogant, who boast of their financial, political or military power or whatever they believe they possess in the way of merit, material or moral power which makes them see themselves as above the rest of the people. The haughty person, therefore, is a person who denies his equality with other people and claims a sort of superiority. The oppressed are those who suffer from the arrogance of the haughty, as they have no wealth or any other means of power at their disposal, like the haughty. In other words, the oppressed are those deprived of their rights in a society which is not based on equality and justice.

The Qur'ān enumerates all types of weak oppressed people and enjoins special care for them, repeatedly confirming their rights and warning whoever forfeits those rights. Of these are the old (of the fathers, mothers and kin), the poor, the needy, orphans, the wayfarer, slaves and prisoners. The following is a conclusive verse in this respect:

> Righteousness is not that you turn your faces towards East or West; but righteousness is to believe in Allāh, and the Last Day, and the angels, and the Book, and the Messengers, to spend of your wealth, though loved. For your kin, for orphans, for the needy, for the wayfarer, for those who ask, and for the ransom of slaves; to be steadfast in prayer, and practice regular charity, to fulfil the contracts which you have made; and to be firm and patient, in pain [or suffering] and adversity, and throughout all periods of panic. Such are the people of truth, the God-fearing and pious (2, al-Baqarah, 177).

Four points must be highlighted in this verse. First, the address here is to the People of the Book, namely, the Jews, who face Jerusalem, located to the west relative to the Hijaz, in their worship, and the Christians, who face the East. This means that righteousness and good deeds are not limited to prayer and worship, but include, also, observing the rights of the oppressed. Second, the verse couples the belief in Allāh and the Last Day with giving out money, which is cherished, to the oppressed mentioned in the verse. This stresses the importance of the rights of the oppressed and puts them on a par with the rights of God, namely, worship. Third, the verse specifies that payment of money to the oppressed is separate from *al-zakāt*, which means that the right of the oppressed to the riches of God, which are in the hands of the wealthy, is not limited to *al-zakāt*. Fourth, as the verse lists payment of money to the oppressed with the basic principles of Islam such as testifying to the oneness of God, prayer and *al-zakāt*, it raises the observance of the rights of the oppressed to the level of a religious duty. The Qur'ān confirms this meaning in another verse: "And in their wealth and possessions is the right of the [needy] who beg and for the deprived' (51, al-Thairiyāt, 19). There is a *ḥadīth* which states, 'In their wealth there is a right other than *al-zakāt*'.

The oppressed in the verse are first the needy of the kith and kin, then the orphans whose parents did not leave them enough to fulfil their needs, then the needy who do not have enough to live on: 'It is reported that the Prophet said, "The needy is not the one who is given a meal or two, a morsel or two, a date or two." They said, "Who is he then?" He answered, "He is the one who has no means and the one whom none has given in charity."' In modern terms, he is the 'unemployed' who cannot find work to help him make a living for himself and his family. The wayfarer is the traveller who lost his way and may be compared with the 'political refugee' in the modern sense. Those who beg are the needy who ask for alms, either because they are poor or due to an emergency. The ransomed are the slaves to be liberated, through buying them from their masters. But their need for food and clothes is the responsibility of their master. In addition to these, there are other types of the oppressed mentioned in the Qur'ān: 'Then eat [of the sacrifice] and feed the distressed impoverished one' (22, al-Hajj, 28). The distressed person is the one in dire straits; the one in want is the poor person who does not have enough food for himself and his family. *al-zakāt* is payable to eight types of people mentioned in the Qur'ān:

> Alms are for the poor and the needy, and those employed to administer the [funds]; for those whose hearts have been [recently] reconciled [to the truth], for those in bondage and in debt; in the way of Allāh; and for the wayfarer; [thus it is] ordained by Allāh (9, al-Tawbah, 60).

Some of these categories have been mentioned above. But 'Those employed to administer the funds' are the collectors of alms who convey them to the 'ones in charge' (the treasury). These are paid out from *al-*

*zakāt* money as a compensation for their work. The ones 'whose hearts have been recently reconciled' were some of the Arab chieftains who were paid by the Messenger to encourage them to embrace Islam. The 'debtors' are the ones who were overwhelmed to a degree that they no longer have anything to pay for what they owe. The category 'in the way of Allāh' covers the poor among the fighters and the pilgrims who cannot return home.

This shows that 'the rights of the oppressed' are of two types: one is the right to *al-zakāt*; another the right to charity. The difference is that *al-zakāt* was made by God a basic principle of Islam, like *al-shahādah* (bearing witness to the faith), *al-ṣalāt* (prayer), *al-ṣiyām* (fasting), and *hajj*. Without accepting *al-zakāt* as a duty imposed by God, a person's Islam is not complete. I believe that it has a symbolic political function, which makes the symbolic equal to the holy. *Al-shahādah* symbolizes the relation which should exist between man and God (belief in the unicity of God – *al-tawḥīd* – and faith in the message of Muḥammad). *Al-ṣalāt* is a religious rite to pray and make supplication for God's help and to avoid shameful and evil deeds. *Al-ṣiyām* symbolizes the elevation of the soul above material passions and the sharing of hunger with the poor. Hajj is the pilgrimage which symbolizes the unity of the Muslims and provides the chance for this unity to move from the wishful level to an actual congregation under equal living conditions, represented by the unity of 'attire' in its simplest form in addition to the unity of ritual. *Al-zakāt* is also a symbol of the Muslim's allegiance to the Muslim society as a whole. It is well-known that Abū Bakr, the first caliph, did not fight the apostates who denied him the payment of *al-zakāt* out of need for money. He fought them because *al-zakāt* was a token of allegiance to him as head of state and successor to the Prophet. *Al-zakāt* in modern terms is the government tax, which, in its legal sense, represents the allegiance of the individual to the state and the fulfilment of his obligations towards it in return for the services which the state undertakes towards the community as a whole, such as providing security and funding projects of development in all fields.

In this context, we have to look at the rights of the non-Muslims within Islamic society, especially the question of *al-jizyah*. This is nothing but the tax which represents the allegiance of the individual to the state and secures his interest. It is a symbol of political allegiance and a participation in the state's expenditure for the public good, like the provision of security and development, enjoyed by all citizens, irrespective of their religion. *Al-jizyah* is different from *al-zakāt* because the protected non-Muslim, *al-dhimmī*, from the People of the Book is not required to participate in *jihād*, neither in the fighting nor in providing finance for it.

Yet he is under the protection of the state like all other citizens. But in 'charity' justice and all other rights, Muslims and non-Muslims (*ahl al-dhimmah*) are alike:

> Allāh does not forbid you, with regard to those who do not fight you for [your] faith, nor drive you out of your homes, from dealing kindly and justly with them; for Allāh loves those who are just. Allāh only forbids you, with regard to those who fight you for [your] faith, and drive you out of your homes, and support [others] in driving you out, from turning to them [for friendship and protection]. It is such as turn to them [in these circumstances] that do wrong (60, al-Mumtaḥinah, 8–9).

The Messenger emphasized respect for the rights of the non-Muslim: 'Whoever does injustice to a covenanter, or undermines his due or charges him more than he can afford, or take away something from him against his will, shall have me as his contender on the Day of Judgment.' Some *fuqahā'* say that oppressing a *dhimmī* is a greater sin than oppressing a Muslim.

## Chapter 31

# Social Security in Islam: Necessity of Development

The rights of the oppressed are stressed in the Qur'ān, not only in the verse on 'righteousness' alone, but also in other verses. At times, this comes as a direct command, at times only by implication: 'And render to the kindred their due rights, as [also] to those in want, and to the wayfarer; but do not squander [your wealth] in the manner of a spendthrift' (17, al-Isrā', 26). Also, 'Give them out of the wealth which Allāh has given to you' (24, al-Nūr, 33). The commentators say that this verse was revealed about '*al-mukātib* – the 'contracted slave'. This is a slave who signs a contract with a master who bought him on condition that he will be manumitted upon payment of a certain sum of money, which the slave can pay by instalments. To help this slave in attaining his freedom, the verse orders the rich to pay the slave what will expedite his manumission.

In another *sūrah*, we read, 'And those in whose wealth is a recognized right for the needy and the deprived' (70, al-Ma'ārij, 24–5). These verses occur immediately after 'Man was created very impatient, except those devoted to prayers, those who remain steadfast in their prayers' (70, al-Ma'ārij, 19–23). This juxtaposition between steadfastness in prayers and giving money to the needy and the deprived makes them two qualities which characterize the genuine believer. We find a similar juxtaposition in another verse which describes the bliss of dwellers of paradise, referring it to the fact that those are the ones who, in their worldly life, were steadfast to their prayers, and often gave money to the poor and the needy:

> As for the righteous, they will be in the midst of gardens and springs, taking joy in the things which their Lord gave them, as before that they were benefactors. They hardly slept during the night, and in the hours of early dawn they [were found] praying for forgiveness; and in their wealth [was remembered] the right of the needy and the deprived (51, al-Dhariyāt, 15–19).

There are several verses which indicate this meaning: the bliss of paradise dwellers is connected to paying money to the poor and the needy; the torment of the hell-dwellers is related, in a way, to their holding on to their money and to their avarice.

There is a verse which has a special significance in this connection: 'They ask you how much they are to spend, say, "What is beyond your needs (*al-'afw*)"' (2, al-Baqarah, 219). Al-Nasafī explains 'What is beyond your needs' as 'surplus' (*al-faḍl*), and he adds that:

> ...paying the surplus – *al-'afw* – as alms was a duty in the early years of Islam. A man who owned a land to cultivate used to set aside what he needed for a year then he paid the surplus as alms. If he was a craftsman, he would keep what he needed for the day and pay the surplus as alms. Then the verse on *al-zakāt* abrogated the one on surplus.

This means that when the Islamic society had meagre revenue, each member had to pay to the poor and needy whatever exceeded his need in order to establish a balance of livelihood. But when the resources of that society increased through trade, agriculture, cattle-raising, etc., *al-zakāt* replaced the surplus. This is an indication that recourse to sources other than *al-zakāt* was quite legitimate when *al-zakāt* could not fulfil the needs of the poor and provide a minimum of balance in livelihood. Thus, the right of the poor to the property of the rich includes the surplus in case of need. The legitimacy of this measure is endorsed by a *ḥadīth* reported by al-Tirmidhī: 'There is a right to the riches of the wealthy other than *al-zakāt*.' In another *ḥadīth* the Prophet says, 'No man is a true believer in me if he sleeps his night having eaten enough while his neighbour is hungry and he is aware of it,' as reported in *al-Ṣiḥāḥ of* Aḥmad bin Ḥanbal.

Is it, then, not our right, or even a duty on us, to look at the above verses and *ḥādīth* on the rights of the oppressed in the light of what is nowadays called 'social security'?! This covers the right to medical care, unemployment benefit, and the right to pension benefit. These rights are guaranteed for the benefit of the oppressed through deductions from the income of the rich and the state employees. It is a modern arrangement quite in keeping with righteousness, *al-zakāt* and surplus (*al-'afw*). Ibn Hazm explained 'giving money' in terms similar to the modern concept of 'social security':

> God imposed on the rich of every country to provide for the poor. The ruler is to compel them to do that if zakat revenue was not sufficient for that aim. They have to be provided with their sustenance, clothing for winter and summer, lodging to protect them from rain and sun and the eyes of the

> onlookers. Then he added, the proof to that is the holy verse, 'So give what is due to kindred, the needy, and the wayfarer' (30, Al-Rūm, 38).

I have to point out in this connection that what Ibn Hazm specified as a duty on the ruler (the state) towards the poor, in general, had previously been applied by Khālid bin Walīd to the non-Muslims. In the treaty he concluded with the Christians of Hira, in Iraq, we read the following:

> Any elderly person who has become too old to work, or afflicted with some ailment, or who was rich and has become impoverished and supported by people of his own religion will be exempt from paying his *jizyah*, and will be supported by the *bayt al-māl* (public treasury) of the Muslims together with his family [MC159].

It is well-known that such treaties are considered a source of legislation in Islam. This covenant was concluded in the time of Abū Bakr, who endorsed it, and no one of the Companions objected to it, which makes it approved by consensus (*al-ijmā*ʿ). Needless to say the description of the non-Muslim in the treaty applies as well to the Muslim who 'becomes too old to work, or afflicted with some ailment, or who was rich and has become impoverished'. Hence, social security in the modern comprehensive sense is one of the human rights in Islam, as seen in the texts of the Qurʾān and the *ḥādīth*, and in the conduct of the Companions.

However, this extreme care for the weak oppressed does not, in any way, relieve the people of their need to work, if they can, in order to satisfy their needs. Islam urges people to work, and this encouragement occurs as an order in several verses: 'It is He Who has made the earth manageable for you, so traverse through its tracts and enjoy of the sustenance which He furnishes, as to Him is the Resurrection' (67, al-Mulk, 15); 'And when the prayer is finished, then disperse through the land, and seek of the bounty of Allāh' (62, al-Jumuʿah, 10); and 'Others travel through the land, seeking of Allāh's bounty' (73, al-Muzzamil, 20). One *ḥadīth* says, 'No one has ever eaten better food than what he himself prepares. Prophet David used to eat the food he himself prepared.' Another *ḥadīth* says, 'The most savoured food one can have comes from the hand of a craftsman (*ṣāni*ʿ) faithful to his calling.' So, Islam urges people to work for gain in agriculture (the first verse) and trade (the next two verses), and by the work of one's own hands (the two *ḥadīth*). This is the building of the land entrusted to man as the basis of civilization and a special honour to the human being.

The 'building' of the land, or what today is simply called 'development', may be engrafted in our conscience by the employment of some texts from our tradition. In addition to the texts which make land development a duty of man in general terms, there are other texts which transfer this duty to the state, which can do more to support the rights of the oppressed. One outstanding text in this connection is by Ibn Hazm:

> The sovereign leads people towards development and increase of agriculture. He allots them portions of undeveloped land as their own and supports their efforts of development and cultivation in order to reduce prices, for people and livestock have a better life. The greater the reward, the more wealthy people there will be and the greater the amount of *al-zakāt* which will be accrued.

CHAPTER 32

# The Rights of God, the Rights of People: Application of *al-Sharīʿah*

We have seen how human rights can be viewed through the basic Islamic texts (the Qur'ān and *ḥadīth*). But in their modern connotation, now that these rights include the right to comprehensive development, human rights are not among 'what is thought of' in the past, neither in Arab-Islamic civilization, nor in any other, as they are the product of the economic, social, political and cultural development achieved by modern European civilization in the eighteenth century or in later times.

If human rights in the modern sense did not belong to the field of 'what is thought of' in the past Arab-Islamic texts, it was and still is apt to be so, especially as seen in the Qur'ān and *ḥādīth*. Needless to say, what kept those rights within the limits of 'what is not thought of' is the failure of Arab-Islamic thought, due to certain objective, historical, economic, social and cultural conditions, to disregard the concept of ruler and subjects, which regulated the social hierarchy and controlled the relation between the ruler and the ruled. That was a concept which limited political thought to finding ways and means to make the 'subjects' obedient to the ruler 'willingly'. This is why political thought in Arab-Islamic culture revolved around *al-adāb al-sulṭānīya* (*Mirror for the Magistrates*) or *al-siyāsah al-mulukīyah* (*Royal Polity*) literature, which recommended certain qualities in the ruler and advised him of the conduct to secure the obedience and 'satisfaction' of his subjects.

However, in the field of politics the *fuqahā'* focused on the axis of the ruler and the ruled in what some of them called 'Islamic politics' (*al-siyāsah al-sharīʿah*). This was nothing but jurisprudential discussion dealing with the 'rights of God' and the 'rights of people', and the provisions which put those rights in force.

The rights of God include belief (*al-īmān*), prayer (*al-ṣalāt*), fasting (*al-ṣawm*), and the other religious duties which have a purely devotional nature, and their accompaniments, such as atonement for breaking the fast in Ramadan, and paying the various land-taxes, and the *ḥudūd* penalties for adultery, theft and the atonements. The 'rights of people' in that jurisprudential sense covered the rights of the relatives of a murdered person to blood money or killing the murderer; the right of wounds in kind (a hand for a hand, and a tooth for a tooth); the rights of a man whose honour had been insulted through libel and abuse; marital rights of both husband and wife; and the rights of inheritance.

These are the issues that were covered by the 'thought of' in the field of rights in Islamic jurisprudence. The *fuqahā'* classified those rights in a more general and abstract manner. They looked at them and at the entire *sharī'ah* rulings from the viewpoint that their intents were to secure 'the good of the people in this world and the hereafter'. They classified those intents or public interests into three categories: necessities, needs and improvements. The first are 'indispensable to the good of both faith and worldly affairs, and if missed, the worldly affairs will not go right, and the otherworldly life will be bereft of bliss and salvation, and plagued with utter loss'. These necessities are the protection of faith, self, mind, progeny and property. This means that *al-sharī'ah* was intended for the protection of these five elements. The needs are 'what is required to alleviate hardship', such as the dispensation to break the fast for the traveller or the sick in Ramadan. The improvements mean 'to observe propriety and choose commendable habits and to avoid what is shunned by sane minds, namely all that come under ethics and morals'.

Human rights in the modern sense as the backbone of comprehensive human development could have been based on the three major intents of *al-sharī'ah* – necessities, needs and improvements – and by considering the five necessities (preservation of self, mind, religion, progeny and property) as the solid basis for human rights and the focusing of thought on human development on preserving these necessities, needs and improvements. However, this would have meant the projection of what is thinkable now on what was neither 'thought of' nor thinkable in traditional *fiqh*. The *fuqahā'* addressed the intents of *al-sharī'ah* in order to lend rationality to the *sharī'ah* rulings which deal comprehensively with the actions of the culpable human being from a consideration of duties, not of rights. Hence, the jurisprudential texts in this connection are not open to interpretation, nor can they serve as a starting point for dealing with human rights. Contrary to that are the Qur'ānic and *ḥadīth* texts, which are open to such thinking, as we have seen. Therefore, we prefer to refer to these texts only.

However, despite the importance of the concept of intents, according to which al-Shatibi tried to rebuild *fiqh*, conceiving of rights through these intents remained, even after al-Shatibi, within the scope of *al-ḥudūd*: such as the *ḥudūd* of God – the punishment for adultery and theft, and human punishments such as blood money. Punishments are the same as rights in the minds of *fuqahā'*. Similarly, those who call for 'the application of *al-sharī'ah*' nowadays generally think of these rights/punishments as specified in Islamic penal law.

I believe that human development in the Arab and Islamic world should concentrate on developing first and foremost human rights as specified by the Qur'ān and *ḥadīth*, as explained above. These rights are: the right to life and its enjoyment, the rights to belief, to knowledge, to disagree, to *al-shūrā* (consultation), to equality and justice, in addition to the rights of the oppressed. And these are the basic rights which, if they are not enjoyed by people, means the *sharī'ah* punishments cannot be applied equitably. Without putting an end to poverty, ignorance and the injustice of the rulers and the injustices of the strong against the weak, the *ḥudūd* will remain exposed to doubt. And, the Prophetic *ḥadīth* says, 'Avoid the *ḥudūd* [penalties] when in doubt.' The Prophet and the Rāshidūn Caliphs did that on various well-known occasions.

The starting point, then, in the application of *al-sharī'ah*, must be to enable Muslims and non-Muslims in Islamic society to enjoy the basic rights specified by the Qur'ān and *ḥadīth* for people as human beings, from the right to life to the rights of the oppressed. Without this, the *sharī'ah* *ḥudūd* will be applied only to the oppressed, who are forced by hunger, ignorance and the injustice exercised against them to commit violations and crimes. As for the arrogant who possess power, wealth and prestige, they always know how to conceal their crimes and avoid punishment.

# Index